20.99

Comparative Health Policy

Second Edition

Robert H. Blank
New College of Florida and University of Canterbury

and

Viola Burau
University of Aarhus

First edition 2004
Second edition 2007

Published by
PALGRAVE MACMILLAN
Houndmills, Basingstoke, Hampshire RG21 6XS and
175 Fifth Avenue, New York, N.Y. 10010
Companies and representatives throughout the world

PALGRAVE MACMILLAN is the global academic imprint of the Palgrave
Macmillan division of St. Martin's Press, LLC and of Palgrave Macmillan Ltd.
Macmillan® is a registered trademark in the United States, United Kingdom
and other countries. Palgrave is a registered trademark in the European
Union and other countries.

ISBN 13: 978–0–230–00139–8 hardback
ISBN 10: 0–230–00139–4   hardback
ISBN 13: 978–0–230–00140–4 paperback
ISBN 10: 0–230–00140–8   paperback

This book is printed on paper suitable for recycling and made from fully
managed and sustained forest sources. Logging, pulping and manufacturing
processes are expected to conform to the environmental regulations of the
country of origin.

A catalogue record for this book is available from the British Library.

A catalog record for this book is available from the Library of Congress.

10   9   8   7   6   5   4   3   2   1
16   15   14   13   12   11   10   09   08   07

Printed in China

To **Lynton Keith Caldwell, 1913–2006**
a true visionary, scholar and friend

Contents

List of Boxes, Figures and Tables

Boxes

Figures

Tables

Preface to the Second Edition

We wrote the first edition of this book to fill a gap in comparative health policy. Although there have been numerous books about the health policies of specific countries and a handful of books that compare a few nations, our own research in a variety of countries convinced us that a more inclusive comparative coverage would be helpful in elucidating the issues and problems surrounding health care. Therefore, we pooled our shared knowledge of a diverse set of health care systems and wrote an introduction to the health policy of nine countries. Although it was written primarily with students in mind, we are gratified that the first edition has been read by academics involved in scholarly research and health policy makers as well as graduate and undergraduate students in many countries.

Based on many favourable reviews in journals and on input from scholars and from teachers and students who used the first edition, we have thoroughly updated the text, statistical tables and references to reflect the many changes that have taken place in the last few years in this dynamic area of health policy. We have restructured four of the chapters to cover better the elaborate comparative content and further elucidate the themes; and we have added new topical material, boxes and case studies throughout in order to complement the analytical discussion in the chapters.

In order to establish the extent to which the problems facing health care systems have common roots or spring from specific national circumstances, our assessment of health policy focuses on key themes, issues and tensions that run through the book Thus, chapters are organized on a thematic basis rather than a country one. How do the main types of health systems in the developed world address health care problems, and do diverse systems make a difference in policy outcomes? Is health policy in all developed countries converging due to globalization as some commentators argue? The book analyses what lessons can be learned about public/private mixes, policy and funding frameworks, professional organizations, and acute and preventive services across disparate health systems. In order to accomplish this, the systems of Australia, Germany, Japan, New Zealand, the Netherlands, Sweden, Singapore, the UK and the USA are methodically covered. In addition, discussions of France and Italy are incorporated where we feel it facilitates a better understanding of the topic.

Throughout the book, we put health care in a broader social context and reveal its interdependence with factors often excluded from analysis. Health care, we argue, cannot be separated from other issues that impinge on health such as economic inequalities, the environment and social services. Thus, we include analyses of home care for the elderly and an array of public health issues that cumulatively impact on health outcomes more than medical services. We also explore whether the medical model and the heavy emphasis on curative medicine is the most effective way to address the health of populations.

Chapter 1 introduces health policy and the impact of global trends of population ageing, technology diffusion and heightened public expectations on the health systems of developed nations. It also discusses the importance of comparative health care analysis and presents the typologies conventionally used to classify health systems. Chapter 2 looks at the institutional, historical/cultural and economic context of health care and proposes an integrated model of health that accounts for the variation across our countries. It also discusses differences over the definition of health, the role of alternative forms of medicine and the relationship of health status to the socio-economic milieu.

Chapter 3 shifts attention to the provision, funding and governance of health care and to the nature and scope of health reforms across the countries. Our countries show considerable diversity, both among different health systems and across the sub-systems of each health system, and only a few countries neatly fit existing typologies. Chapter 4 continues and expands this discussion by examining priority-setting in health care. It illustrates the problematic allocation and rationing issues facing all health systems and discusses how these countries have responded to these challenges. Chapter 5 examines the organization and power of doctors in these health systems with special emphasis on how this role has changed through recent health care reforms. Although the face of medical practice has altered, doctors in particular have retained considerable power and remain key players in health policy.

Chapter 6 moves the discussion to home care to illustrate the interdependence of health with other care services as countries face the dual challenges of ageing populations and social transformation in an era of cost containment. Despite diverse approaches, common trends are apparent, most notably the enhanced support for women as informal carers. Chapter 7 shifts focus from individual, patient-centred acute care to public health with its emphasis on the health of populations. It demonstrates that health outcomes for populations are more closely tied to health promotion and disease prevention efforts, income distribution, public services, housing, social conditions and the environment than with medicine. The concluding chapter returns to the broader themes introduced in Chapter 1 and assesses the appropriateness of existing typologies of health systems. The discussion demonstrates the continued importance of country-specific differences within overall trends of convergence, as well as to the complexity of health systems. Complexity arises from differentiation of health systems into often quite distinct sub-systems and from the fact that health care encompasses more than health systems.

This edition offers a genuinely cross-country comparative analysis where we as co-authors have worked across the boundaries of our respective country and thematic expertise. For us this has been the most exciting part of our collaboration, but this has of course required a fair share of coordination. Having offices opposite each other greatly facili-tated this process while working on the first edition, whereas the spatial frame of our collaboration has been more global this time round, spread-ing across three countries in as many continents. We are therefore partic-ularly grateful to our respective universities for the different ways in which they have supported our collaboration. At the University of Aarhus, Viola Burau received a part-time research fellowship from the university's Research Foundation that provided valuable space for think-ing and writing. Viola would particularly like to thank Carsten Daugbjerg for his support of the initial application.

In terms of the revisions for this second edition we have greatly bene-fited from the constructive comments we received from colleagues whose valuable feedback has helped us sharpen our analysis. We also want to acknowledge the helpful reviews in many journals which were largely highly supportive of our efforts. Some of the changes in this edition were responses to suggestions raised by reviewers. Moreover, teaching in comparative health policy has offered a welcome test bed for new ideas and we are grateful to our students for their patience and input. At the University of Aarhus, Søren Uhre provided invaluable research assistance with updating the statistical material, while Lone Winther edited the bibliography with her usual care. We would also like to thank our publisher Steven Kennedy for his strong support and encouragement on this project over the years and for the excellent production team at Palgrave Macmillan and to the outside reviewers for their constructive suggestions. Finally, we are fortunate to have supportive family and friends, and Viola would like to thank especially Ruth, Vicki and Henrik for their open ears and encouragement.

A searchable version of the Glossary and periodically updated version of the List of Websites in this book can be found at www.palgrave.com/politics/blank where any other updated materials or corrections will also be posted as necessary.

New College of Florida/University of Canterbury   Robert H. Blank
University of Aarhus   Viola Burau

List of Abbreviations

ACC	Accident Compensation Commission
AHB	Area Health Boards (New Zealand)
AMA	American Medical Association
BMA	British Medical Association
BMI	Body Mass Index
CAT	computerized axial tomography
CDC	Centers for Disease Control and Prevention (USA)
CHE	Crown Health Enterprise (New Zealand)
CPF	Central Provident Fund (Singapore)
DHBs	District Health Boards (New Zealand)
DRGs	diagnosis-related groups
EPR	Epidemic and Pandemic Alert and Responses
EU	European Union
GATS	General Agreement on Trade in Services
GDP	gross domestic product
GMC	General Medical Council
GP	general practitioner
HACC	Home and Community Care Program (Australia)
HCFA	Health Care Financing Administration (USA)
HCQI	Health Care Quality Indicator Project
HFA	Health Funding Authority (New Zealand)
HMO	Health Maintenance Organization
HTA	health technology assessment
IMC	Inter-Ministerial Committee on Health Care for the Elderly (Singapore)
IPA	Independent Practice Association (New Zealand)
JMA	Japanese Medical Association
MBS	Medicare Benefits Schedule (Australia)
MHCs	Municipal Health Centres (Japan)
MOH	Ministry of Health
MRI	magnetic resonance imaging
MSA	Medical Savings Account (Singapore)
NHI	National Health Insurance
NHS	National Health Service
NICE	National Institute for Clinical Excellence (UK)
NIH	National Institutes of Health (USA)
NZMA	New Zealand Medical Association
OECD	Organisation for Economic Co-operation and Development

PACE	Program for All Inclusive Care for the Elderly (USA)
PET	positron emission tomography
PHI	private health insurance
PHO	Primary Health Organisations (New Zealand)
PHS	Public Health Service (USA)
PPO	Preferred Provider Organization
RHA	Regional Health Authorities (New Zealand)
QALY	quality adjusted life years
QWB	Quality of Well Being
SARS	Severe Acute Respiratory Syndrome
SCHIP	State Children's Health Insurance Program (USA)
SES	socio-economic status
TCM	traditional Chinese medicine
UVB	ultraviolet B
WHO	World Health Organization

Chapter 1

Comparative Health Policy: An Introduction

Health care has always been a controversial policy issue, but over the last decades it has become a major area of concern in all developed nations. Ageing populations, the proliferation of new medical technologies, and heightened public expectations and demands, among other factors, have elevated health care to the top of the political agenda. Intensifying pressures on political leaders to meet rising public demands for expanded service conflict directly with the need to constrain health care costs and to manage scarce societal resources. Thus, despite major differences among countries as to how health care is funded, provided and governed, no government has been able to escape the controversy and problems accompanying health care in the 21st century, although some seem to be coping significantly better than others. Why is that so?

Given the universality of health care as a problem, one must question whether what governments do about it – the policies they adopt – makes a difference. And if it does matter, what approaches and strategies offer the most hope of resolving or managing the dilemmas of health care? Does simply spending more money improve the health of a population? If not, what does? This book addresses these questions by examining health care policy across a collection of countries that have taken divergent approaches and established a variety of mechanisms for covering the health needs of their populations. It also analyses trends within and across these countries in order to determine whether or not there is a convergence in health policy among developed nations, as argued by some observers.

Health care as public policy

The term 'policy' has a wide range of meanings in current English usage. Politicians and parties present their intended actions as policies to be pursued and they defend past actions as policies to be extended. Political commentators often talk about a government's housing policy, crime policy or drug policy in general terms, while others debate a specific government action. Policy, then, can be used to refer to general statements

1

of intention, past or present actions in particular areas, or a set of standing rules to guide actions. Although all organizations have policies, at least in the latter sense, the focus of this book is on the policies of government. 'Public policy' is defined here as a decision taken by the government or on behalf of it. Although usually viewed as an action, a decision not to act could also be a policy. All health policies then involve a fundamental choice by a government as to whether to take a specific action or to do nothing (see Howlett and Ramesh, 2003).

Only the government has the legitimate authority to make decisions that are binding and carried out in the name of the people as a whole. Other organizations, such as medical associations and nursing societies, often make decisions that affect many individuals as well as the health care system as a whole. While their decisions might indeed have a bearing on what the government ultimately does, they are not binding by force of law. Although this book includes a discussion of actions by private and voluntary organizations that impact on health care where fitting, the focus of attention is on governmental action or non-action.

It is useful here to distinguish between health policy, health care policy, and health care politics. Health policy is defined here as those courses of action proposed or taken by governments that affect the health of their populations. As we will see in Chapter 7, health policy overlaps with economic, social welfare, employment and housing policy, among other areas. Health policy, then, is a broad term encompassing any action that has health implications. On the other hand, 'health care' policy is a more narrow term that refers to those courses of action taken by governments that deal with the financing, provision or governance of health services. Although we use the term health policy throughout the book, given its prominence in Western countries, most attention is placed on health care policy. Only in Chapters 6 and 7 does this emphasis widen to health policy in the broader sense. Finally, 'health care politics' comprises the interactions of political actors and institutions in the health care arena in each country. It will become apparent in Chapter 2 that politics is a crucial dimension of all attempts to frame health policy; but politics is very country specific and it is impossible to cover systematically all the intricacies of health care politics of each country. Therefore, while we do not purport to analytically cover country-specific health politics, further readings that offer such detailed analyses are provided in the Guide to Further Reading.

It is also important to note that while health policy conceptually can be distinguished from other areas of public policy, in reality it is highly interrelated with a wide range of social and economic policies. In fact, there are health dimensions in virtually all policy areas including national defence and security, law enforcement and labour policy. It will become apparent in the following chapters that health and health policy cannot be understood in isolation from social welfare, unemployment, poverty, housing and immigration policies. In fact, it will be argued in Chapter 7 that the health of a population can be as dependent on these policies as it is on prescribed health care policy.

Public policy can be categorized as one of three basic types: regulatory, distributive and redistributive (see Lowi, 1966). Regulatory policies impose constraints or restrictions on the actions of groups or individuals: they provide rules of conduct with sanctions backed up by the authority of government. Distributive policies provide services or benefits to particular segments of society. Often distributive policies are based on the notion of public entitlements, which are normally defined as those goods and services that will benefit all individuals but which are unlikely to be produced by voluntary acts of individuals, in part because they lack the resources. In other words, societal-wide effort is needed to effectuate these goods for the population. Public entitlements are defined by each society differently depending upon how broadly government responsibility is interpreted. Much activity of all governments centres on this provision of public services and it is often accomplished without undue controversy until scarcity forces tradeoffs to be made as to what groups get what goods. Redistributive policies, in contrast, are controversial in principle because they represent deliberate efforts by governments to alter the distribution of income, wealth or property among groups in society. The reallocation of resources through progressive taxes and other mechanisms is present in all democracies, but it is the foundation of the welfare state.

Health care encompasses all three types of policy. The regulation of the health care sector through fee scales, licensing requirements, approval of drugs for use and other constraints on medical practice is extensive. Health care is one of the most regulated sectors in all developed countries in spite of their divergent types of health systems. The distributive policies of health care are most obvious under national health services, but occur to some degree in all countries through medical education programmes, the funding of health care research, the provision of public health services and health promotion activities. Finally, redistributive health care policies are based on the concepts of need and entitlement and encompass a range of efforts by government to shift resources from healthy to non-healthy citizens. They are usually based on a society's conception of equality. Mechanisms for such policies include the use of general revenues to provide services to those who lack resources, means-tested social insurance schemes for the poor, and programmes that redistribute societal resources from general revenues to the elderly or indigent.

Health policy is an amalgamation of these various types of policy as governments attempt to influence the provision of health care to their citizens. Of all areas of public policy, health care is one of the most controversial because it always entails conflicts, especially in the regulatory and redistributive modes. This is not surprising given the high emotional and economic stakes involved in any policy involving life, death and huge amounts of resources.

In addition to the potential life/death stakes inherent in any policies regarding health care, health policy is distinctive because the health care profession has by virtue of its specialized knowledge a privileged status of experts in shaping and constraining it. Because of the centrality of health professionals to the delivery of health care, a policy can only be successful if it has at least the tacit support of the medical community. Furthermore, since medical professionals largely define health need and the means necessary to meet it, any attempts by a government that are perceived as imposing constraints on the profession risk condemnation from these key stakeholders. The complexity of providing health care and the inherent uncertainty surrounding medicine further reinforces the power of the health care providers to influence the delivery of medical services and thus shape health care policy.

Complicating the policy context, in part because of the shift towards sophisticated curative care over the second half of the 20th century, is the fact that health care spending has become concentrated in a relatively small number of patients in acute care settings. Table 1.1 demonstrates the extent of this concentration in the USA, but similar patterns in systems as diverse as Canada and France have been documented. In 1996, the top 1 per cent of users accounted for 27 per cent of all health care expenditures; the top 5 per cent used 55 per cent; and the top 10 per

Table 1.1   *Distribution of health expenditures for the USA by magnitude of expenditures for selected years 1963–1996*

Percentage of population ranked by expenditures	1963	1970	1977	1980	1987	1996
Top 1%	17%	26%	27%	29%	28%	27%
Top 2%	–	35%	38%	39%	39%	38%
Top 5%	43%	50%	55%	55%	56%	55%
Top 10%	59%	66%	70%	70%	70%	69%
Top 30%	–	88%	90%	90%	90%	90%
Bottom 50%	5%	4%	3%	4%	3%	3%

Source: Adapted from Berk and Monheit (2001).

cent used 69 per cent. In contrast, only 3 per cent of payments go to those patients in the bottom half of the population. Those in the bottom 50 per cent incurred an average annual expenditure of $122 in medical costs in 1996 compared with an average expenditure of $56,459 for those in the top 1 per cent! Thus, the majority of citizens are responsible collectively for a very small proportion of health care spending. Moreover, there has been a 'remarkable stability in this concentration pattern over the last three decades' (Berk and Monheit, 2001: 12).

It is possible, of course, that these figures reflect the fact that while a few people become seriously ill each year and use significant resources, they are replaced by others in following years. Anecdotal evidence from emergency rooms, however, reveals that a small number of repeat patients consume substantial resources over a longer term. Moreover, a systematic analysis of high users by Monheit (2003) found that a sizable majority of high users exhibit persistently high expenditures from one year to the next. Critically, the heaviest users of health care come predominantly from two groups: the elderly and those persons who engage in high risk behaviour, thus causing or contributing to their own ill health. This concentration of need for health care, therefore, necessitates the redistribution of significant resources from young to old and from those who live healthy lives to those who do not and raises questions of equity and fairness in times of scarce resources (see Chapter 4).

Many of the most challenging dilemmas in democracies surface as governments struggle to find the proper mixture of these policy types in the light of conflicting interests. Because of the heavy emphasis on rights to health care in many countries, the distinction between negative and positive rights is important (see Heywood, 2002). Negative rights are those rights which impose obligations on governments and other citizens to refrain from interfering with the rights bearer. They relate to the freedom to be left alone to use one's resources as one sees fit. Under negative rights, each person has a sphere of autonomy that others cannot violate; but no one is further obliged to take positive action to provide that person with the resources necessary to exercise that right. The only claim on others is a freedom from intrusion. Health care as a negative right would allow patients with adequate personal resources to maximize their use of health care. Negative rights are always in conflict with redistributive social welfare policies which deprive individuals of the free use of their resources.

In contrast, positive rights impose obligations on others (society?) to provide those goods and services necessary for each individual to exercise her or his rights. Although the level of positive rights is generally ill defined, this additional dimension requires the presence of institutions that guarantee a certain level of material well-being, through governmental redistribution of resources where necessary. Positive rights imply a freedom from deprivation, the entitlement to at least a decent level of human existence. The welfare state is based to a large extent on this more expansive notion of positive rights. One question of health policy is whether all citizens have a positive right to health care and, if so, what it should entail. How far does a right to the freedom from ill health go in requiring societal provision of health care resources to all citizens? What limits can justifiably be set on these entitlements to health care? For instance, could treatment be denied to an individual who causes his own ill health and who refuses to change his self-destructive behaviour despite repeated warnings?

Comparative health policy

Comparative policy analysis has become a growth industry. Advances in information technology have expanded the availability and dissemination of data across countries, while at the same time many policy fields have become increasingly internationally oriented. The interest in information about policies in other countries has also been fostered by the perception of shared policy challenges arising from economic and welfare state crises. Deleon and Resnick-Terry (1999) refer to this development as the 'comparative renaissance'. The comparative perspective is now widely used in both the academic field of public policy analysis and in more applied policy studies (see, e.g., Castles, 1999). Parallel to discussions about the insights generated by comparative analyses is a debate about the methodologies of cross-country comparison (for comparative politics, see, e.g., Peters, 1998; for comparative social policy, see, e.g., Clasen, 1999; Hantrais and Mangen, 1996).

This book places health policy in a comparative context in order to demonstrate the similarities and differences in approach among various countries as they attempt to resolve health care problems. Although it can be dangerous to transfer policies that work in one country to another, comparative public policy is useful in expanding policy options and demonstrating the experiences of a wide range of applications. Øvretveit argues that travel and information systems are making it both easier and more necessary to understand cultural and national differences. Moreover, he argues that comparative health research has a role in building relations among different communities 'by creating knowledge that helps people understand their differences and similarities' and that 'health managers can improve their services by sensitively adapting ideas that have worked elsewhere' (1998: 15). Harrop agrees that 'by examining policies comparatively, we can discover how countries vary in the policies they adopt, gain insight into why these differences exist, and identify some of the conditions under which policies succeed or fail'

(1992: 3). Comparative public policy is, therefore, a source of generalizations about public policy, that, in turn, are valuable for understanding policy in any particular country.

In addition, comparative policy analysis can demonstrate that factors viewed as overriding in one country, such as the attitudes of the medical profession or the uniqueness of its liberal tradition, might actually produce contrasting outcomes in other countries. According to Immergut, the 'comparative perspective shows that some factors are neither as unique nor as critical as they appear, whereas others stand out as truly significant' (1992: 9). Ham (1997a) adds that an examination of international experience can illuminate both the difficulties faced by and the wide range of strategies available to policy makers. It can also elucidate the institutional context and the importance of the process by which decisions are made (Klein and Williams, 2000). Comparative studies, then, give us cross-cultural insights as to what works or does not work under an array of institutional and value contexts. Given the complexity of health care and the plethora of potential health care systems, only comparative studies can generate the evidence necessary to consider the full range of policy options.

Against a background of common policy problems, many comparative studies highlight the significance of policy convergence for understanding how health care policies are being shaped (cf. Harrison *et al.*, 2002; Wessen, 1999). Health policy convergence suggests that there are global trends in the formation of health policies, and that the objectives and activities of national health systems are becoming more alike. Based on an examination of trends across industrialized democracies, Chernichovsky (1995: 340) contends that despite the diversity of health care systems, health system reforms have led to the emergence of a 'universal outline or paradigm' for health care financing, organization and management that cuts across ideological (private versus public) lines and across conceptual (market versus centrally planned) frameworks. Other authors point to medical knowledge and technology as drivers of health policy convergence. Field (1999), for example, suggests that the means of medical production are becoming universal and that the social organization of medical work is becoming strikingly similar across systems, leading to health systems sharing more common elements. Similarly, Gibson and Means (2000) argue that restructuring has led to convergence of the long-term care policies of Australia and the UK, despite quite dissimilar goals and strategic emphases. Harrison *et al.* (2002) also found a policy convergence in approaches regarding the management of medical care in the US and the UK during the 1990s.

The argument underlying convergence theory is that as countries industrialize they tend to converge towards the same policy mix (Bennett, 1991). The convergence thesis suggests that health policy across disparate country environments has a tendency to become similar over time as they develop economically. Moreover, since all countries face comparable dynamics of demographic changes and the proliferation of expensive technologies (discussed later), the pressures towards convergence are extenuated. Convergence is further bolstered by globalization and by the development of an international health forum through the Internet where people anywhere can shop around for different kinds of comparison (Stone, 1999). In addition, explicit efforts by international organizations such as the OECD, WHO and the EU help prepare the foundations for what Harrison *et al.* (2002) in their study of evidence-based medicine refer to as 'ideational convergence'. For instance, the World Trade Organization's General Agreement on Trade in Services (GATS) could lead to homogeny of health services such as health insurance, hospital services, telemedicine and the acquisition of medical treatment abroad. These common driving forces, then, suggest a convergence in relation to the framing of policy problems and the intellectual underpinnings of policy solutions.

There is, however, growing criticism of initiatives such as GATS that are viewed by some as forcing convergence at the expense of country and culturally specific health policy. Critics argue that GATS requires the *privatization* of health services, prevents governments from regulating the health sectors, and hinders a government's ability to determine the shape of its domestic health systems in a democratic way. Although Belsky *et al.* (2004: 138) conclude there is 'little clear evidence of such adverse consequences', it is too early to tell what if any impact GATS and similar EU initiatives will have. While GATS at present does not seem to be significantly affecting health care services, Sexton (2001) contends that if current proposals are implemented, GATS could be used to overturn almost any legislation governing health services. Although the controversy surrounding GATS and its imposition on national autonomy and democratic legitimacy are bound to escalate, it is most likely that such issues concerning autonomy will be concentrated in low and middle income countries which are most vulnerable to outside pressures to adopt models that may not be responsive to the health needs of their populations.

Convergence is intuitively attractive because similar problems potentially make for similar solutions, and under these circumstances it becomes more likely that health policies will converge. This assumption is also supported by the fact that ultimately there are only a limited number of policy instruments available to address a certain policy problem, thus suggesting that function rather than politics informed by historical legacy or culture shapes health policies. As Gibson and Means (2000) argue, policy levers are limited and there are simply relatively few 'good ideas' around to solve a specific problem. Policy convergence is also encouraged by the fact that all health systems must fulfil similar types of functions, for example raising public funds to pay for medical care and organizing the delivery of these services. Without doubt, equity/access, quality and cost containment are the common goals of health policies across vastly different health systems and countries. Only the relative importance that individual countries attach to each goal differs (see Chapter 4).

In contrast, critics of convergence theories argue that the proponents oversimplify the process of development and underestimate significant divergence across countries (Howlett and Ramesh, 2003). Convergence, they argue, downplays the importance of country-specific factors other than economic development, and most studies that find evidence of convergence do not find it applicable across the board, thus allowing for divergence in other areas. Furthermore, most studies that have found evidence of convergence have failed to demonstrate that it is applicable across all domains, thus allowing for significant divergence in other areas (Blank and Burau, 2006). Therefore, while one can selectively find evidence of convergence, it is by no means certain, inclusive or consistent and has not necessarily translated into similar health policies or policy directions across countries.

Although convergence of health systems has become a focus of scholarly debate, the underlying conceptual framework of the studies of health policy convergence are often vague, relying on diffuse variations of 'soft determinism' (Field, 1999), which assume that comparable conditions produce comparable problems which result in comparable policies (cf. Jacobs, 1998; Saltman, 1997; for a similar argument in relation to public management reform, see Pollitt, 2002). In other cases, policy convergence is often the by-product of studies which are designed to explain policy differences across countries (cf. Freeman, 2000; Ham, 1997b). Such studies frequently build on a most similar case design using varieties of institutionalism and as such are not always equipped for analysing policy convergence in its own right. Irrespective of where they put the emphasis, cross-country comparative studies of health policy largely agree on the coexistence of policy divergence and convergence (cf. Field, 1999; Lian, 2003; Mechanic, 1999; Rico *et al.*, 2003). However, the conceptual fuzziness of health policy convergence makes it difficult to capture this coexistence in a systematic way.

The concept of convergence is important for health policy because if it is viewed as inevitable that there will be accompanying pressures on policy makers to converge in areas that might be counterproductive to the unique needs of their particular countries. In other words, there is a danger that a belief in policy convergence becomes a self-fulfilling prophesy, possibly to the detriment of health care programmes in many countries. Convergence theories also beg the question of convergence to what: privatized health care, national health services, or social insurance?

Although this book is not designed to test the convergence theory directly, its current prominence in the literature dictates that where appropriate its assumptions be addressed later (especially Chapter 4) and that its explanatory power across these countries be explored more fully.

Classifications of health care systems

At its base, health policy is, of course, a political matter. The most obvious dimension of the political context comprises the formal institutions that have been created for making public policy decisions. The institutional setting in which policy making takes place is termed the policy arena, which includes not only the formal political institutions such as legislatures, executives and courts but also regulatory agencies, semipublic bodies and specialized committees and commissions. These institutions define the distribution of power and the relationships among the political players by setting the rules of the game regarding access and interaction within arenas. As such they give distinct advantages or disadvantages to various groups in society. Equally important to understanding public policy, then, are the informal practices and structures that have evolved within a particular formal institutional framework. These traditions and rules of the game define a different political logic in each country. They are also critical to the environment within which interest groups, political parties, bureaucrats and individual politicians vie for influence over policy.

Together these formal and informal political institutions shape how politics is conducted and create a strategic context for political conflict within the arena. 'Political factors help to determine whether a problem is defined as a public policy that requires action, they shape the way in which the problem is defined, and they intervene in the resolution of that problem' (Immergut, 1992: 10). Although institutional variables are not the only ones to matter, variation in institutional conditions across countries yields different opportunities for the actors involved in policy making in each country (Timmermans, 2001). The health system represents a set of sector-specific institutions. However, while health politics is big business for states, it remains characterized by strong private-interest government by medical professionals.

Although no two political systems are identical, many share characteristics that allow us to develop *typologies* or ideal models. The use of typologies is central to the comparative turn in policy analysis and they have been used to conceptualize the (institutional) context in which policies are embedded. Prominent examples include: Castles' (1999) notion of 'families of nations', which describes different clusters of cultural, historical and geographical features of nations; Esping-Andersen's

(1990) welfare state regimes, which identify distinct welfare state logics; and Lijphart's (1999) and Blondel's (1990) typologies of democratic and state regimes. Cross-country comparison generates an abundance of information, and ordering this information through typologies is central to using comparison to build, review and revise explanations about policy emergence, policy making and policy cycles.

Despite widespread variation among health care systems, at root they represent variants or combinations of a limited number of types. As with political systems, the comparative analysis of health policy often uses typologies of health systems to help capture the institutional context of health care and contribute to explaining health policies across different countries. While typologies can be valuable in simplifying a multifaceted set of cross-cutting dimensions, one must be cautious when interpreting them because they do represent ideal types of specific macro-institutional characteristics. As will be demonstrated in this book, the real world of health care systems is considerably more complicated.

Because of their importance in the literature, several typologies that have been used to classify health care systems are summarized here. The initial typology developed by the OECD (see Figure 1.1) is a descriptive categorization of how health care is organized in different countries and reflects its specific origins in applied policy analysis. At one extreme is the potential for a completely free market system with no government involvement, while at the other extreme is a tax-supported government monopoly of provision and funding of all health care services. Though in reality neither of these extremes exists and public involvement in the funding and provider roles may be at variance, along this continuum are three core types of health care systems that operate across all countries.

As illustrated in Figure 1.1, the *private insurance* (or consumer sovereignty) *model* is that with the least state involvement in the direct funding or provision of health care services. This type is characterized by the purchase of private health insurance financed by employers and/or individual contributions that are risk oriented. This system is also largely based on private ownership of health care providers and the factors of production, although it might include a publicly funded safety net for the most vulnerable groups such as the poor, the elderly or the young. The

Figure 1.1   *Types of health care system by provision and funding*

Source: OECD (1987: 24).

basic assumption of this approach is that the funding and provision of health care is best left to market forces.

The second basic type of health system as to state involvement is the *social insurance* (or Bismarck) *model*. Although there is significant variation as to organization, this type is based on a concept of social solidarity and characterized in effect (though not always by design) by a universal coverage health insurance generally within a framework of social security. As a rule, this compulsory health insurance is funded by a combination of employer and individual contributions through non-profit insurance funds or societies, often regulated and subsidized by the state. The provision of services tends to be private, often on a fee-for-service basis, although some public ownership of the factors of production and delivery is likely.

The third type is the *national health service* (or Beveridge) *model*. This model is characterized by universal coverage funded out of general taxation. Although this model is most identified with the UK, New Zealand created the first national health service in its 1938 Social Security Act which promised all citizens open-ended access to all the health care services they needed free at the point of use. The provision of health care services under this model is fully administered by the state, which either owns or controls the factors of production and delivery.

Freeman (2000) observes that the OECD typology emerged from a search for better solutions to common problems, thus corresponding to a focus on the internal workings of health care rather than on its political and social embeddedness. However, this situation changed with the wide use of this basic typology in the comparative analysis of health policy (see, e.g., Freeman, 2000; Raffel, 1997; Scott, 2001; Wall, 1996). Together with the mounting interest in neo-institutionalism, the typology has been a facilitator for critical analyses of the health system as the institutional framework in which health policies are embedded and how the institutions of health care (among others) shape health policies (and politics). Scott (2001), for example, uses the typology as part of her framework to analyse public and private roles and interfaces in health care across different countries while Ham (1997b) focuses more explicitly on health reform.

However, these analyses also have in common their consideration of other aspects of the institutional context of health care in addition to the typology of health systems. Freeman (2000), for example, explicitly includes in his analysis the mechanisms by which health care is coordinated (health care governance). This inclusion clearly demonstrates that applying the typology of health systems to a wider range of cases has also led to its adaptation. As Collier and Levitsky (1997; also Collier and Mahon, 1993) note, such a process is characterized by a tension between increasing analytical differentiation in order to capture the diverse forms of the phenomenon at hand, while avoiding the pitfalls of conceptual stretching and applying the concept to cases that do not fit. The literature on comparative health policy has addressed this tension by adding, although more or less explicitly, new attributes to the definition of the health system.

An overlapping scheme used to categorize health care systems is based on the dimension of the method and source of financing. At one extreme are those systems fully dependent on private sources of funding, and at the other are those fully funded by public sources. Based on this criterion there are four main types of funding:

- direct tax/general revenues
- social or state insurance
- private insurance
- direct payment by users.

Within each type, however, there are many potential variants. For instance the direct tax might be levied by the central government, by sub-units such as states or provinces, or by a combination of governments. Similarly, the social insurance system might be based on a single national scheme or on multiple insurance schemes more or less rigidly regulated or controlled by the government. Furthermore, there is a wide array of possible combinations both of basic types and their variants that are used often within a single health care system, such as in the USA where only the elderly have social insurance. According to Appleby, 'all health-care systems are pluralistic with respect to financing (and organisation) with tendencies to one method rather than another' (1992: 10).

In addition to the wide variety of combinations of these funding methods in each country, different countries apply them in different ways. Some, such as the USA (and, to a much lesser extent, Australia), use general taxation for particular groups such as the poor and elderly, but depend on private insurance or direct payments for the remainder of the population. Other countries distinguish between specific forms of health care. For instance, New Zealand funds hospital care through general taxation but until recently relied heavily on direct user payment for most primary care, except for specified categories of patients such as children whose care was subsidized. When examining health care policy, then, it is critical to examine not only how health care is financed based on these types, but also under what circumstances it is targeted from particular sources.

A similar classification of health systems, based on a distinction among institutions related to the governance of consumption, provision and production is offered by Moran (1999, 2000) who constructs four different types of health care states, three of which are especially relevant here. In entrenched *command and control* health care states, the governance of consumption consists of extensive public access based on citizenship and extensive control of resource allocation through administrative mechanisms. In contrast, in the *corporatist* health care state, funding through social insurance contributions makes for de facto public access to health care and gives public law bodies (such as statutory, non-profit insurance funds) an important role. This limits the public control over health care costs. The role of providers is even greater in the *supply* health care state, where funding through private insurance limits public access to health care as well as the public control of costs.

Another way of categorizing countries is to rank them on a single variable considered appropriate for the comparisons being made. For instance, one simple measure of state involvement that is often used to compare countries is the extent to which health care is publicly funded. Table 1.2 shows a country ranking on that criterion, ranging from over 85 per cent in Sweden and the UK to just over 30 per cent in Singapore (see also Box 1.1). It should be noted that this ranking can tell us nothing about whether one system is better or worse than another; it simply illustrates how the countries array themselves on this dimension. Another use of this data is to trace changes, both for particular countries and collective patterns, and to compare the comparative rankings over time.

It must be noted that while typologies are helpful for teaching purposes because they allow us to simplify a complex reality and focus on the most important aspects, they must always be viewed as a heuristic

Table 1.2   *Public funding as a percentage of health expenditures, 1970–2003, ranked by 2003*

	1970	1980	1990	1998	2003	% change
UK	87.0	89.4	83.6	80.4	85.4	−6.4
Sweden	86.0	92.5	89.9	85.8	85.4	−0.2
Japan	69.8	71.3	77.6	80.8	81.5	+11.7
New Zealand	80.3	88.0	82.4	77.0	78.3	−2.0
France	75.5	80.1	76.6	76.0	78.3	+2.8
Germany	72.8	78.7	76.2	78.6	78.2	+6.0
Italy	86.9	80.5	79.3	71.6	75.1	−11.8
Australia	62.3	63.0	67.1	67.4	67.5	+5.2
Netherlands	61.0	69.4	67.1	64.1	63.0	+2.0
USA	36.4	41.3	39.7	44.3	44.6	+8.2
Singapore	70.1	68.0	n/a	26.0	31.6	−38.5

Sources: Data from OECD (2006), except Singapore – Singapore Ministry of Health (2006).

Box 1.1   The Singapore system: low in public funding, high on individual responsibility

Of all the systems discussed here, Singapore is most unusual as reflected in its low level of public funding. The main reason that Singapore registers low public funding is because in 1984 it instituted a compulsory savings scheme that shifted primary health financing responsibility from the state to individuals (Lim, 2004). Funds are then deposited in an individual savings account in each contributor's name which can then be drawn on to pay for health insurance or hospital expenses incurred by that person or his immediate family. While the scheme is compulsory in the form of a tax on income, because each account is private it is considered to be privately financed. This health care system is based on a unique interpretation of individual responsibility and is designed to provide incentives to reduce consumption and offer protection against 'free-rider' abuses while guaranteeing affordable basic health care through government subsidies. Individuals can also choose the level of subsidy they wish to receive in public hospitals – if they opt for a fancy ward the subsidy is low or non-existent whereas if they go for a less fancy ward the subsidy is higher. The key principle is that patients are expected to pay part of the cost of medical services that they use, and pay more when they demand a higher level of service.

Sources: Singapore Ministry of Health (2002b) and Ham (2001).

tool, not a full representation of reality. Even in those cases where the health system of a country is dominated by one of the types identified in these models, traces of many variations are identifiable. Most countries reflect mixes of characteristics in finance, provision and governance across the various types and there is often variation across time and space within a single country. The specific configuration of any health care system depends on a multitude of factors including the political system, the cultural framework, the demographic context, the distinctive historical background, specific events and social structures inherent to that country (see Chapter 2). Societal goals and priorities develop over time and shape all social institutions and values, which themselves are fluid and changeable.

Countries selected for study

In order to provide a constructive cross-country analysis of health policy, we have selected nine countries for primary coverage in this book (with the addition of examples from France and Italy, where appropriate, for

Britain	Germany	United States
New Zealand	Japan	(Australia)
Sweden	Netherlands	
	(Singapore)	

| ――――――――――――――――――――――――――――――――――― |

| **National Health** | **Social Insurance** | **Private Insurance** |

Figure 1.2   *Types of health care systems*

illustrative purposes). The core countries were selected to give the reader systematic exposure to the full range of health systems (see Figure 1.2). Although all three have moved away from this pure model in varying degrees, Britain,* Sweden and New Zealand are examples of the national health service model. Likewise, Germany, Japan and the Netherlands are often viewed as examples of the social insurance type, while Singapore, with its compulsory Medisave system, is a variation on that theme, but with a heavy private component. Finally, the private insurance type is most clearly represented by the USA and (until recently) by Australia, although many systems contain some elements of the private market-place. Additionally, these countries represent a wide spectrum of political, cultural and economic environments for illustrating the vagaries of health care.

Our country selection includes some, such as Germany, Sweden, the UK and the USA, that are frequently included in comparative policy studies, and others, such as Australia, the Netherlands and New Zealand that are less often included. Also covered in the analysis here are Japan and Singapore, which offer valuable insights into health care policy that are regularly overlooked in the largely US/European-based studies. Individually, each of the countries has a unique contribution to make to the study of health policy. In combination, they serve as a good sample upon which to analyse the dynamics of health care policy in the 21st century.

Obviously, even the relatively large number of countries covered here does not exhaust the vast array of variation in health care systems found across the world. All of these countries are developed countries with Western-type medical systems. Even Japan and Singapore, the two non-Western countries, have highly sophisticated medical systems and affluent

---

* In the following, when we refer to Britain or the UK we often specifically focus on the organization and policies of health care as they exist in England. Following political devolution in the late 1990s the health systems in the four countries of the UK have developed in different ways (for an overview, see Baggott, 2004).

populations with similar levels of expectations and demands. Excluded from this analysis are cases from Africa, Asia, the Middle East and Eastern Europe which collectively represent over 5 billion people. Although inclusion of a selection of these countries would be illuminating, it would also be unwieldy and complicate the level of analysis. One of the drawbacks in trying to cover even nine countries is that it is not possible to provide a thorough analysis of any one of their health care systems. As regards specific countries, then, the objective of this book is to be an introduction, not a comprehensive analysis, and to provide a context within which to study individual countries. To this end, readers with an interest in a particular country or countries should make use of the Guide to Further Reading at the end of this book which should provide a valuable basis for building on the foundational knowledge offered in this book. In addition, the Guide to Websites provides links to the most recent information and data on these countries.

Types of health care

Another distinction that is crucial in understanding health policy relates to the types of health care. Table 1.3 describes three categories that largely define the range of activities normally incorporated under health care. Although the terms used to define these categories vary, *primary care*, *curative medicine* and *chronic care* are used here. Primary care normally encompasses visits to general practitioners (GPs), ambulatory care and health education efforts, and includes a strong health promotion/disease prevention element discussed in Chapter 7. In contrast, curative medicine, which represents the core of modern health care discussed in Chapters 3 to 5, centres on acute care in hospitals and relies on specialists and technologies to restore health to those acutely ill. Finally, as illustrated in Chapter 6, chronic care constitutes the wide range of services provided to people in long-term residential and hospice

Table 1.3   *Categories of health care*

Primary care	Curative medicine	Chronic care
General practitioners	Acute/hospital care	Long-term facilities
Well-patient physicals	Outpatient clinics	Nursing home
Ambulatory care	Technology based	Hospice
Health promotion	Specialists	Respite care
Education/prevention	Intensive care	Home care

facilities, home care and so forth, many of which have significant social as well as medical dimensions.

Although the health policy of any country will comprise a mixture of these types, there is considerable variation in the weight given to each dimension depending on the assumptions and goals of the policies pursued. As illustrated by the scope of coverage in this book, health care today is dominated by curative medicine. When one thinks about health care, hospitals and highly trained specialists, it is the latest technologies that often come to mind. As noted below in the discussion of the expansion of biomedical technology, health care is often equated with medicine despite evidence that such an unbalanced approach has limits. Even the term 'curative' is misleading because in many cases the patient is not cured, but is rather rescued or maintained, often in a state of health that is lower than it was before the person became ill. Instead of 'curing' the person, these interventions support or preserve a particular level of personal health by creating a continued dependence on further medical treatment or medications.

Prior to World War II, health care was normally limited to performing 'public health' and primary care functions, in part because its curative capacities were limited and frequently ineffective. Hospitals were primarily designed to protect the public health, often by quarantining patients rather than treating them individually, and largely served only persons who could not afford a private physician. Those with private resources would avoid hospitals like the plague because often plagues were there. Families were the primary long-term care givers and most people died at home rather than in the intensive care wards of high-tech hospitals.

During the 1950s and 1960s, the emphasis on health care shifted perceptibly towards curative medicine even in health care systems in countries such as the UK, Japan and New Zealand which had strong roots in primary care and prevention. Although other countries have not bought into curative medicine to the same degree as the USA, as will be evident in the chapters that follow, there are strong pressures for aggressive medical interventions in acute care settings. The increased demands of the public for higher levels of technological medicine, as mentioned earlier, produced indelible alterations in the health care community, most clearly manifested in the growth of medical specialities at the expense of primary care physicians and, especially, public health workers. As a result, the modern medical profession has developed primarily around the search for finding cures to disease rather than promoting health, preventing disease and protecting the public health. The growth of high-tech medical centres, the expectation of ever more sophisticated diagnostic capacity and the expansion of dramatic life-saving procedures has changed the nature of medical care.

Growing problems in health policy

Despite variation in health care across countries, there are several factors endemic to all developed nations that make health policy ever more problematic. In the wake of falling national incomes and increasingly scarce resources for social spending, all countries, no matter how much they vary politically or socially, face growing difficulty in the financing and delivery of health care. Table 1.4 clearly demonstrates that while countries differ considerably as to the percentage of their gross domestic product (GDP) they devote to health care, in virtually all cases it has increased appreciably over the last three decades. This means that health care costs are increasing at rates exceeding that of economic growth, a pattern that is not sustainable in the long run.

The increase in health care costs is not by itself a problem. As Duff (2001) points out, an expansion of spending on other goods is welcomed as contributing to economic well-being; why, then, should increased consumption on health care be a problem? Furthermore, every country spends 100 per cent of its GDP on something, so if countries spend considerably more on health care that is their choice. The main reason we should care about growing health care expenditure is that the extra spending might not be providing as much value as if those funds were used for education, housing, environmental protection or other private or public consumption or investment (Fuchs, 2005: 77). In economic terms, the 'opportunity costs' might be too high when excessive money goes to health care and is thus diverted from more effective spending

Table 1.4   *Health expenditure as a percentage of GDP, 1970–2003*

	1970	1980	1990	1998	2003	% change
Australia	5.7	6.8	7.5	8.3	9.2	3.5
France	5.3	7.0	8.4	9.1	10.4	5.1
Germany	6.2	8.7	8.5	10.4	10.9	4.7
Italy	5.1	7.0	7.7	8.2	8.4	3.3
Japan	4.5	6.5	6.1	7.4	7.9	3.5
Netherlands	7.2	8.0	8.5	8.7	9.3	2.1
New Zealand	5.1	5.9	6.9	7.8	8.0	2.9
Singapore	n/a	n/a	2.8	2.9	3.8	1.0
Sweden	6.8	9.0	8.3	8.3	9.3	2.5
UK	4.5	5.6	6.0	6.9	7.9	3.4
USA	7.0	8.8	11.9	13.1	15.2	8.2

Sources: Data from OECD (2006) and Singapore Ministry of Health (2001 and 2006).

areas. Another reason for this concern over heightened spending on medical care centres on the critical role of the state in funding it because governmental spending does not respond to normal market forces. A final cause for deep concern is that ageing populations, rapid advances in medical technology, and expanded public expectations and demands promise to exacerbate the problems. Recent reform efforts in virtually all countries are largely a reaction to these major forces and although there is variation by degree across countries, these trends represent ominous signs for the funding and provision of health care in the coming decades.

Ageing populations

As indicated in Table 1.5, demographic projections show that most countries will experience substantial ageing of their populations over the next 30 years. Although the ageing process is taking place earlier and more rapidly in some countries, all will experience it. The primary cause of the ageing of Western societies is the precipitous decline in fertility rates since the 1970s that has increased the proportion of elderly. This trend is exaggerated because the sharp upturn in birth rates after World War II produced a bloated age cohort in the baby boom generation, the first wave of which is now reaching retirement age. Even if life expectancy is unaltered, this wave of ageing baby boomers, along with declining fertility rates, guarantees an increasing proportion of the elderly.

The second factor contributing to the ageing of populations is increased life expectancy. In the years between 1950 and 1980, life

Table 1.5   *Percentage of population aged 65 and over*

	1960	1980	1990	2000	2020	2030	2040
Australia	8.5	9.6	11.1	12.2	15.4	18.2	19.7
France	11.6	13.9	14.1	15.9	19.5	21.8	22.7
Germany	10.8	15.5	15.3	16.8	21.7	25.8	27.6
Italy	10.5	13.2	14.9	17.6	19.4	21.9	24.2
Japan	5.7	9.1	12.1	16.7	20.9	21.0	22.7
Netherlands	9.0	11.5	12.8	13.6	18.9	23.0	24.8
New Zealand	8.7	9.7	11.1	11.7	15.3	19.4	21.9
Singapore	n/a	4.9	6.0	7.0	18.5	19.0	22.0
Sweden	11.8	16.3	17.8	17.8	20.8	21.7	22.5
UK	11.7	15.0	15.7	15.7	16.3	19.2	20.4
US	9.2	11.2	12.4	12.3	16.2	19.5	19.8

Sources: Data from OECD (1988) for all but Singapore (Singapore Ministry of Health, 2001).

Box 1.2   A warning: 'profound consequences' as the EU grows older

EU-wide, the share of the elderly in the total population is expected to rise from 21% now to around 34% by 2050. Those 80+ are predicted to rise from 4% of today's population to some 10%. By 2050, 37 million people are expected to be octogenarians+. Eurostat says these big rises in the elderly will have 'profound consequences' for social protection systems – particularly pensions, which are funded mostly by workers and employers. Health spending is also likely to 'increase significantly' (Eurostat News Release, 29 July 1999).

---

expectancy at birth increased by 8.5 years for females and 6.0 years for males. These significant gains reflect improved social factors, health habits and the new capacities of medicine to reduce infant mortality and extend the life span. It is important to note that in the past gains in life expectancy have been underestimated, meaning that there could be even more significant increases in average life span in the coming decades. Moreover, substantial differences in average life expectancy in Organisation for Economic Co-operation and Development (OECD) countries at present strongly suggest that further gains could be made in a number of countries. Ironically, these health-improving steps, together with continued low fertility rates, could exacerbate population ageing and complicate funding problems (Box 1.2).

These ageing trends are accompanied by two critical changes in the population structure. First, within the overall trends towards older populations is the ageing of these elderly populations themselves. At present the most rapidly growing segment of the elderly population is the cohort aged 80 and over. As illustrated in Table 1.6, this proportion is expected to climb to over 30 per cent in most countries, and over 40 per cent in Japan, by 2040. These increases are particularly significant for health policy because those over 80 are by far the heaviest users of health care. The second trend within a trend relates to the sex composition of the elderly population. As a result of their longer life expectancy, women outnumber men significantly in the elderly age cohorts. Furthermore, the sex imbalance increases with age, meaning that as the very elderly cohort expands, the proportion of elderly women will grow. Even though this imbalance is projected to narrow over time, especially at the younger end of the elderly age group, women will continue to constitute a substantial majority of the elderly, particularly among the most elderly. As with the other trends, this has considerable impact on health care needs of the population.

Table 1.6   *Share of very old persons (80+) among the elderly,*
1960–2040

	1960	2000	2040
Australia	14.3	23.6	31.8
France	17.2	23.3	34.6
Germany	n/a	22.3	29.9
Italy	14.6	22.2	30.6
Japan	12.6	22.0	41.1
Netherlands	15.2	23.5	30.0
New Zealand	17.1	23.8	30.5
Sweden	15.9	29.0	31.5
UK	16.4	25.4	29.1
US	15.2	26.4	33.3

Source: Data from OECD (2005).

What does it matter for health care if the populations age? It matters because at present a disproportionate share of health resources go to the elderly, particularly those over 80. As illustrated in Table 1.7, in most countries those over 65 account for at least double the expenditures their size alone would indicate, and in most cases at least triple. In the extreme case of the USA the 12.4 per cent of the population aged 65 and older consumed nearly 48.8 per cent of total health care expenditure in 2000. How can governments possibly continue this spending pattern as the proportion of the elderly swells? Although improvements in the health conditions of the elderly might serve to delay the highest expenditure which occurs near the end of life for most people, cumulatively ageing populations demand ever greater expenditures.

As the projections in Table 1.7 illustrate, the estimated increases in health spending on the elderly are staggering in some countries, especially Sweden and the USA. Although there is variation by country, the trend towards a heightened concentration of health care resources in the elderly is universal with most countries registering over 50 per cent by 2040. The ageing population not only increases health care spending and shifts it towards the elderly, but it also has considerable potential impact on the type of health care provided. Obviously, the growing number of old people will generate a higher demand for geriatric care and thus a proportionate increase in geriatric facilities and personnel and long-term care (see Chapter 6).

Several additional aspects of the ageing of populations are critical to

Table 1.7   *Percentage of health expenditures and persons aged 65 or more, 2003 and estimated 2020 and 2040*

	% 65+	% Total expenditure	Projections 2020	Projections 2040
Australia	12.8	40.2	46.4	56.0
France	16.3	30.0	35.8	41.1
Germany	18.6	34.1	40.0	49.4
Italy	18.2	34.3	38.9	46.8
Japan	19.0	42.4	52.5	55.9
Netherlands	13.8	41.2	49.6	60.1
New Zealand	11.9	42.1	n/a	n/a
Sweden	17.2	54.2	59.6	63.3
UK	16.0	43.0	45.6	54.1
USA	12.4	48.8	56.9	62.9

Source: Data from OECD (2006).

an understanding of the full range of implications for health policy. Although attention here has focused on the increased expenditures generated by the growing proportion of the elderly, there is also the issue that as populations age the size of the productive sector decreases, thus raising concern over the capacity of society to support the new demands. The ability of any country to finance increased costs associated with the ageing population depends upon the relative size of the productive population (usually measured by dependency ratios of some type), as well as unemployment rates and productivity. As the workforce and the tax base is reduced through ageing and continued low levels of fertility, the pressures on the remaining working age population will intensify.

Finally, just at the time where there is an increased need for long-term care-giving, social changes have undermined traditional, largely informal care mechanisms for the elderly. The decline in the extended family, the increased mobility and the trends towards more working women and fewer children have in many countries reduced the willingness and ability of families to care for the elderly. Although women continue to provide significant levels of long-term care for family members, coverage is saturated and as a proportion will decrease (see Chapter 6 for details). As a result, the demands for formal long-term care services will intensify and such services will depend increasingly on public funds. Those countries without adequate planning and funding infrastructures for long-term care are most vulnerable to severe problems.

Medical technology and health policy

Another force impacting on all health systems is the rapid expansion of medical technology. Simply put, there are a lot more technologies available today for intervention – and many of these new techniques are very costly on a per-case basis. Vast improvements in surgical procedures, tissue matching and immuno-suppressant drugs are making repair and replacement of organs routine. Likewise, innovations in diagnostic machinery continue to push the boundaries. Computerized axial tomography (CAT) scanners and magnetic resonance imaging (MRI) have been quickly followed by positron emission tomography (PET) and other specialized diagnostic machines – but at high cost. Moreover, human genetic technology, stem cell research and pharmacology dramatically promise an expanding array of costly diagnostic and therapeutic applications that will increase both the range of intervention options and the pressures on health care systems to deliver. These innovations can enhance care but they tend to cost considerably more than older forms of treatment.

This proliferation of new medical technologies and pharmaceuticals over the past several decades has been one of the most important drivers of health care spending growth, if not the most important (Bodenheimer, 2005). According to one study, new medical technologies account for up to one-third of the rise in annual health care costs (Zwillich, 2001). Medical technology affects outlays by adding to the arsenal of feasible treatments and by reducing the invasiveness of existing interventions, thus increasing the number of patients who might enjoy net gains from diagnosis and treatment. Although not every technological advance leads to increased expenditure, the net effect has tended to raise costs due to extensions in the range and intensity of care. Thus, even relatively inexpensive advances, such as antibiotics, which appear to reduce health care costs by treating common diseases at a lower cost than conventional treatments, add significantly to medical spending.

Virtually all scholars agree that the biomedical revolution persistently drives up health care spending (Aaron, 2003). Baker *et al.* (2003) found that increases in the supply of technology tend to be related to both higher utilization and spending on the service in question. Thorpe *et al.* (2004b) found that a small number of medical conditions were associated with much of the increase in health care spending between 1987 and 2000, with the top 15 conditions accounting for approximately half of the overall growth in spending (see also Skinner *et al.*, 2006). Moreover, the problem of priority setting is destined to become more acute in the coming decade because we are seeing the rapid proliferation of costly 'last chance' therapies: technologies that represent the last chance for prolonging life for individuals. These are very expensive and typically

Box 1.3 The cost of technology

After helping to develop some of the hottest new drugs, Memorial Sloan-Kettering cancer doctor Leonard Saltz has come down with a bad case of sticker shock. The price tag for treating patients has increased 500-fold in the last decade. Ten years ago, doctors could extend the life of a patient who had failed to respond to chemotherapy by an average 11.5 months using a combination of drugs that cost $500 in today's dollars. Now, new drugs are able to extend survival on average to 22.5 months, but at a cost of $250,000, not including pharmacy markups, salaries for doctors and nurses, and the cost of infusing the drugs into patients in the hospital. That kind of cost is unsustainable. 'Sooner or later the bubble is going to pop,' according to Saltz. The question is simple: How many $20,000 cancer drugs can society really afford to stack on top of one another? 'Absent a thoughtful national discussion, the answer is none,' says Michael A. Friedman, chief executive of City of Hope, a cancer center in Los Angeles. 'We will quickly run out of resources, leading to de facto rationing.' The rising costs, he says, are 'utterly insupportable'.

Source: Herper (2004).

yield what might be judged as marginal benefits relative to their costs (see Box 1.3).

The impact of technological advances will be heightened by the increase in the very elderly since advances in technology enable the prolongation of life for persons with illnesses that until recently would have been untreatable – but at high cost. Moreover, while curative treatment may be beneficial to individual patients, the marginal gain in terms of length of survival and quality of life is difficult to judge. This uncertainty is complicated by the fact that most medical procedures have not been subject to controlled assessment to determine their effectiveness in particular cases and how they compare in outcome to less expensive alternative approaches. According to Eddy (1991), in the USA alone the difference between the attitude of 'when in doubt do it' and that of 'when in doubt stop' could add up to $100 billion annually.

Despite the fact that medical technology is global and contributes to cost escalation in all health systems, there is evidence that policies adopted by countries can have a significant impact on the use of new technologies. Although all countries feel the impact of new technologies, many try to limit the diffusion of expensive new drugs and equipment by instituting controls and requiring physicians and hospitals to work within fixed budgets (Fuchs, 2005: 76). McClellan and Kessler, for example, found 'enormous differences in how quickly and widely treatments diffused into medical practice' (1999: 253), especially those high-technology treatments with high fixed costs or high variable costs per use. They also found more modest differences in the times it takes new drugs, procedures or devices to become available. So while the approach of the USA in particular reflects the view that new technologies should be made available quickly, other countries have been more cautious. The result is that medical spending growth across nations has diverged as some countries implement cost-containment policies designed to curb the diffusion of medical technology.

Rising public expectations and demands

The primary forces behind technological medicine come from the providers of the health care community who instil a demand in the public. Health professionals are trained to do what is best for their patients and in some countries this has produced a do-everything, 'maximalist' approach (Fuller, 1994). Health care is big business with huge financial stakes. The health care industry itself is a powerful shaper of perceived needs and it benefits significantly from an ever-expanding notion of health care. Not surprisingly, any attempt to place limits on access to the newest technologies risks condemnation from practitioners, their patients and the public. As noted by Altman and associates, any limitation on health spending will be met by strong resistance from groups negatively affected. If the past decades have taught us anything, it is that the pressure to use medical technologies up to the point that they have no marginal value is very strong, and as a result the long-term spending growth trend may appear to be inevitable (Altman *et al.*, 2003). Such cases of denial of access result in dramatic news stories and tough questioning of those officials who dare to deny such care (see Box 1.4).

These public expectations and perceptions of medicine have resulted in an over-utilization of and reliance on technology (Ubel, 2001). Patients demand access to the newest technologies because they are convinced of their value. Popular health-oriented magazines and television shows extol the virtues of medical innovations. Physicians are trained in the technological imperative, which holds that a technology should be used despite its cost if it offers any possibility of benefit. Furthermore, third-party payment provides no disincentive against the over-utilization of medical technology. Any limits on the allocation of medical technologies, then, must come from outside the health care community itself. The only agent with the power to enforce such limits is the government, but it can do so only within the context of rising public expectations. Also, since it is natural for politicians to want to please their constituents and be re-elected, they are beholden to those interests with political power and to the demands of their constituents. As a result, they tend to over-promise and avoid talking limits whenever possible.

Box 1.4   Media campaigns for treatment denied

In the UK, multiple sclerosis sufferers are furious and go to the media when the National Institute for Clinical Excellence, the government's cost-effectiveness agency threatens to ban a new drug on the grounds that at £10,000 per year per patient it is simply too expensive for its relative benefits. One mother of two children with the disease is quoted in the press as saying: 'My children are dependent on me – how can you put a price on that?' Should the government step in and fund the drug for these young children and, if so, where will the money to do so come from? Meanwhile, in New Zealand a 76-year-old man is denied kidney dialysis by the public hospital. The man and his family take his case to the media accusing the health authorities of denying his rights to life-saving treatment. The media portray him as a wronged war veteran and include emotional interviews with family members and his MP. Unrelenting media pressure forces political officials to overrule the hospital authorities and give him dialysis despite their argument that he was a very poor medical risk for reasons they could not disclose due to patient confidentiality. He received kidney dialysis but died within five months due to heart failure. Were the politicians right in bowing to public pressure?

The expectations and demands of the public for health care are potentially insatiable and they are fuelled by a medical industry that has much to gain by the continual expansion of the scope of medicine. Health care costs have increased partly because citizens expect and often demand higher and higher levels of medical intervention, levels undreamt of several decades ago. Moreover, patients have become less deferential and more informed as to their options through the Internet and the media (Scott *et al.*, 2005). This exaggerated view of health care often is nurtured by politicians who place heavy emphasis on the rights of individuals to health care with few limits. It also reflects the fact that every person is a potential patient or a family member of one who at any time might need health care. Furthermore, since World War II there has been a shift towards the notion of positive rights to health care that places a moral duty on society to provide the resources necessary to exercise those rights. The long-term effect, within the context of ever more sophisticated technological options, is that setting limits has become progressively more difficult politically as the population takes health care entitlements for granted.

In many countries, the proposition that one should limit the medical expenditure on one particular patient in order to benefit the community contradicts the traditional patient-oriented mores of medicine. Thus, there are strong pressures for intensive intervention on an individual basis even in the last days of life, often in spite of the enormous cost for

Table 1.8   *Views of the elderly about their health care systems (%)*

	Australia	Canada	NZ	UK	USA
System works well	34	38	22	39	25
Needs fundamental change	38	40	45	44	44
Needs complete rebuilding	24	18	31	15	26

Source: Data from Schoen *et al.* (2000).

very little return in terms of prolonging the patient's life. In countries with more communal or collectively grounded cultures, this maximalist approach to health care is more malleable and the public less disparaging of limits. Public opinion studies, for instance, have found that public support for specific health care systems varies considerably across countries and seems to have little correlation with the amount spent on health care (Table 1.8). One must look closely at the cultural factors and value systems of the specific countries to explain these differences in support in which systems delivering fewer services are rated more highly by the public than those with much higher provision levels.

Public expectations may be elevated unrealistically because of a tendency to oversell medical innovation and overestimate the capacities of new medical technologies for resolving health problems. At the centre are the mass media, which are predisposed to unrealistically optimistic and oversimplified coverage of medical technology. Frequently, the initial response of the media, often encouraged by medical spokesmen, is to report innovations as medical 'breakthroughs'. Because most health care is routine and not newsworthy, the media naturally focus attention on techniques that can be easily dramatized. By and large, media coverage solidifies public trust in the technological fix and 'stimulates their appetite for new, expensive, high technology procedures' (Kassler, 1994: 126). Moreover, media coverage, along with a freedom of information climate that has emerged in many countries, has forced the rationing process out into the open. Users of health care are less willing to accept a gate-keeper role for their general practitioners, especially when they read in the papers of inconsistencies and problems in the health care system. As a result, many politicians find it difficult not to join in the call for expanded access to new technologies, while the media seems to relish uncovering and sensationalizing cases where treatment is denied.

Arguments in favour of containing the costs of health care, while acceptable at the aggregate, societal level, are often rejected when applied at the individual level. Thus, while a large proportion of the population in theory supports the need for cost containment, when one's own health or that of a loved one is at stake, constraints on the availability of health care resources are viewed as unfair: 'I know the government needs to control health care costs but not when my child needs an expensive new drug.' It is little wonder that many elected officials are unwilling to make decisions that jeopardize these emotionally held values. Again, it is important to note that although there are global forces working to increase public demands and expectations, these are stronger in some countries than in others.

It has been observed that no matter to what extent health care facilities are expanded, there will remain a steady pool of unmet demands (Cundiff and McCarthy, 1994). Despite the policy statements of some officials, there is little evidence that additional facilities and money alone will resolve the health care crisis (Box 1.5). Although wealthier countries devote substantially higher proportions of their resources to health services than poorer countries, the demand for services does not abate; instead, the public comes to expect a level of medical care that could not be imagined by citizens of less affluent countries. Moreover, as more of these expectations are met, demand for expanded health services actually escalates.

Box 1.5   Does more high-technology medicine improve health outcomes?

Findings from various studies confirm the notion that US health care makes extensive use of technology. For instance, a study comparing care for heart attack patients in 17 countries over the past decade showed that, while treatment in all countries has become more intensive, the USA had a pattern of early adoption and fast diffusion of new technologies. By contrast, other countries showed either a late start/fast growth pattern of technological diffusion (Australia and Belgium) or a late start/slow growth pattern (the UK and Scandinavian countries). The patterns of diffusion for new, very high cost drugs were similar to those for intensive procedures, but no such patterns were observed for low-cost, easy-to-use medications (Docteur *et al.*, 2003: 23). Despite this pattern, the USA consistently rates below the top 20 nations in health outcomes. A recent study, for example, found that the USA ranked near the bottom of industrialized nations for the survival rates of newborns despite high spending on neonatal medicine (Tanner, 2006). Similarly, other studies have found that Americans aged 55 to 64 are much sicker than their British counterparts even though the USA spends twice as much per person on health care (Banks *et al.*, 2006) and that Canadians are healthier than their USA counterparts on almost every measure of health (Lasser *et al.*, 2006). Despite this massive spending on the newest technologies, Americans have higher rates of diabetes, hypertension, heart disease, stroke, lung disease and cancer.

Conclusions

Health systems of all countries face major problems as regards the issues raised here. Whether health care represents a crisis in a particular country depends on one's perspective but certainly there is much variation in severity across nations on more objective measures as well. To what extent are these differences the product of health policies of the countries and to what extent are the problems beyond the direct control of policy makers? Put another way, what steps can governments take, if any, to maximize the chances of framing sustainable health care systems that can weather the ageing population, the proliferation of technologies, the heightened public expectations and other forces driving up the costs?

What should be already evident from the discussion so far is that there are significant differences as to how well countries are doing in constraining costs, providing universal and quality care and protecting the public health. It has yet to be demonstrated convincingly whether universal, global forces are moving the health policies of industrialized countries towards convergence. Even if that is the case, it is imperative to examine closely the variations and similarities of the health care systems of countries and to appreciate the implications for the provision of health care to populations. Chapter 2 begins this task by describing the political, cultural and historical context of the health systems of these countries in order to get a better understanding of how and why each country's health system has evolved the way it has. It presents three different sets of explanations for the divergent approaches to health care found in our countries. As such, the chapter provides a framework for studying the intricacies of the systems and the substantive issues raised in the chapters that follow.

Chapter 2

The Context of Health Care

The health policy of any country at a particular point in time is the product of a multitude of factors, the most important of which are displayed in Figure 2.1. These factors include the intrinsic social, cultural and political fabric of a country, including its social values and structures, political institutions and traditions, the legal system and the characteristics of its health care community. For instance, policy-making authority might be highly centralized or widely dispersed across multiple levels. Moreover, in some countries unions and/or corporate structures are strong factors in determining social policy and might, in effect, have a veto power over proposed policy changes made by the government. Likewise, the influence of the medical industry and medical associations varies widely, as does the power of the insurance providers in shaping health policy.

The practice of medicine also can be strongly affected by the legal system and its role in compensation claims and the definition of legal rights to health care services. Moreover, in some countries the courts can challenge and even negate government policies, while in others the government is supreme and its decisions are the law. Social values, too, are important forces, with some traditions emphasizing individual rights and entitlements and others putting heavy emphasis on collective or community good. The boundaries as to what is a 'public' good and what should remain in the private sphere also impacts on health policy. Countries with stronger socialist roots are likely to define public goods and services much more broadly and include universal coverage. In some societies, the extended family still plays an important role in health care, while in others even the nuclear family has a diminished importance in the delivery of health care.

In addition to the values and institutions of a country, health policy is also shaped by the composition of its population and by demographic patterns. Heterogeneous, multi-cultural populations require more complex health systems than more homogeneous ones. Likewise, older populations have different needs from younger ones. Health policy and the way in which medical resources are distributed also reflect the current state of medical technology and the public expectations and demands that accompany it. For example, a survey of attitudes about length and quality of life among adults conducted by the UK International

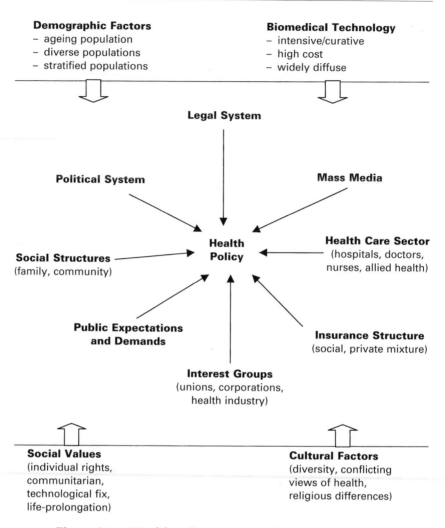

Demographic Factors
– ageing population
– diverse populations
– stratified populations

Biomedical Technology
– intensive/curative
– high cost
– widely diffuse

Legal System

Political System

Mass Media

Social Structures
(family, community)

Health Policy

Health Care Sector
(hospitals, doctors,
nurses, allied health)

**Public Expectations
and Demands**

Insurance Structure
(social, private mixture)

Interest Groups
(unions, corporations,
health industry)

Social Values
(individual rights,
communitarian,
technological fix,
life-prolongation)

Cultural Factors
(diversity, conflicting
views of health,
religious differences)

Figure 2.1   *Health policy context of developed nations*

Longevity Centre in 2002 found significant differences between the French, the Americans and the British. While 64 per cent of Americans and 55 per cent of the British wanted to live as long as possible even if that entailed pain, nearly two-thirds of the French opted to live a shorter than average life if it meant dying without being in pain or dependency on others (Carvel, 2002a).

The mass media and its coverage of medical stories clearly influence how medicine and health care policy are perceived by the public. Countries with 'tabloid' traditions are likely to emphasize the more sensational aspects of medicine and those with more investigative traditions are

Table 2.1   *Public satisfaction and percentage of GDP spent on health care*

	Satisfaction level[a]		% GDP	
	1991	*1996*	*1990*	*2003*
Australia	34	n/a	7.5	9.2
France	41	65	8.4	10.4
Germany	41	58	8.5	10.9
Italy	12	20	7.7	8.4
Japan	49	n/a	6.1	7.9
Netherlands	47	70	8.5	9.3
Sweden	32	58	8.3	9.3
UK	27	57	6.0	7.9
US	10	40	11.9	15.2

[a] 1991 measured by statement, 'On the whole, the health care system works pretty well, and only minor changes are necessary to make it work better' (Blendon *et al.*, 1990). 1996 is percentage saying they were 'fairly or very satisfied' with their health system (Blendon *et al.*, 2001).
n/a = not available

Sources: Data from OECD (2006); Blendon *et al.* (1990); Blendon *et al.* (2001).

likely to look for faults in the health care system. In general, however, the mass media in these countries has tended to dramatize medicine, heighten expectations and place more demands on health managers and politicians.

Public support for policy, of course, is an important factor in democratic societies and is critical in explaining how governments with similar problems cope differently. Interestingly, levels of public support for health services across countries seem to have little correlation with levels of health spending or any objective level of services provided. Table 2.1, for instance, compares for each country the public satisfaction with their health care system with the percentage of GDP spent on health care: and it finds little relationship between higher spending and satisfaction. Spending more does not necessarily increase satisfaction levels.

There have been numerous statistical analyses to explain aggregate health expenditure of countries and investigate the impact of institutions and other possible explanatory variables. Studies across developed and developing countries commonly find that the per capita income of a country is the single most important factor explaining health expenditure variation (Gerdtham *et al.*, 1998). Total health spending rises from around 2 to 3 per cent of GDP in the poorest countries to 8 to 9 per cent in the highest, with of course some like the USA substantially higher (Musgrave *et al.*, 2002). Since all of our countries are quite similar in wealth, however, we suggest that differences in spending reflect a combination of economic, cultural and historical factors. Wealth might be the most important single factor but it is only one of many that must be considered. Moreover, these statistical modelling studies cannot explain variation in how aggregate expenditure is distributed nor how funding and provision of health services are organized.

Although health care on one level might reflect universal challenges for all countries, the political, historical and cultural context of health and health care varies from country to country as well as within countries. A main argument in this book is that variation in health policy from one country to the next can be explained only by understanding the unique combination of these variables and their interaction in each nation. This chapter examines three underlying and complementary explanations for country diversity: the institutionalist, the cultural and the functionalist (or structuralist) explanations. First, institutionalist contextual factors, specifically the political structures and institutions of these countries and their legal systems, are surveyed. Second, attention is directed toward the historical and cultural context of health care. After discussing the defining cultural characteristics of each country, different approaches to defining health and the role of traditional medicine are examined. Third, functionalist explanations are presented. These include population size and diversity, the wealth of a country, and social/ economic determinants of health.

Institutionalist explanations: contrasting political systems

Although the political systems of no two countries are identical and each nation has a unique combination of formal and informal structures, the characteristics of political systems can be categorized along several overlapping dimensions (Lijphart, 1999). The major distinguishing factor is the extent to which political power is concentrated or dispersed. As a rule, *unitary* systems concentrate political authority in a central government while *federal* systems constitutionally divide powers between the central government and states, provinces or other sub-national governments. Although the central government in a unitary system might choose to delegate specific administrative functions and responsibilities to lower units, final authority rests at the national level. In contrast, states in a federal system have constitutionally based powers that most often include health policy. Unitary governments include most European countries and Singapore, while Germany, the Netherlands, Australia and the USA are examples of the federal model.

Another institutional configuration that relates directly to the continuum of centralization is the distribution of power within each level of government. For instance, many democracies, such as New Zealand and the UK, concentrate power in parliament where the distinction between executive and legislative power is obscured or virtually non-existent. Moreover, although many parliamentary systems have upper and lower houses (e.g., the House of Lords and House of Commons in the UK), in effect most power rests in the lower houses.

In stark contrast to other countries is the USA with its deliberate constitutional separation of powers among a separately elected president, two houses of Congress, and a relatively active judicial system. Despite a great deal of variation in dispersion of policy-making authority in parliamentary systems, when compared to the USA they all have considerably more concentrated bases of power. Figure 2.2 presents a rough distribution of our countries in terms of centralization of institutional power along these dimensions. This distribution corresponds closely to the findings of Lijphart (1999: 189) who classifies Australia, Germany and the USA as 'federal and decentralized'; the Netherlands as 'semi-federal'; Japan and Sweden as 'unitary and decentralized'; and France, Italy, New Zealand and the UK as 'unitary and centralized'. Singapore, a city-state of 4 million people in which all political power rests in the central government, is by far the most centralized of the countries discussed here.

The implications of these formal government types for health policy are significant. Where power is centralized, the government has the formal capacity to make more rapid and comprehensive policy changes. Singapore, for instance, was able to initiate a major change in funding with little contest, and successive New Zealand governments introduced unimpeded a range of major restructuring initiatives of the health system during the 1990s. In contrast, the more fragmented the political authority, the higher the probability of deadlock and inaction or at best mere incremental change. The USA is the prime example of a system in which making even minor changes in health policy represents a long-term struggle. Even in a relatively narrow area such as payment of prescription charges for the elderly on Medicare where almost everyone agreed

| Singapore | UK | Italy | Japan | Germany | Australia | |
| | New Zealand | | France | Sweden | Netherlands | USA |

Concentrated   **Fragmented**

Figure 2.2   *Institutional power in political systems*

something must be done, little has been accomplished after over two years of political wrangling (Abrams, 2002). Australia and the USA are both federal systems, but their approaches to health care are quite divergent. Although not as static as the USA, however, reform in Australia over the years has been very measured compared to that of neighbouring New Zealand.

In Germany health policy making also tends to be highly incremental, to the extent that health policy is often locked into 'reform blockades'. As decision-making powers are dispersed among a multitude of mainly non-state actors (the insurance funds and provider organizations) across federal, state and local levels, the federal government has little direct influence on health care. This is particularly pertinent in the case of medical reform (Burau, 2001). Through the joint self-administration with insurance funds, doctors are at the heart of health governance, and it is difficult to address the relationship between economic and medical rationality.

Moreover, in fragmented political systems where competing political parties are able to control particular institutions, there is more likely to be a divided government where one party controls one or several branches or levels and the other party controls others. Although this might contribute to a more deliberative policy-making process, it can also easily degenerate into stagnation and gridlock as has been common in US health policy. Conversely, it might be expected that a highly centralized system, as in the UK or New Zealand, results in a policy arena characterized by more frequent and inclusive changes such as major restructuring, often to the detriment of programme stability. For instance, instability and insecurity have been major charges made by opponents of the near-continuous reforms of the New Zealand health system in the 1990s (Martin and Salmond, 2001).

Another dimension that Lijphart (1999) sees as important in distinguishing among democracies is the strength of judicial review (the extent to which a high court can overrule the elected representative bodies). Figure 2.3 demonstrates a wide range across our countries regarding the power of the courts to influence health policy. In recent decades, the German and American courts in particular have become highly activist,

Germany	Australia	France	Netherlands
USA	Italy	Japan	New Zealand
		Sweden	UK
Strong	**Medium**	**Weak**	**None**

Figure 2.3   *The strength of judicial review*

Source: Lijphart (1999: 226).

invalidating many laws on constitutional grounds, thus earning them the label of being an 'imperial judiciary' (Franck, 1996).

In contrast, the Netherlands, New Zealand, the UK and Singapore do not have systems of judicial review. In these countries, the will of parliament is supreme and cannot be challenged or overridden by a high court. The remaining countries have provisions for judicial review but for a variety of reasons the courts have exercised their power with restraint and moderation. The role of the European Court of Human Rights is likely to influence health policy in affected countries but its powers are still metamorphosing.

Legal systems

Figure 2.1 also suggests that the legal framework can have significant influence on health care. It can do this in many ways, ranging from regulating the medical professions to influencing the distribution of health care resources, to constructing liability systems that impact on both. While some countries have opted for no-fault accident compensation systems and for sanctions by medical bodies, others turn to the courts to various degrees to determine liability and the allocation of medical resources and to punish wrongdoers in the medical professions.

Not surprisingly given its emphasis on negative rights, the USA has the most extensive civil liability system imaginable and health care is no exception. Many states are considered to have a crisis with medical malpractice insurance affordability or even availability, and doctors in some states have had work stoppages or slowdowns out of protest (Reiss, 2003). Insurance rates for the riskiest medical specialities have skyrocketed with annual insurance coverage for obstetricians averaging over $210,000 and for general surgery $175,000 in Florida for instance. Consequently, physicians are leaving the state to practise elsewhere or leaving medicine entirely (Reiss, 2003).

The malpractice crisis has been blamed on larger claims and more lawsuits: the average jury award increased from $700,000 to over $1,000,000 from 1999 to 2000 alone (INSWorld, 2002). The doctors' argument is that medical liability awards for the elusive categories of pain and suffering, and punishment awards, which often reach tens of millions of dollars, must be capped (a usual figure given is $250,000) as they have been in California, which has escaped the crisis. However, trial lawyers and consumer groups argue that the real problem is the failure of the medical profession to discipline bad doctors and that any attempt to limit awards runs counter to the rights of individuals to redress wrongs against them in a court of law (Public Citizen, 2003). All sides agree, though, that the current system is inequitable and unsustainable as most patients who go to court lose and get absolutely nothing while in some cases persons who have suffered little or no harm receive huge monetary settlements.

There can be no doubt that the US liability system contributes heavily to inflated health care costs although the two sides offer substantially different estimates. The system adds to the costs in two ways. The direct cost increases come from the cost of malpractice insurance itself, most of which is passed on to patients and third-party payers. The indirect impact is even more profound, because virtually every medical decision is made within a legal context and under threat of potential litigation. This environment leads to what is termed *defensive medicine* under which doctors order all available diagnostic tests and therapeutic measures, even those that are of marginal or no benefit to a patient, in order to avert a lawsuit (e.g., the doctor did not do everything possible) or, if sued, to provide documentation that all that was possible was done for the patient. Although there are no reliable cost estimates for defensive medicine, it represents a significant portion of overall health spending in the USA and helps explain why US costs are so out of line with other countries (see Chapter 3).

Other countries have tended to depend on alternative systems to deal with medical misadventure and compensation. New Zealand, for instance, created an accident compensation system specifically to avoid the problem of costly litigation. Under this system, individuals suffering harm, medical or otherwise, are compensated by an Accident Compensation Commission (ACC) according to a standardized formula. In return, legal action is severely limited, although in recent years the incidence of legal action has increased. Moreover, over the past several decades as more people have pursued medical misadventure claims, the ACC cost for health care has multiplied, as has compensation.

Although accident compensation systems are more successful in ensuring that all victims are compensated, often the compensation is small in comparison to the possible awards granted in a liability based system. It makes sense that countries with national health services would want to avoid an unpredictable but costly liability system and opt for a predictable less costly system even if critics argue it violates the rights of individuals to go to court. That these health systems tend to be in countries with traditions of solidarity and community rather than individual rights gives them legitimacy they would not enjoy in the USA.

In the absence of civil liability, accident compensation systems normally are linked with stricter professional self-regulating systems for medical negligence. Medical societies are given responsibility to sanction and, where appropriate, prevent such members from practising. European countries in general have traditionally put emphasis on preventing medical malpractice and disciplining problem doctors through professional self-regulation. In Germany, for example, professional chambers at state level are responsible for licensing doctors, controlling medical ethics, organizing disciplinary processes and offering specialist training. The chambers are public bodies regulated by law (Moran, 1999).

However, the case of Britain shows the limitations of this approach. In recent years, there have been a number of high-profile cases of medical malpractice. One involved a pathologist who had removed organs from the bodies of dead children during post-mortem examinations without the prior consent of parents (Boseley, 2001). In another case, a GP was convicted of murdering 15 of his elderly patients though a subsequent inquiry suggested that the actual number of victims exceeded 200 (Carter, 2002). Both cases strongly throw into doubt the ability of the General Medical Council (GMC), the doctors' professional body, to protect patients from medical malpractice. Mounting pressure from the government and the public, as well as from within the medical profession, led to substantial reforms of the Council, including reduction in size, increased lay membership, tightened fitness-to-practice procedures and the introduction of revalidation (Batty, 2001). At the same time, liability claims in the UK have risen sharply. According to the National Audit Office, NHS hospitals in England face massive liabilities totalling £3.9 billion. The rate of new claims rose by 72 per cent between 1990 and 1998, and, as of March 2000, around 23,000 claims of clinical negligence were outstanding (Woodman, 2001). The average value of settlement in 2000 was £87,000, excluding brain damage and cerebral palsy where courts have at times awarded more than £1 million. The report found that the current system for handling litigation is 'fraught with delays', and often lawyers benefit far more than do the patients (Woodman, 2001). Despite divergent legal systems, then, the problems facing the UK are reminiscent of the malpractice debacle in the USA.

Cultural explanations: cultural/historical factors shaping health care

It is argued here that each country brings to health a distinctive combination of historical and cultural factors that are crucial in explaining its proclivities and characteristics. Political culture is the complex of beliefs, values and attitudes held by the public concerning the proper role of government. To what extent is health care a public as opposed to a private good and, if a public good, on what grounds should health services be distributed to individuals? What is the perceived role of the state as opposed to the citizen? To focus on those elements of culture which influence health policy, one must look at beliefs concerning definitions of health, the role of the government in the health arena, and the extent to which health care represents an individual right or a privilege granted by

Table 2.2   *Distribution by type of health political culture*

Communitarian	Egalitarian	Individualistic
Germany	Sweden	USA
Netherlands	New Zealand	Australia
Japan	UK	Singapore

society. In order to provide a basis for more in-depth comparison throughout later chapters, we will look briefly at one of the key defining cultural characteristics that shapes health care across countries and then provide an overview of the most defining aspects in each country.

One key dimension focuses on how the individual in the society relates to the whole. Table 2.2 illustrates a rough distribution of these countries showing whether they are classified primarily as communitarian, egalitarian or individualistic cultures. Countries with communitarian traditions, based either in the family or other groupings, have designed various mechanisms to ensure the interests of the various communities. Germany, for instance, has a strong tradition of self-administration, the Netherlands guarantees empowerment of the various pillars to reach consensus, and Japan puts strong emphasis on the family and on tradition itself.

In contrast, egalitarian cultures such as those of New Zealand and Sweden, although having divergent political systems, place emphasis on the entitlement to health care and on a societal commitment to provide health care on those grounds. Interestingly, countries such as the USA and Australia due to their rugged individualism have a tendency to elevate individual rights above the welfare of the community. For such countries, it is difficult to limit these negative rights to health care even for the common good. While rights and entitlements are often used synonymously, entitlements suggest a concern for equality that can be found only in the notion of positive rights, while the individualistic version of negative, self-centred rights lacks the social dimension found in egalitarian and communitarian societies.

Although they are placed in Table 2.2 as to their predominant orientation, some countries have tended to combine aspects of these types into unique hybrids. For instance, Singapore has merged communitarian and common good features with a very strong view of individual responsibility for health and health care. Similarly, the UK culture combines a pragmatic approach to collective action with a very generous entitlement philosophy reminiscent of egalitarian cultures such as New Zealand and

Sweden. In Japan (and, to a lesser extent, Singapore), meanwhile, Western medicine has introduced a form of individualism foreign to communitarian culture and created friction between generations as well as among social classes, as illustrated by the discussion of traditional medicine later in this chapter.

Germany

Germany has a strong tradition of voluntarism, self-help and family support, embedded in Christian social teachings and the idea of 'subsidiarity'. The 1873 social health insurance, the first of its kind, built on these traditions and incorporated them in a statutory system of social solidarity. The conservative underpinnings of this vision of social solidarity contrast with the egalitarian orientations characteristic of New Zealand and Sweden. The organization of health care in Germany is marked by profound continuity and is shaped by a number of principles, among them social solidarity, freedom of choice for patients and nearly full coverage of services (Bäringhausen and Sauerborn, 2003).

In the social insurance context, access to health care is an entitlement that individuals 'earn' by virtue of paying insurance contributions. This, together with a strong legalistic approach typical of Germany, turns access to health care into the right of individuals to a defined range of services. Patients literally have 'ownership' of health services. This helps to explain why the freedom of patients to choose their doctors remains a fundamental principle of health care provision. Not surprisingly, Germany is one of the few countries, which does not operate a British-style GP gate-keeping system. The individualized right to health care also goes hand in hand with the expectation that the social health insurance system provides full coverage. In conjunction with the structural features of the health system this makes cost containment and restrictions of services covered by social insurance very difficult.

The Netherlands

Another example of a communitarian country is the Netherlands, which resembles Germany in that private initiative has been a guiding principle in the organization of society. Dutch society has traditionally been organized in separate segments or pillars that represent different religious and political orientations. According to the Roman Catholic notion of subsidiarity and its Protestant counterpart of sovereignty the different segments in society should be empowered to provide for their members (Björkman and Okma, 1997). However, the 'pillarization' of Dutch society began to weaken in the 1960s and state intervention in health care increased (Maarse, 1997).

This marked the modernization of the Dutch health system and a 'universalist turn'. The introduction of insurance for exceptional medical risks in 1967 is indicative here. This insurance is compulsory for all employers irrespective of income and, together with relatively generous entitlements, such insurance has helped to establish a culture of care which gives preference to formal care. However, elements of universalism do co-exist with the legacy of pillarization. The provision of health care continues to be predominantly in the hands of private non-profit organizations and health policy making still requires the consensus of a large number of interest groups, to the extent that health reform almost becomes impossible.

Japan

Although for many Westerners Japan is an enigma, its health care context borrows much from Germany and is similar to the Netherlands, because at its base Japan has a communitarian, extended-family-based culture with veneration for the elderly. For health care, this has meant that universal coverage for health care is widely accepted socially as a given, although long-term care has until recently largely rested with the family, particularly women. However, during the last half-century traditional Japanese values have come into conflict with the infusion of Western, largely American, individualistic culture, thus causing significant distress, particularly among the older Japanese population.

As a result, Japanese views of medicine are an amalgamation of Buddhist, Confucian and Shinto influence, combined more recently with Hippocratic and Christian influences (Macer, 1999). During the 5th and 6th centuries, for instance, the medical profession was restricted to the privileged classes. During centralization of government in the 7th and 8th centuries, a bureau of medicine was established creating an official physician class. After the Heian period in the 9th to 14th centuries, the government-sponsored health service was replaced by professional physicians, and in the 16th century, a code of practice similar to the Hippocratic code, the 'Seventeen Rules of Enjuin', was drawn up which emphasized a priestly role for the physician. Although modern Western medicine took hold in the 19th century and the rapid progress of medical technology challenged the way medicine is practised, there remains a very strong paternalistic attitude on the part of doctors and a lasting reliance on traditional practice (see below, p. 49).

Sweden

Perhaps the clearest example of an egalitarian type of culture is Sweden, which is notable for the very early provision of medical care by the state dating back to the 17th century (Glenngård *et al.*, 2005). Towns and cities employed doctors to provide public health care and municipalities also operated hospitals. In rural areas the central state paid physicians to provide basic care. State involvement in health care was consolidated in the middle of the 19th century with the creation of county councils, which had primary responsibility for health care. However, a considerable expansion of health services only occurred in the post-war period, paving the way for the universal health care system as we know it today.

The historical legacy of public involvement in health care is combined with the principle of equality, which is deeply embedded in Swedish society. People have a right to health care regardless of income and where they live (Håkansson and Nordling, 1997). The right to health care is part of people's citizenship and not an individually earned entitlement, as in the case of Germany and the Netherlands. Public funding and provision of health care are key features of the health system in Sweden, as is a strong emphasis on public health and concern for equity.

New Zealand

Although its national health system compares most closely with that of the UK and its political culture retains many features of its Commonwealth heritage, like Sweden, New Zealand has a strong tradition of egalitarianism. This was clearly reflected in the Social Security Act of 1938 that promised an open-ended provision to all citizens based on need. It is also demonstrated by the strong belief in the public consultation process and the view that office holders are holders of the public trust, not above it. New Zealand's egalitarian foundation is also illustrated by the 'tall poppy' belief which holds that people who get too successful, wealthy or powerful must be cut back to size. New Zealand politicians embraced the new, right, market-centred philosophy in the 1980s and 1990s, but the public rejected attempts to restructure the health system in ways that were seen as destroying its egalitarian foundations. The result has been a series of rather bold attempts by governments of both parties to make major changes in the health care structure, only to pull back from more extreme and unpopular tactics once the public felt threatened and demanded a return to a more egalitarian system.

Britain

In comparison to Sweden, Britain not only has had a much shorter history of public involvement in health care, but the approach to collective action has typically also been pragmatic rather than principled (Johnson and Cullen, 2000). This also helps to explain why after World

War II a universal health service was introduced in what was traditionally a liberal state regime. However, the NHS did not resolve the tension
between laissez-faire liberalism and collectivism and instead a generous
entitlement philosophy has co-existed with rationed service provision
(Moran, 1999).

The NHS enjoys high public support. The generosity of the NHS entitlement philosophy contrasts with both the failure of the earlier National
Insurance arrangements and the austerity of post-war Britain, and it is
deeply entrenched in the public's mind. Not surprisingly, reforms have
focused on the organization of health services, and even the extensive
changes under the Conservatives in the late 1980s were prefaced with the
assurance 'the NHS is safe in our hands'. Universalism, together with a
centralist political system, also generates expectations that health
services are the same (or at least comparable) across the country.
Concerns about inequities in access are prominent and are reflected in
debates about the 'postcode lottery', whereby services vary significantly
from one locale to the next.

USA

The USA is the prototype of an individualistic society. Although individual rights have some emphasis in all the nations examined here, in the
USA rights have been elevated to a status of supremacy over collective
interests. Moreover, by rights Americans mean negative rights, and, as a
result, they are hesitant to sacrifice perceived individual needs for the
common good. Thus, there is no guaranteed universal coverage but also
no limits on what health care individuals can buy if they can afford it.
This cultural tenet goes a long way to explain why the USA expends so
much more of its GDP on health care than other countries, without
providing universal access. The USA is simply unwilling to institute policies that place limits on the amount of medical resources that an individual can acquire, or even which doctor they can see. Cost containment
measures such as Health Maintenance Organizations (HMOs) that
attempted to set limits on individual care are widely attacked as counter
to patient rights and led to calls for a 'Patients' Bill of Rights'.

In the USA, when individual rights and the common good conflict, the
individual's claims take precedence. 'Our premium on individual rights
and our emphasis on the differences between us is a far cry from the social
beliefs that back the health systems of Europe, Canada, and Japan, in
which more homogenous societies band together for the common good'
(Kassler, 1994: 130). Moreover, in direct contrast to the UK and New
Zealand, in the USA there is a strong aversion by the medical community
to serve as gatekeepers and professional codes of ethics refuse to acknowledge the existence of scarcity of resources. The idea that limits on medical

expenditures for an individual patient could be set in order to benefit the wider community contradicts the traditional patient-oriented customs of medicine. Although Americans complain about high costs and high taxes, when their health or life is at stake they expect no expense to be spared and believe that medicine should not have a price tag (Ubel, 2001).

American patients also expect a higher standard of care. In contrast to Japan, where physicians spend little time with patients, such conduct is unacceptable in the USA. Moreover, one is struck by the comparatively Spartan conditions in hospitals in other nations. In the USA, amenities commonly include satellite television, DVD libraries, bedside phones, wide menu choices and tastefully decorated rooms. These extras have little appreciable impact on health but add substantially to the costs. This value setting has led to the inability to control health care spending. In 2006, over $2.0 trillion was spent on health care, an average of $5,848 per person. In 2002 alone, health spending increased 9.1 per cent, the biggest increase in a decade. Although the rate of increase 'dipped' to 6.6 per cent in 2005, it is expected to quickly rebound (Borgor *et al.*, 2006). Many observers warn that this pattern necessitates drastic policy changes to put the brakes on spending growth, but given the US culture this is highly unlikely (Anderson *et al.*, 2006).

Reinforcing the predominance of negative rights, US culture is also predisposed towards progress through technological means (see Box 2.1). The result has been an unrealistic dependence on technology to fix health problems at the expense of non-technological solutions. High-quality medicine is equated with high-technology medicine and the best health care is that which uses the most sophisticated new techniques. This demand for medical technology is reinforced by the dominance of medical specialists who extend the indications for use of new innovations, thus leading to a very aggressive form of medicine, under which, for example,

---

Box 2.1   Health care in the USA

It is sometimes said that the USA has the best *medical* system but one of the worst *health care* systems among developed nations. The heavy dependence on intensive and expensive diagnostic and life-saving interventions has resulted in a system where those with adequate third-party coverage have quick access to a broad range of technologies and specialists unmatched in any other country. It has, however, also spawned a system for which the control of costs has been elusive and 45 million people have no health care coverage. The extreme contrasts of the system are illustrated by the expenditure of $5 million over 34 days to treat a 69-year-old patient who in the end died (Winslow, 2001) but the failure to guarantee pre-natal care for pregnant women.

the USA carries out four operations for every one performed in Japan (Drake, 1994: 138).

Australia

Although Australia shares the far South Pacific and a similar British heritage with New Zealand, the two cultures have diverged since independence in the 19th century, with New Zealand opting for a more egalitarian and collectivist political culture and Australia adopting a much more individualistic, US-type approach to defining the scope of public goods and the role of government in promoting equality. Australia's unique welfare state places it in a hybrid category value-wise, though the fragmented Australian health care system with its strong private component is closer to the USA than it is to its neighbour New Zealand (Rix *et al.*, 2005). The decentralized Australian health delivery system reflects a rugged individualism needed to survive in a hostile environment (even though Australia is now the most urban of countries) as much as it does the fragmented federal system that defines Australian politics.

Thus, while there has been an inevitable British influence in Australia since the beginning of the first prisoner settlements and this continues to be reflected in some aspects of its health care system, the 'tendency to look to North America as a source of technology, of funding and organizational initiatives and the inspiration for new policies has continued to the present time' (Palmer and Short, 2000: 6). Australian culture, then, represents a unique combination of its European heritage with a heavy dose of individualism.

Singapore

Of all the countries, Singapore is the most difficult to classify as to cultural orientation, in part because, unlike other Asian countries, its history is short and it is thus a unique mixture of several blends of culture, East and West. Singapore has risen in the last 40 years from a Third World territory with appalling health and human conditions to a highly modern society that ranks high on health and economic measures (Ham, 2001). Its political leaders are proud of their success and angered by criticism by some Western nations that they have accomplished this by violating individual freedom. In fact, health officials argue that their health funding system based on personal savings accounts maximizes freedom of choice by focusing on the individual's responsibility for his or her own health care. Individual responsibility, not rights, is at the centre of the Singapore value system and is clearly exhibited in the health system. Thus, Singapore represents a hybrid form of individualism often at odds with that of the USA and Australia.

Singapore's approach to health policy is a distinctive combination of free-market principles and careful government control (Lim, 1998). Its philosophy is to build a healthy population through innovative preventive programmes and promotion of healthy lifestyles which individuals have a civic duty to embrace. As a result, the system de-emphasizes high-cost curative technologies, thereby explaining the low rates of intensive medical procedures performed in Singapore relative to other countries and the low proportion of its GDP that it spends on health care. According to Yeo Cheow Tong, the then Minister of Health: 'Our medical system is based on individual responsibility . . . no Singaporean has enjoyed or expects to enjoy health services for free. When hospitalized he pays part of the bill . . . His Medisave is his own money. This gives him the incentive to be healthy, minimise[s] the need for medical treatment, and save[s] on medical expenses.' According to Lim, Singaporeans readily accept this social contract based on individual responsibility and co-payments because of their willingness to place the common good above self-interest, the absence of any tradition of state largesse, their 'spirit of self-help' and their pragmatic nature that understands that 'trade-offs are an inevitable fact of life' (2004: 89).

As noted in Chapter 1, the convergence theory suggests that any subsequent differences in health policy will tend to fade over time as health systems of all shapes face the same problems. While this theory might or might not be borne out in the substantive discussions that follow, the presumption here is that the underlying values and beliefs of a population will be reflected in how they view health, health care and the distribution of health care resources. In that regard, we see considerable variation across these countries and it will be interesting to see how it will play out in the analysis of health care systems in the coming chapters. National culture and history might help explain health policy, but as populations become more diverse through immigration many nations are finding health delivery increasingly problematic due to the new cultural diversities within their populations. Not only health care needs, but also perceptions of health itself, vary among cultures.

Different approaches to defining health

A critical question for health care policy is what is meant by the term 'health'. There are several competing models, each of which has important implications for how we organize health care. The prevailing Western medical model is primarily founded on defining health as the *absence of disease or illness*. People are healthy under this definition if they are not suffering from an illness or disease. The goal of curative medicine is to diagnose an illness and restore the health of the patient, who by definition is unhealthy. Inherent in medicine is the continual expansion of categories of disease to account for a broadening range of conditions deemed unhealthy. Such labelling of a condition as a disease has tended to ingrain in medicine the notion that disease is the enemy (Seedhouse, 1991: 43).

A competing definition of health is the *coping* model where health is essentially an ability to adapt to the problems life gives us. Under this definition, individuals can be healthy even if they are diseased or ill so long as they have the personal strength and resilience to cope with life. The tension with the not-ill theory is manifested in a concern that the latter interferes with individuals' ability to cope with their internal states and environment. Under this definition people without identifiable disease or illness are still unhealthy if they are unable to cope.

The third definition of health, that of the World Health Organization (WHO), defines it as 'a state of complete physical, mental and social well-being and not merely the absence of disease or infirmity' (1946). This ambitious ideal has been widely criticized because, if taken literally, it means that individuals are unhealthy if they are unhappy with their lot in life or even if they just feel unfulfilled. Moreover, in conflict with the coping theory, individuals with any defined disease, illness or disability cannot be healthy. Although this definition is so broad as to make it meaningless, this is unfortunate because it does incorporate the need to expand the definition of health beyond the situation where a person has a medically defined illness or disease. To the extent that it does broaden ill health beyond the notion of biological dysfunction, the WHO definition is useful despite its operational problems.

One problem with all of these definitions is their failure to bring in the social and cultural dimensions of health and ill health explicitly. Health has both a personal and a public dimension. Although pain, suffering, disappointment and regret are personal under the WHO definition, their effect on the lives of others might be severe. Moreover, because health and illness are social constructs and culturally defined, health and disease have to be considered within a cultural context. For Callahan (1990: 103), illness itself is as much social as individual in its characteristics because tolerability will depend on the kind of care and support provided by others and by the social meaning of the disease. Good health, therefore, requires social networks and systems that are obscured by all of these definitions of health.

Even within particular social systems health can be a very relative term. Seedhouse (1991: 40), for instance, sees disease and health akin to the analogy of weeds and flowers. As with plants, what we perceive as undesirable in one case might be desirable in another. Pneumonia in an otherwise active 20-year-old is undesirable and it is appropriate to say she is suffering from a disease. In contrast, pneumonia in a 90-year-old victim of a severe stroke might be welcomed as offering an easier death.

Although in clinical terms pneumonia in both cases is termed a disease, the ambiguity of the disease label requires clarification of the specific context. Increasingly, it is evident that health must encompass not only the physical and mental aspects of personal well-being but also the social (Babcock and Belotti, 1994: 209).

Putting health into this broader context also raises the question of why we value health in its narrow sense as freedom from disease. Although health should be highly valued since it is central to the completion of one's plan of life, health is better viewed as a means to broader goals and purposes in life. Good health is not a substitute for a good life, and good health does not guarantee a good life. Good health in itself cannot guarantee achievement of our goals, give us a reason to live, or maximize our potential to the highest order. Good health in the physical sense but without the other three dimensions of health, then, is unlikely to ensure contentment. One area in which these ideas take form is in what is often termed 'alternative' or 'holistic' medicine.

Culture and traditional medicine

Although the Western medical model enjoys dominance in all of the countries examined here, traditional values continue to shape how it is practised. Therefore, although most attention in this book centres on the analysis of the similarities and differences of these countries within that broader framework, it is imperative to examine features that might be unique to, or more dominant in, particular countries. One area that offers useful insights is the extent to which various forms of traditional medicine continue to be practised alongside modern Western medicine.

Until 1875, when Western medicine became the official form of medicine in Japan, kampo and acupuncture were dominant. Kampo means 'Han Method' in Japanese because it was the Chinese who introduced the use of herbal products for medical therapy during the 7th to 9th centuries at the time of the Han Dynasty. The Japanese health care system remains an amalgamation of modern Western medicine and traditional Eastern practices, and kampo is still an important feature of medical practice. The great majority of Japanese physicians (72 per cent of all Western-style doctors in a 2000 survey) use at least some kampo formulae in their practice. Moreover, almost all pharmacies have staff trained in traditional methods of prescription and most health insurance companies recognize and support its use (Kenner, 2001). From 1974 to 1989 there was a 15-fold increase in kampo medicinal preparations in comparison with only 2.6-fold increase in the sales of mainstream pharmaceutical products in Japan (WHO, 1996). Acupuncture and other holistic practices are also integrated into the Japanese health system, in part a reflection of its Shinto/Buddhist roots.

Similarly, while Singapore's health care services are based on Western medicine, it has been common practice among the various ethnic groups to contact traditional practitioners for general ailments. Although Western medicine is the main form of health care, a variety of traditional practices continue to serve as complementary forms of medical care (for implications of this clash of 'ethos', see Quah, 2003). Given the large proportion of Chinese in Singapore, traditional Chinese medicine (TCM) has been of special importance. TCM is an important part of Singapore's heritage and enjoys considerable popularity. Although its practice is confined to outpatient care, two acupuncture clinics are affiliated with public hospitals. The Ministry of Health estimates that about 12 per cent of daily outpatient attendance is through TCM practitioners, the majority of whom are trained locally by specialist TCM schools (Singapore Ministry of Health, 1995). In its report, the Ministry concluded that there should be no forced integration of TCM and Western medicine and that only those persons properly trained to practise TCM should be allowed to do so. Therefore, some government regulation of TCM was necessary to safeguard patients' interests, which meant legitimizing it as a facet of health care.

Perhaps because of their location in the South Pacific and ties to Asia the health care systems of both Australia and New Zealand, although emerging out of significantly different political systems, have heavy links to holistic medical practices. In Australia, for instance, where TCM has been practised since the 19th century, it has been estimated that over 48 per cent of the population use at least one form of alternative medicine (Maclennan *et al.*, 1996). Between 1992 and 1996, imports of Chinese herbal medicines increased 4-fold in Australia, accounting for approximately A$1 billion of business (Bensoussan and Myers, 1996). In 1995, the Australian State of Victoria, in response to the 'rapid expansion of the practice of and demand for TCM in this country', created a Ministerial Committee on Traditional Medicine (Victorian Department of Human Services, 1996). In 1998, the Committee issued an extensive report on the risks and benefits of TCM and a wide range of other traditional approaches used in Australia, and a consideration of the need for regulation. A major recommendation of the Committee to the Australian Health Minister's Advisory Council was that occupational registration of the profession of TCM 'proceed as a matter of urgency' (Victorian Ministerial Advisory Committee, 1998: 1).

As in Australia, oriental medicine is well established in New Zealand with schools of acupuncture, TCM and holistic healing. Many general practitioners are trained in acupuncture, and the use of herbal products, including New Zealand native plants, is common. Although Chinese and other Asian traditional approaches are available, the most unique influence on New Zealand health policy comes via Maori and Pacific Island cultures. Considerable effort over the past decades has been directed at accounting for cultural differences in the perception of health and health care between the European and Maori populations and to integrate this into the health delivery system.

In contrast with these systems, the dominance of the American Medical Association and other mainstream medical organizations has marginalized the scope of alternative medicine in the USA. Although recently some insurance carriers and HMOs have begun to partially reimburse selected non-traditional treatments, this practice remains the exception. Moreover, unlike even Australia and New Zealand, few medical practitioners in the USA have training in acupuncture or other alternative regimes. The predominance of the medical model even as portrayed in the media has resulted in a very closed notion of health care among most Americans. As a result, when they feel unwell they expect to be seen post-haste by a medical specialist, thus again driving up expectations and costs.

Although conventional medicine remains at the centre of the health service in Britain, there are moves to integrate complementary and alternative medicine into the NHS. In 2000 a report by the House of Lords called for patients to have access to unconventional medicine and to be given more and better information about existing therapies (Boseley, 2000). Here, tighter regulation was identified as a key issue and the report argued that only those therapies which were properly regulated should be accessible through the NHS. In response to this report, there have been moves to strengthen the regulation of alternative practitioners and to standardize the myriad of training schemes in alternative therapies that currently exist. The Department of Health is also providing funding to develop the research capacity in alternative medicine as part of the drive towards evidence-based health care practice.

Functionalist explanations: population, wealth and economics

The third explanation for country-by-country variation is termed functionalist or structuralist because it centres on quantitative characteristics such as demographics and wealth. Problems facing a small highly concentrated population like Singapore are on a different scale than those facing a large, diverse population like the USA, or even those of the similar sized population of New Zealand sprawled across two large islands. Moreover, we would expect that wealthier nations have an easier time meeting the health needs of their populations as reflected in their higher levels of spending (Musgrave *et al.*, 2002). This section examines these functionalist contextual factors for our countries.

Population size and diversity

Not surprisingly, health policy can be significantly influenced by the demographic characteristics of a country. Moreover, because these characteristics change over time, such as the ageing or the diversification of the population through immigration, the health system must adapt to those changes. To some extent, the reform efforts of countries over the last several decades represent attempts to deal with changing needs brought about in part by demographic trends, especially population ageing. One might expect, therefore, that some of the differences in health policy among these countries described in the following chapters can be traced in part to differences in the size of the respective populations, their age and ethnic diversity, and their degree of social stratification in terms distribution of wealth.

Table 2.3 summarizes key demographic variables across our countries. Most obvious is the vast difference in the size of population. It is not surprising that the USA struggles to devise a workable health system for almost 300 million people. The State of California alone, with over 33 million people, is larger than half the countries examined here. Certainly, it can be argued that countries with smaller populations ought to be better able to design a workable health policy. Since the total populations of New Zealand and Singapore are smaller than at least five metropolitan areas in the USA, perhaps it would be more appropriate to compare

Table 2.3   *Population characteristics, 2005*

	Population	% growth rate	Net migration	% over 65	% under 14
Australia	20,090,437	0.87	3.91	12.9	19.8
France	60,656,178	0.37	0.66	16.4	18.4
Germany	82,431,390	0.00	2.18	18.9	14.4
Italy	58,103,033	0.07	2.07	19.4	13.9
Japan	127,417,244	0.05	0.00	19.5	14.3
Netherlands	16,407,491	0.53	2.80	14.1	18.1
New Zealand	4,035,461	1.02	3.83	11.7	21.4
Singapore	4,425,720	1.56	10.30	8.1	16.0
Sweden	9,001,774	0.17	1.67	17.4	17.1
UK	60,441,457	0.28	2.18	15.8	17.7
USA	300,000,000	0.92	3.31	12.4	20.6

Source: Data from *The World Fact Book* (2006).

their systems with a large US city or a small state. Large population size might also contribute to efforts in the UK to decentralize decision making in the National Health Service (NHS) to health authorities, or (more recently) Primary Care Trusts.

However, population size is but one important variable for health policy. Population growth rates are crucial because they point to future health needs and relate to the composition of that dynamic population. A high growth rate calls for planning for expansion of services and, depending on where the growth is coming from (e.g. births, immigration), a change in types of services needed. In contrast, a low or negative growth rate might indicate difficulties in funding services even at the existing level. Singapore, New Zealand and Australia display the highest percentages of growth, indicating a need for expanded services just to take care of the increased numbers. However, most of the European countries demonstrate smaller rates of growth, and in Sweden's case near zero growth (Box 2.2). Combined with the ageing of their populations, these low growth rates signal difficulties in maintaining existing spending patterns without increasing the tax load on the shrinking proportion that is employed.

One way of counteracting low growth rates is to increase immigration rates, which at least several countries (Italy, Germany and the Netherlands) appear to be doing. Net migration per 1,000 ranges from zero in Japan to almost 27 in Singapore. Again, it is important to know more details about the immigrants before estimating their impact on health policy. Are they skilled or unskilled, destitute or wealthy? Are they members of compatible cultures and religions or those likely to cause friction with the existing community? Although diverse cultures and ethnic groupings can strengthen countries in the long run, they can put severe pressures on health and social service

Box 2.2 Policies for older people in Sweden

Together with low rates of net migration and low growth rates of the population Sweden has one of the highest percentages of old people. Together, these factors make Sweden something of a test bed for coping with the challenges of ageing. In the area of care of older people Sweden has responded with a combination of decentralization, service integration and de-institutionalization and targeting. In 1992 municipalities became responsible for providing health and social care to older people living in institutions; and in half of the county councils this has been extended to home-based services. In addition, the number of long-term beds has been reduced significantly, while home-based services are increasingly targeted to highly dependent older people.

Box 2.3   Asylum seekers and the National Health Service in Britain

Asylum seekers impact on the NHS in two ways. In an already tightly cash-limited health service any increase in the number of patients puts considerable additional strain on existing services. This particularly applies to GPs as the first point of contact for patients. The NHS also struggles to cope with the scale and nature of health problems of asylum seekers. In part, this reflects special needs arising from asylum seekers coming from countries with a high prevalence of infectious diseases, or having been tortured (Dunne, 2002). However, health problems are often exacerbated by the poor living conditions of asylum seekers once they arrive in the country (Casciani, 2002). Their vulnerable and very marginal position is also a major barrier to accessing health services.

system upon arrival (see Box 2.3). Often, they bring with them disease patterns that require shifts in resources. Just as infusions of immigrants of different backgrounds can produce challenges for the health system, countries that are more homogeneous are likely to have an easier time meeting the health needs of their population than highly ethnically diverse populations.

As was noted earlier, diverse cultures can have vastly different views of health, health care and health service delivery. These differences can be heightened when the values of a group are in conflict with those of the medical profession (e.g. female genital mutilation). With the clear exception of Japan, the countries examined here all reflect relatively high degrees of ethnic or religious diversity (Table 2.4), or (in many cases) both. While religious diversity in some cases might be a significant factor beyond simply reflecting other cleavages in society, ethnic differences can be more crucial, particularly where newer immigrants are predominantly from minority groupings. Ethnic groups not only challenge the health system because they have a varying prevalence of particular diseases and conditions, but also because they bring with them divergent views about the medical community, health and political authorities.

Although most countries have a single dominant majority, except for Japan they have significant ethnic/racial minorities that complicate delivery of health care services. The problem is aggravated because health services often have not embraced diversity. An exception is Singapore, which seems to have been largely successful in integrating the Malay and Indian minorities into the health system. In contrast, blacks in the USA continue to be significantly less well served by the health care system than whites as measured by access or health

Table 2.4   *Ethnic and religious composition*

	Ethnic composition	*Religious composition*
Australia	Caucasian 92%; Asian 7 %; Aboriginal and other 1%.	Catholic 26.4%; Anglican 20.5%; other Christian 20.5%; Buddhist 1.9%; Muslim 1.5%; other or unaffiliated 28.0%.
France	Predominantly Celtic and Latin with Teutonic, Slavic, North African, Indochinese and Basque minorities.	Roman Catholic 83–88%; Protestant 2%; Jewish 1%; Muslim 5–10%; unaffiliated 4%.
Germany	German 91.5%; Turkish 2.4%; other 6.1% (mainly Greek, Italian, Polish, Russian, Serbo-Croatian and Spanish).	Protestant 34%; Roman Catholic 34%; Muslim 3.7%; other or unaffiliated 28.3%.
Italy	Predominantly Italian with clusters of German-, French-, and Slovene-Italians in the north and Albanian- and Greek-Italians in the south.	Predominantly Roman Catholic and Protestant with mature Jewish communities and growing Muslim immigrant community.
Japan	Japanese 99%; other 1% (mainly Korean, Chinese, Brazilian and Filipino).	Shinto and Buddhist 84%; other (including Christian 0.7%) 16%.
Netherlands	Dutch 83%; other 17% (of which 9% are of non-Western origin, mainly Turks, Moroccan, Antilleans and Indonesians).	Roman Catholic 31%; Dutch Reformed 13%; Muslim 5.5%; other 2.5%; none 41%; Calvinist 7%.
New Zealand	European 69.8%; Maori 7.9%; Asian 5.7%; Pacific Islander 4.4%; mixed 7.8%; other 0.5%; unspecified 3.8%.	Anglican 14.9%; Roman Catholic 12.4%; Presbyterian 10.9%; Methodist 2.9%; other 6.3%; unspecified 17.2%; none 26%.
Singapore	Chinese 76.8%; Malay 13.9%; Indian 7.9%; other 1.4%.	Buddhist 42.5%; Muslim 14.9%; Christian 9.8%; Hindu 4%; Catholic 4.8%; Taoist 8.5%; other 0.7%; none 14.8%.
Sweden	Indigenous population Swedes and Finnish and Sami minorities; foreign-born or first-generation immigrant Finns, Yugoslavs, Danes, Norwegians, Greeks and Turks.	Lutheran 87%; others include Roman Catholic, Orthodox, Baptist, Muslim, Jewish and Buddhist.
United Kingdom	English 83.6%; Scottish 8.6%; Welsh 4.9%; Northern Irish 2.9%; black 2%; Indian 1.8%; Pakistani 1.3%; mixed 1.2%; other 1.6%.	Christian (Anglican, Roman Catholic, Presbyterian, Methodist) 71.6%; Muslim 2.7%; Hindu 1%; other 1.6%; unspecified or none 23.1%.
United States	White 81.7%; black 12.9%; Asian 4.2%; Native American 1%.	Protestant 52%; Roman Catholic 24%; Mormon 2%; Jewish 1%; Muslim 1%; other 10%; none 10%.

Source: Data from *The World Fact Book* (2006).

Table 2.5   *Health indicators by race, USA*

	White	Black
Low birthweight/1,000 births	7.0	13.5
Neonatal deaths/1,000 births	3.86	9.22
Infant deaths/1,000 births	5.72	13.49
Life expectancy (at birth)		
Male	75.0	68.6
Female	80.2	75.5

Source: Data from National Center for Health Care Statistics (2006).

outcomes (see Table 2.5). Similarly, the Maori minority in New Zealand has traditionally had a difficult assimilation into the health care system. As more asylum seekers are coming into specific European countries, they will complicate health delivery and will bring with them unique new health problems with which the health care systems must deal.

The comparative wealth of countries

As discussed earlier, the most obvious determinant of health care funding and provision across all countries is wealth. Rich countries on average put considerably more resources into health care simply because they have more discretionary funds. Unfortunately, very poor countries cannot compete with wealthier countries in health care spending and cannot afford the kind of medicine affluent countries take for granted.

The most used comparative measure of wealth is the GDP per capita. In 2005, the average GDP per capita of all countries worldwide was $9,500, with a low of $400 in East Timor and a high of $55,600 in Luxembourg. Seventeen countries had per capita GDP below $1,000 and an additional 68 between $1,000 and $4,000. From the data presented in Table 2.6, it is clear that all of our countries are relatively wealthy; in fact, they are clustered at over $25,000. The variance in wealth among these nations might help to explain minor economic limits on those nations near the bottom as compared to those at the top. However, the relatively small differences in wealth among these countries means that differences in health provision and spending found among them here are not likely to be explained simply by this factor.

Table 2.6 *GDP per capita, 2005, in US dollars*

Country	GDP/capita
USA	41,800
Australia	31,900
Japan	31,500
Netherlands	30,500
Germany	30,400
UK	30,300
France	29,900
Sweden	29,800
Italy	29,200
Singapore	28,100
New Zealand	25,200

Source: Data from *The World Fact Book* (2006).

Social and economic determinants of health

In addition to the overall wealth of a country, there is evidence that the degree of inequality or disparity in social and economic conditions at the national level is a determinant of population health. Countries with greater inequality tend to have poorer health outcomes overall as well as a more unequal distribution of health. Navarro investigated the association between political economy type and socio-economic conditions in various countries and found that, compared to social democratic or Christian democratic political economies, liberal political economies had higher income inequality and unemployment, lower wage and salary levels and a higher proportion of people living in poverty (1999). Moreover, Navarro and Shi (2001) found that countries with liberal political economies had the largest income and wage differentials, the least redistributive impact of the state, and the lowest rate of improvement in infant mortality between 1960 and 1996. In their study of infant mortality rates in OECD countries, Navarro and associates at the International Network on Social Inequalities and Health found that political variables play an important role in defining how public and social policies determine the levels of inequalities. 'In general, political parties more committed to re-distributional policies, such as social democratic parties, are the most successful in reducing inequalities and improving infant mortality' (2003).

While our country data largely support this thesis, there are exceptions. For example, Japan ranks near or at the top for most population health indicators, even though it is a liberal political economy. As Boxall and Short (2006) point out, however, many features of Japan's political economy closely resemble those of social and Christian democratic political economies, and it has a relatively equitable income distribution and high pension commitments and practices 'stakeholder' rather than 'shareholder' capitalism. They also found that Australia runs counter to the hypothesis of the relationship between political economy, inequality and population health, but they suggest that its unique welfare state model may partly account for its exceptionalism in terms of population health outcomes.

Although there is variation in health status across nations, often the variation among groups within a particular nation is even higher. Because this variation cannot be attributed to differences in the health system of the country, other factors must be important. Key factors are social and economic, which in turn might be reflected in differences in health by race, religion or ethnic background. Lower social class, as measured by income, education or other socio-economic status (SES) indicators, is related to higher death rates overall and higher rates of most diseases that are the most common causes of death (Fuchs, 2004; Fukuda *et al.*, 2004; Marmot and Wilkinson, 1999). Moreover, social class differences in mortality and morbidity continue to widen (Mackenbach *et al.*, 1997).

If a primary goal of health policy is to improve the health status of the population, it is essential to understand the economic and social determinants of health at the individual level as well. For instance, according to an Australian study, 'the prevalence of chronic disease varies across the socioeconomic gradient for a number of specific diseases, as well as for important disease risk factors. Therefore, any policy interventions to address the impact of chronic disease, at a population level, need to take into account these socioeconomic inequalities' (Glover *et al.*, 2004). A workable model of health requires a shift away from the dominance of the medical care system towards this more inclusive model of health. 'Social problems are resolved primarily through non-medical means, signifying a shift away from the current practice of defining and treating them as medical illnesses' (Hurowitz, 1993: 132).

Health status disparities linked to SES are probably the result of a complicated mix of factors suggested by three distinct theories. The first, *natural and social selection,* contends that one of the key determinants of social class is health status. This theory assumes that those with poor health, high-risk behaviour and social pathologies naturally concentrate in the lower social class. If good health is indeed necessary in order to pursue life goals and affords one the opportunity to succeed in meeting them, it should not be surprising to find that persons in poor health would tend towards a lower SES. Although this might explain the disparity at the margins, however, it is not generally seen as a major explanation.

A second theory, the *structuralist*, attributes class differences in health to structural factors such as the production and consumption of wealth. Lower SES persons generally exist in less healthy environments, both at home and work. For example, a recent study concluded that there is 'widespread evidence that the poor in the US, UK, and perhaps other countries as well, face a disproportionate burden of environmental risks' (Huggins, 2002). They face more exposure to air pollution, poor water, ambient noise, sub-standard housing and overcrowding. In contrast, higher SES persons enjoy healthier homes, safer appliances and vehicles, and less hazardous jobs.

The third theory, a *cultural and behavioural* one, sees disparities in health among social classes as the result of differences in behaviour. Often the culture of the lower classes leads to engagement in multiple high-risk behaviour that, in turn, leads to poor health. Smoking, alcohol and drug abuse, violence, sedentary lifestyles, obesity, poor diet and other unhealthy behaviours are disproportionately present in lower SES groupings. Many observers have concluded that this last theory is the most explanatory, but most conclude that it must be accompanied by the structuralist theory because the behaviour occurs within this broader social context. As noted by Mechanic, SES is 'perhaps the single most important influence on health outcomes, in part through its direct influence, but more importantly, through the many indirect effects it has on factors that directly shape health outcomes' (1994: 149). These indirect factors are most apparent when one examines the several components of SES: income and education.

Income has been found to be a critical variable in determining health status at two levels. At a cross-national level, research consistently shows that the distribution of income has more to do with the health of the population than does the level of medical spending. The best health results are achieved in those societies that minimize the gap between the rich and the poor, that place more emphasis on the values of equity. Wilkinson (1997) suggests that healthy, egalitarian societies are more socially cohesive, they have a stronger community life, and they suffer fewer of the corrosive effects of inequality. He also found that approximately two-thirds of the variation in mortality rates within developed nations is related to the distribution of income in the population. This includes the UK where, despite universal access to health care, mortality rates among the working-class population increased as income distribution widened in the 1980s (Wilkinson, 1992). In contrast, Japan has the most equal income distribution and the highest life expectancy despite relatively low levels of health care spending (Kawachi *et al.*, 1999).

At the individual level as well, low income is consistently related to ill health. Low-income families are more likely to assess their health status as 'poor'. Low-income persons are significantly more likely to have preventable hospitalizations than high-income persons, with one study finding that the lowest income group was four times as likely to be hospitalized as the highest-income group (Angell, 1993). The most likely explanation of these disparities is to be found in some combination of the theories discussed above, but its implication for health policy is significant. The impact of any efforts to constrain health care costs will hit most severely those groups which are not only most likely to need the care but also least likely to have other options. Despite greater need, larger proportions of the poor have difficulty in gaining access to health services that might avert poor health.

Not surprisingly, given its close association with income, education is also significantly related to health status. Persons with less education have more frequent short-stay hospitalizations, they have a higher prevalence of chronic conditions and are significantly more limited in activity due to such conditions, and they have significantly lower self-assessment of their health. One study found that of all indicators, education had the strongest and most consistent relationship with health and was the single most consistent predictor of good health (Winkleby *et al.*, 1992).

Health status, then, is intimately related to various measures of SES, particularly education and income (Marmot and Wilkinson, 1999). These differences are critical in understanding the social and cultural context of health and require considerably more research on how these factors operate. The interactive model of health care attributes poor health outcomes to a broad range of social factors that are bound up in the SES construct. Although SES might have a direct impact on health, it is more likely that it operates indirectly through other factors. In addition to inequitable access to primary care, health promotion and disease prevention efforts, other critical factors include unemployment, violence, breakdown of family support structures and inadequate housing.

Unemployment can influence health by reducing income level and standard of living. Moreover, the importance of work to one's well-being, over and above the financial aspects, is well-documented (Hummelgaard *et al.*, 1998; Turner, 1995). The unemployed have lower self-esteem and experience significant psychological stress which is linked to higher levels of both subjectively and objectively assessed levels of physical and mental ill health. Heightened unemployment rates are associated with heightened death rates. A recent study concluded that 'increases in the unemployment rates in European Union countries are related to deteriorated health as measured by elevated mortality rates over the following 10 to 15 years' (Brenner, 2001). Interestingly, the relationship was strongest in the UK, Sweden, Germany and Finland. Suicide and deliberate self-harm are more prevalent among the unemployed, as are smoking and alcohol and drug abuse, particularly among the unemployable youth. At the community level, death rates have been found to increase during times of economic depression and joblessness, and to decrease during times of economic growth (Barwick, 1992). Although the full dynamics are unclear, the assumption that employment is crucial to both mental and physical health is supported by a broad array of studies. Reduction of unemployment has significant health benefits for the population as well as the individual.

The family has traditionally played an important role in integrating health-promoting routines into the daily lives of its members. It has also served as an important facilitator of self-esteem and a social setting that provides critical contributions to psychological and physical development. While reality has often fallen short of this ideal, the decline first of the extended family and more recently the nuclear family has had adverse effects on health. Studies consistently find that marriage is associated with lower levels of mortality, better overall health status and healthier behaviour patterns (Stanton, 2003). A study from the Netherlands, for instance, concludes that married people have the lowest morbidity rate, while the divorced show the highest (Joung *et al.*, 1994). Another study from the UK found that even when the effects of smoking, drinking and other unhealthy activities were factored in, married men had a 9 per cent lower risk of dying as compared to unmarried men (BBC News, 2002). Although the reasons for this are unclear, a likely factor is the 'social support' of having a wife or husband nearby. Another explanation is that both single men and women tend to have a less healthy lifestyle including sleep, diet and work habits, and to be more prone to loneliness and depression. Family relationships, however, in whatever form do appear to encourage good health practices and provide strong social links that reduce the likelihood of ill health. Thus, one would expect that health outcomes would be better in those countries like Japan and Italy where close family structures remain a more resilient feature of society.

The context of health care

This chapter has placed health care in its broader context in each of our countries. We suggest that one cannot understand the dynamics of a health care system without understanding the political and legal institutions and practices of the country and the cultural and historical environment from which it emerged. The size and mix of the population, its ethnic, racial and religious composition, and the level of economic equality, all help shape the health care system of a country. Each of our countries has its own character, a certain combination of features that sets it apart. Although far from an in-depth analysis of each country, this overview demonstrates that each provides a distinct setting for the emergence of a health care system over time.

Chapter 1 suggested that there are strong forces that might be leading by necessity to a convergence of policies across countries. In this brief overview of the context of health policy in these countries, it is obvious that although they are all affluent, developed countries, they bring with them a divergent set of structural and value systems that will be useful for comparative purposes in the following substantive chapters. While these factors certainly cannot explain all the differences or similarities among the countries, they can help us understand some of the anomalies that will arise out of the more in-depth analysis of these health care systems in the following chapters.

Chapter 3

Funding, Provision and Governance

Health care is often thought of as a system. A health system is a highly complex entity and consists of a range of sub-systems. Among these, the sub-systems of *funding, provision* and *governance* are central for understanding health policy comparatively.

The sub-system of *funding* is concerned with raising financial resources and allocating monies to the providers of health care. Health care can be funded from a range of sources, from taxes and social insurance contributions to private insurance premiums and out-of-pocket payments by patients. Funding, however, is about more than the technicalities of raising and allocating financial resources; funding is also a pointer to power, and control of funding is a major resource in health policy. The sub-system of *provision* focuses on the delivery of health services. Health systems provide a range of services, and patients have varying levels of choice when using health services, such as among individual doctors or different care settings. The delivery of health services is in the hands of different types of providers including public and private, profit or non-profit, hospitals. The mix of providers makes the provision of health care more or less publicly integrated. The sub-systems of funding and provision form the basis of the sub-system of *governance*. Governance describes the modes of coordinating health systems and their multiple actors. Governance is underpinned by tensions between public and private as well as between the centre and localities. As governments tend to play an important role in health systems, governance can also be thought of as government capacity or authority.

In a comparative context, health systems are often grouped under specific typologies of health systems, as discussed in Chapter 1. The typologies present models of funding, providing and governing health care in the form of distinct ideal types (Burau and Blank, 2006). The implicit assumption is that certain models of funding are directly associated with certain models of provision. For example, the funding of health care from taxation is said to make for public provision of health care. As the analysis below shows, this is the case in the health systems in some countries. In others, however, individual health systems combine different models of funding and provision, and even rely on a mix of several models of funding or provision. This directs the attention to the country-specific political contexts in which health systems are embedded and which were introduced in Chapter 2.

For example, in Britain and Sweden, where health care is predominantly publicly funded and provided, government looms large in the governance of health systems. At the same time, the specific features of health governance also reflect the fact that the wider political system and health governance in Britain is much more centralized than in Sweden. The factors which lead to differences between countries coexist with common pressures across health systems including ageing populations, advances in medical technology and increasing demands from patients. This chapter provides an overview of the funding, provision and governance of health care and shows how they are shaped by country-specific contexts as well as by universal pressures. An important aim will be to assess the relative usefulness of the typologies of the different types of health systems.

Comparing funding of health systems

Funding offers a good starting point for looking at health systems comparatively. Funding provides a first indicator of the relative size of health systems and the role of governments in health systems. Not surprisingly, there is some variation among these countries. Table 3.1

Table 3.1   *Per capita expenditure on health care in US dollars, 2003*

USA	5,711
France	3,048
Germany	3,005
New Zealand	2,909
Australia	2,876
Sweden	2,745
UK	2,347
Italy	2,261
Japan	2,249
New Zealand	1,902
Singapore	950[a]

[a] The figure for Singapore is from 2004.

Sources: Data from OECD (2006); Singapore Ministry of Health (2006); United Nations Statistics Division (2005).

Table 3.2   *Changes in health care expenditure as a percentage of GDP*

	1974	1979	1984	1989	1994	1999	2004[a]
Australia	6.1	6.8	7.0	7.1	7.9	8.4	9.2
France	n/a	n/a	n/a	n/a	9.3	9.2	10.5
Germany	7.9	8.4	8.9	8.6	9.9	10.5	10.9
Italy	n/a	n/a	n/a	7.5	7.5	7.6	8.4
Japan	5.1	6.1	6.6	6.1	6.7	7.4	8.0
Netherlands	6.5	7.1	7.2	7.6	8.1	8.0	9.2
New Zealand	6.0	6.4	5.6	6.5	7.1	7.6	8.4
Singapore	n/a	n/a	n/a	2.8	3.1	2.9	3.8
Sweden	7.2	8.6	8.9	8.3	8.1	8.4	9.1
UK	5.3	5.3	6.0	5.9	7.0	7.1	8.3
USA	7.6	8.3	9.9	11.3	13.2	13.1	15.3

[a] The figures for Australia, Germany, Japan and Singapore are from 2003.
n/a = not available

Sources: Data from OECD (2006) and Singapore Ministry of Health (2000 and 2006).

ranks the countries according to their per capita expenditure on health care. The USA is in first place and spends over six times as much per head as Singapore, which is the lowest spender. However, this is not typical of the entire range because these two countries are outliers. The upper mid-range is represented by France, Germany, the Netherlands, Australia and Sweden, which spend between US$2,745 and US$3,048 per capita on health care. Britain, Italy, Japan and New Zealand are in the lower mid-range and spend an average of $2,190.

The picture is similar when looking at health care expenditure as a percentage of GDP in Table 3.2. The majority of countries spend between about 8 and 9 per cent of their GDP on health care. The clear exception is the USA with 15.3 per cent, followed by Germany with 10.9 per cent. Health spending has increased since the 1970s, although less dramatically in some countries than in others. For example, in the Netherlands health spending increased from 6.0 to 8.4 per cent between 1974 and 2004, while in the USA health spending doubled over the same period of time.

Besides the overall level of funding, the sources of funding give an initial indication of the kinds of health system with which we are dealing. Table 3.3 suggests that all the health systems are predominantly publicly funded. As before, Singapore and the USA are the clear outliers with only 26.0 and 44.7 per cent of spending, respectively, coming from public

Table 3.3   *Changes in public expenditure on health care as a percentage of total expenditure on health care*

	1974	1979	1984	1989	1994	1999	2004[a]
Australia	63.4	61.8	71.6	67.8	65.8	69.5	67.5
France	n/a	n/a	n/a	n/a	76.0	76.0	78.4
Germany	78.2	78.5	77.4	76.0	80.2	78.5	78.2
Italy	n/a	n/a	n/a	76.9	74.4	72.0	76.4
Japan	74.1	74.3	72.9	76.6	78.6	81.1	81.5
Netherlands	65.9	69.2	70.8	67.0	72.9	62.7	62.3
New Zealand	74.0	84.4	87.0	85.8	77.5	77.5	77.4
Singapore	70.1	n/a	68.0	n/a	n/a	n/a	26.0
Sweden	89.9	91.7	91.6	89.6	87.1	85.7	84.9
UK	89.7	89.6	86.9	83.2	83.9	80.6	85.5
USA	39.8	40.9	40.1	39.6	45.0	43.8	44.7

[a] The figures for Australia, Germany, Japan and Singapore are from 2003.
n/a = not available

Sources: Data from OECD (2006) and Singapore Ministry of Health (2000, 2006).

sources. For the remaining countries, however, public expenditure as a share of total health care expenditure ranges from 62.3 per cent in Netherlands to 85.5 per cent in Britain. Looking at the figures from the early 1970s onwards, continuity is the most striking feature, although there have been interesting changes in some countries. In Australia, Japan, New Zealand and the USA the share of public funding rose between 3 and almost 7 per cent, while Sweden and Britain saw a slight fall in the percentage of expenditure from public sources. Singapore demonstrates an even more dramatic decrease in public funding as it moved to the Medisave scheme, thus shifting to an individual funding base (to be discussed later).

With the exception of the USA and Singapore, therefore, the health systems are predominantly publicly funded. However, a closer look at the exact sources of funding reveals important differences. Table 3.4 distinguishes between public expenditure by governments and compulsory social security schemes, and private expenditure from out-of-pocket payments, private insurance and other private funds. Government expenditure can come from general taxation or earmarked taxes, whereas out-of-pocket payments are payments made directly by patients themselves. Out-of-pocket payments come in a variety of forms. As part of a social or private insurance patients may have to cover part of the cost of medical treatment (co-payments). Alternatively,

Table 3.4   *Sources of funding as a percentage of health care expenditure, 2004*

	Public funding		Private funding		
	Government[a]	Social security[b]	Out-of-pocket payments[c]	Private insurance	Other funds
Australia	67.5	0.0	21.6	7.4	2.9
France	3.3	75.0	7.6	12.4	1.7
Germany	9.8	68.4	10.4	8.8	2.6
Italy	76.3	0.1	19.6	0.9	3.1
Japan	17.5	64.0	17.3	0.3	0.9
Netherlands	3.0	59.3	7.8	19.1	6.0
New Zealand	77.4	0.0	17.2	5.1	0.3
Sweden	85.5	0.0	n/a	n/a	n/a
UK	83.4	0.0	n/a	n/a	n/a
USA	32.2	12.5	13.2	36.7	5.4

[a] The figures for Australia, Germany and Japan are from 2003.
[b] The figures for Australia and the UK are from 2002. The figures for Germany and Japan are from 2003.
[c] The figures for Australia are from 2002. The figures for Germany and Japan are from 2003.
n/a = not available

Source: Data from OECD (2006).

patients may have to pay a fixed amount before the insurance company gets involved (deductibles). Out-of-pocket payments may also occur as a result of self-medication. This includes over-the-counter prescriptions and medical services not covered by the health insurance.

Looking at the public sources of funding, it is striking that countries seem to rely predominantly either on social security, as in the case of France, Germany, Japan and the Netherlands, or on government funding, as in the case of Australia, Italy, New Zealand, Britain and Sweden. As for private funding, most countries rely on out-of-pocket payments by patients, although the percentage ranges from 10.4 per cent in Germany to 21.6 per cent in Australia. The exceptions are the Netherlands, France and the USA, where private insurance is the main source of private funding. Considering the earlier figures on public expenditure, it is not surprising that the sources of health care funding are more diverse in the USA. Here, one-third of health care expenditure comes from government funds, one-third from private insurance, while the remaining one-third comes from social security and out-of-pocket payments. The reasons for the differences in the sources of funding are analysed in more detail in the following sections.

National health services and the commitment to public funding

National health services are the archetypal example of a publicly funded health system. Health care is predominantly funded from taxation and is available to every resident in the country. Public funding results in universal access. Britain, New Zealand and Sweden, together with Italy as a latecomer, are classical examples of this type of public funding.

In the British NHS well over 90 per cent of funding comes from public sources, over 70 per cent from general taxation and the rest from contributions to National Insurance, which is a specific tax levied on incomes. Co-payments by patients account for about only 2 per cent of funding (Department of Health, 2006a). Prominent areas of co-payments include: drugs, where payments by patients have risen over time, although they remain low in comparison to other countries; dental services, where patients have to cover the majority of the costs up to a maximum; and ophthalmic services, which have been widely deregulated. Another source of funding is private insurance. The market for employment-based private insurance schemes expanded dramatically in the 1980s in response to tax incentives, but has since levelled off (Baggot, 2004). An important reason for taking out private insurance is to compensate for the perceived low quality of NHS services and for the long waiting lists for elective surgery.

The situation in Sweden is similar. Public funding is central and comes from income tax raised by county councils, the regional tier of government, and is complemented by state grants and subsidies from National Health Insurance. Private funding from co-payments and supplementary private insurance play only a marginal role. The universality typical of national health services leads to the socialization of funding, although it is never complete (Freeman, 2000). Whereas over 90 per cent of funding in Britain and Sweden comes from public sources, other national health services rely to a greater extent on private sources of funding.

The New Zealand health care system continues to be financed predominantly through general taxation, although the percentage of public health expenditure has fallen over the last 20 years and is now clearly below that of Britain and Sweden. In 2000, about 77.5 per cent of health expenditure was public, down from 88.1 per cent in 1980 (New Zealand Ministry of Health, 2001). New Zealand citizens contribute to health care revenue through general taxation based mainly upon Pay as You Earn (PAYE) income tax and Goods and Services Tax from which funds are allocated annually to the health system budget.

Out-of-pocket payments account for about 16.4 per cent and private health insurance 6.2 per cent of total health care spending in New Zealand. The remaining small share of health revenue (about 0.4 per cent) is primarily from not-for-profit organizations (New Zealand Ministry of Health 2001). With the exceptions of primary care, where a fee-for-service system operates, and individual co-payments for drugs, most health services in New Zealand are provided free of charge. In 2000, about 37 per cent of the population was covered by private health insurance of some kind, much of this supplemental. Although its proportion of total health expenditure grew from 1.1 per cent in 1980 to 6.2 per cent in 2000, it remains marginal and has been static over the last decade.

Private sources of funding have also played an important role in Australia, which had the distinction of being the only country to have introduced universal national health insurance and then to have dismantled it. By 1981, most Australians relied on private insurance coverage. In 1984, however, Medicare, a compulsory national health insurance administered by the Commonwealth, was introduced. It is primarily funded from general tax revenue, supplemented by a 1.5 per cent identified income tax levy, state revenue and co-payments (Hall, 1999: 96). Private insurance accounts for 11 per cent of total health care expenditure while 19 per cent comes from co-payments by individuals. About one-third of the population has private insurance but this represents a substantial decrease in private insurance from the over 80 per cent in 1970 and the 64 per cent just prior to Medicare in 1983 (Palmer and Short, 2000: 13). In light of this steady decline, Australia has taken measures to increase the population coverage of private health insurance, reduce pressure on public hospital waiting lists and services, and support and improve the viability of the insurance industry. In 1999, under the PHI Incentive Scheme, anyone purchasing private insurance received a 30 per cent subsidy, paid either as a tax rebate or as a reduced purchase price of insurance. Then, in July 2000, the Lifetime Health Cover was introduced which applied a base premium to those purchasing insurance up until the age of 30 (Bertelsmann Foundation, 2003b).

Public funding through social insurance

Social insurance is another form of public funding. It is a hybrid and combines two very different principles of organizing health care: the insurance is paid for by independent institutions but is publicly mandated (Freeman, 2000: 54f). In contrast to private insurance, social health insurance is based on the principle of social solidarity. Contributions are paid as a percentage of the salary rather than according to the specific health risks of the individual and are often shared by employers and employees. This represents a redistributive policy between high and low risk patients as well as between high and low earners. Dependants of employees (i.e. non-earning spouses and children) are also covered, thus in effect ensuring universal coverage of the population.

The German health system was the pioneer among its kind. Health care is funded by contributions paid equally by employers and employees as a fixed percentage of the monthly salary. Membership is compulsory on everyone with annual earnings below a certain ceiling, which in 2005 was 42,300 euros (Bundesministerium für Gesundheit, 2005). The social health insurance is administered by private, non-profit funds, which operate under public law. Employees earning above the ceiling (and the self-employed) are free to make their own arrangements and can choose to stay with the social health insurance or join a private health insurance scheme. However, only 9 per cent of the population are covered by this private insurance. Other sources of private funding are co-payments. Co-payments for drugs were introduced in 1977 and have increased regularly comprising 28 per cent of expenditure on drugs by 1999 (Wendt *et al.*, 2005). With greater cost pressures, co-payments in other areas were added and increased considerably in the late 1990s, now making up 12 per cent of the total health care expenditure (Busse and Riesberg, 2004: 73).

A close variant of the German model is the health system in the Netherlands (and France). An important difference is the greater importance of private sources of funding. About one-third of employees have been covered by private insurance, but this changed in 2006 with the creation of a single, universal insurance for acute risks that is compulsory for all employees and that covers a basic package of ambulatory and hospital medical services (Bartholomée and Maarse, 2006; Ministry for Health, Welfare and Sport, 2005). Insurance contributions are paid by employees and consist of a flat, nominal rate and an income-related component. Employees can choose to take out additional insurance cover and have free choice of insurance funds. In addition, there is an insurance for exceptional medical risks that covers long-term nursing care, psychiatric care and costs for outpatient prescriptions. It is organized along the lines of the old social insurance, covering all employees irrespective of income and funded by contributions from employees and increasingly co-payments. In sum, the new Dutch social health insurance is characterized by strong market elements in the form of insurance competition for employees, provider competition for contracts, and elements of private insurance especially in the form of voluntary complementary health plans.

Another, although more remote, variant of the social insurance model is the Japanese health system, which is built on the German model but is a unique combination of private and public components of funding and provision. Under the universal coverage principle, all registered residents of Japan must enroll in one of the social health care insurance systems. The main social insurance systems for salaried workers in companies and factories in Japan are the Employees Health Insurance (KENKO HOKEN) which can be of either the government-managed type or the society-managed type. Self-employed workers and non-employed people are covered by the National Health Insurance (KOKUMIN KENKO HOKEN) while specific work-based insurances include the Seamens Insurance and the Mutual Aid Associations for public services workers such as national and local government employees. The Employees' Health Insurance is a workplace-based insurance system under the administration and operation of the Social Insurance Agency, an external body of the Japanese Ministry of Health, Labour and Welfare. Within the system, society-managed health insurance is for large-scale companies while other companies are covered by the government-managed health insurance. Under the society-managed system, each society may manage its own health insurance programme with its own benefits and contributions, within the government regulations (Social Insurance Agency, 2006).

There are more than 5,000 independent insurance plans in Japan, thus subsuming the private sector under a government regulatory umbrella. In order to reduce the administrative costs of the health insurance system, the government is moving to promote mergers among insurers of the National Health Insurance so this number will decrease. The sources of funding varies between insurance schemes, but all schemes are characterized by co-payments of between 10 and 30 per cent of charges designed to constrain demand (Imai, 2002: 5). In comparison with the Netherlands, France and Germany, co-payments are high and clearly limit the scope of social solidarity. The emphasis on individual responsibility is partly offset by government subsidies for the community-based insurance scheme and the pool for health care for the elderly. Overall, insurance contributions account for 57 per cent of health expenditure, national government subsidies for 24 per cent, local government subsidies for 7 per cent and co-payments by patients for 12 per cent (Japanese Ministry of Health, 2000).

Private insurance and the emphasis on individual responsibility

Countries that predominantly rely on private insurance put considerable emphasis on individual responsibility. However, here too individual responsibility is never complete and private funding coexists with public funding, particularly for designated groups such as the poor and elderly. The USA is the archetypal example of this system of funding and is characterized by high complexity. Outside of programmes for the elderly and

---

Box 3.1   Medicare in the USA: public insurance in a private system

Medicare is a public insurance for the elderly, administered by the federal government and consisting of three parts. Part A is compulsory and covers hospital care funded through social security taxes paid by all working citizens. Part B is voluntary and covers other costs including doctors' bills and outpatient hospital treatment. It is funded by monthly premiums paid by enrollees and substantial federal subsidies. Under the traditional programme, which covers 86 per cent of Medicare beneficiaries, payments to hospitals, physicians and other providers are determined by complex prospective payment systems which provide the programme with a high level of control over the price component of total spending, but not much leverage over the volume of services. The remaining beneficiaries are enrolled in the Medicare+Choice programme, under which private health plans are paid a monthly capitation payment for each enrollee that is based on the amount Medicare spends per beneficiary in the geographic area served by the plan. Under this system, the total payment by Medicare to plans is fixed, and each health plan establishes its own methods for administering benefits and paying providers within parameters established by federal regulation. In 2003, the Medicare Prescription Drug, Improvement and Modernization Act became law and created Medicare Part D, implemented on 1 January 2006, to provide drug coverage to the elderly, through private, stand-alone drug plans. In contrast, a second public programme, Medicaid, is a joint federal–state health insurance programme covering the very poor funded by a combination of federal and state funds. Although originally Medicaid was designed for children its funding goes to supplement Medicare for the elderly poor.

Sources: State Coverage Initiatives (2002) and Iglehart (1999).

---

some disabled (see Box 3.1) the US health system remains largely market-based. Private insurance covers 58 per cent of the population and accounts for 34 per cent of total health expenditure (Health Care Financing Administration, 2000). It is provided by thousands of largely for-profit insurance companies (with the exception of Blue Cross-Blue Shield and other non-profits). Most private insurance is purchased by employers and many large employers are self-insured. Employers are not required by law to offer coverage to their employees and many do not, although tax considerations encourage them to do so. Only a small percentage of non-elderly Americans (5.3 per cent in 2003) purchase private insurance by themselves which is very costly (Krugman and Wells, 2006). An additional 21 per cent of total health spending comes from co-payments or other private sources. The private insurance coexists with a social insurance system for the elderly, which accounts for 45 per cent of total health expenditure and covers 25 per cent of the population (Bitton and Kahn, 2003). Other public expenditures such as Veterans' hospitals comprise 12 per cent of total health care spending. However, Woolhandler and Himmelstein (2002) recalculated the government share of health expenditure by including tax subsidies for private insurance and public employee private health benefits and concluded that the government-financed share of total health spending is actually 59.8 per cent, equal to $723.8 billion or $2,604 per capita. Importantly, an estimated 45 million people have no insurance coverage.

With its emphasis on individual responsibility, Singapore represents another variant of private insurance (see Box 1.1). Unlike European social insurance schemes, Singapore has opted not to have risk-pooling based on the premise that each generation should meet its own needs rather than build up trust reserves or commitments for future generations (Ham, 2001; Lim, 2004). At the centre of the health system is Medisave, a compulsory savings scheme, which is managed centrally by the Central Provident Fund (CPF), Singapore's mandatory pension fund. Under the scheme, each employee and self-employed person puts aside a percentage (6 to 8 per cent with S$4,500 ceiling) of monthly income into a Medical Savings Account (MSA) to meet future health care expenses. This insurance scheme puts individual responsibility centre stage and medical risks remain largely individualized (Lim, 2004). Solidarity is confined to the immediate family and accounts are transferable to one's spouse, children, parents and grandparents. The very limited redistribution, together with ceilings on contributions, also significantly limits the scope of Medisave, as does the reluctance of individuals to deplete their savings.

Medisave is supplemented by MediShield (and Eldershield for the elderly), a catastrophic insurance programme introduced in 1990 to help people with long hospital stay pay for their hospitalization bills. Approximately 2.7 million people in Singapore have medical insurance in the form of MediShield or private Shield plans within the CPF umbrella with another 200,000 holding private hospital plans outside the CPF. Because MediShield's premiums, deductibles and claims limits had not been adjusted sufficiently to keep pace with rising medical costs, MediShield claims exceeded premiums collected annually (Bertelsmann Foundation, 2005b). This led to a reform of MediShield in 2005 designed to broaden the pool to healthier members and restructure private insurance plans and reduce the sizeable pool of uninsured: approximately 440,000 people are not covered by either MediShield or private plans, many self-employed people or dependent spouses, largely elderly (Lin, 2006). Also in 2005, the government launched an open competitive tender to privatize a key component of MediShield, the MediShield Plus plan, which has 350,000 policy holders. The privatization of MediShield

Plus is part of the overall MediShield reforms aimed at encouraging greater competition in the medical insurance market.

A third source of funding in Singapore is Medifund, a government endowment fund built on surpluses each year, that serves as a safety net to provide financial assistance to individuals who, despite the subsidies and payments from their MSAs and the MediShield scheme, cannot pay their medical bills (Vasoo, 2001). Applications for Medifund assistance are considered by Medifund Committees. In 2002, about 178,209 Medifund applications were considered, 177,949 of which were approved (Singapore MOH, 2006). Despite the view that this '3-M' system is the centrepiece of Singapore's health care financing system, however, it presently accounts for less than 10 per cent of national healthcare expenditure. The rest is made up of employer benefits (35 per cent), government subsidies (25 per cent), out-of-pocket payment (25 per cent), and private insurance (5 per cent) (Lim, 2004).

Control of funding and pressures for reform

As Figure 3.1 suggests, funding is about raising resources from a range of sources (such as taxes, social insurance contributions, private insurance premiums or out-of-pocket payments) and allocating these resources to the providers of health care. Health care tends to be funded by a mix of public and private sources, reflecting predominant types of funding and other, country-specific factors. National health services with their

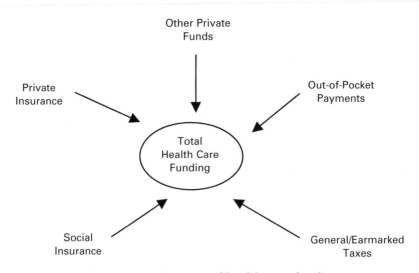

Figure 3.1   *Sources of health care funding*

commitment to universality of access get the majority of their funding from taxes. Britain and Sweden are classical examples of this type of publicly funded health system while Australia and New Zealand combine tax funding with strong elements of private funding with over 20 per cent of funds coming from private insurance and out-of-pocket payments.

Social insurance systems are hybrids: money is raised from independent insurance funds, but are publicly mandated and are based on the principle of social solidarity. Germany is the classical example of this type of funding and social insurance contributions account for the majority of health care expenditure. In comparison with the health systems in the Netherlands and Japan, social insurance coexists with strong elements of private funding, from private insurance and out-of-pocket payments respectively. Finally, health systems where private insurance dominates place individual responsibility first and largely rely on private funds. In Singapore, a highly individualized compulsory savings account is key, whereas the USA relies on a mixture of private and public insurance at the price of leaving over 17 per cent of the population uncovered.

However, funding is about more than raising and allocating financial resources. How funds are raised and allocated is also a pointer to power. Different types of funding result in different types of control, and different types of control lead to different types of pressures for reform. Public funding means public control (Freeman, 2000: 44). Public control can be expected to be strongest in national health services, which are largely funded by taxes. Taxes place control over funding in public hands, leading to concentration rather than fragmentation and allowing for the control of (global) budgets.

The prime example is Britain, where the total NHS expenditure is set by the Treasury and is part of the government's three yearly spending reviews. Once the overall spending level has been set, the Department of Health determines the funds allocated to Primary Care Trusts as providers of primary care and purchasers of acute care and other forms of care. Budgets are based on population size and weighted for other factors that may increase health care needs. Public control over funding is further tightened by the fact that control resides primarily with central government, not least also because about 10 per cent of health care funding is earmarked for national level agencies and initiatives (Baggot, 2004). In addition, the Department also issues guidance on the use of resources, some of which is compulsory, together with priorities and directions relating to the development of health services (Ham, 2004). In contrast, in Sweden public control of funding is more decentralized and rests with the county councils. However, on two occasions the national government has limited the level of taxes that can be raised by county councils (Glenngård *et al.*, 2005).

However, public control of funding comes at a price (Klein, 2001). Inevitably, the interests of government as the payer of health care will be reflected in its approach to raising and allocating funds, and cost efficiency and containment are likely priorities (Fattore, 1999). And, to paraphrase Moran (1999: 61), a uniquely generous entitlement philosophy often goes hand-in-hand with parsimonious practice.

In national health services, problems of controlling total expenditure are practically unknown. Instead the central challenge is to meet the growing demands for health care within a fixed and tight budget. The political price of public control of funding rises when patients become less deferential and more demanding and the heightened mismatch between supply and demand manifests itself in long waiting lists for elective surgery. For example, a WHO study ranked the British NHS eighteenth in the world because of its lack of responsiveness to patients (Laurance and Norton, 2000). Centralization of control adds to the politicization of health care expenditure and in Britain responsibility for the negative consequences of inadequate funding falls back on central government (Ham, 2004). Health care reforms over the last 20 years can be read as attempts to make limited resources go further and have focused on increasing micro-efficiency and competition. Competition promises to provide more and/or better health services without spending more money (Freeman, 1998, 2000). The British NHS, for example, has gone through several waves of major reorganization (Ham, 1999). Yet, there are limits to this and starting in 2000 the government increased the spending on the NHS to match international spending levels. Here, an external review into the funding of the NHS provided a powerful leverage for a sustained increase in NHS funding (Ham, 2004).

In contrast with national health services, public control of funding is weaker in health systems that rely on social insurance and this typically manifests itself in problems of controlling total health care expenditure. A classical case is Germany where health reform has long been seen as an attempt to halt the 'cost explosion'. As a percentage of monthly salaries, social insurance contribution rates make health care expenditure highly visible (Moran, 1999: 74). However, contribution rates have come under pressure not only from rising expenditures but also from falling funding. An increasingly lower proportion of GDP is used for wages, reflecting larger profits by employers, wage increases below productivity as well as high levels of unemployment; also, there is a greater share of wages that is either exempt from contribution or that exceeds the maximum ceiling up to which contributions have to be paid (Amelung et al., 2003). This has been exacerbated by unification, to the extent that shortfalls in funding now are the main reason for the financial problems of the health system (Busse and Howorth, 1999: 331). Traditionally, power over funding has been decentralized and fragmented. In part, this is typical of the organizational complexity of social insurance systems and in the case of Germany is compounded by federalism. Until the mid 1990s, there were over 1,000 different insurance funds, each raising its own funds and setting its own contribution rates. Health care resources were allocated from the bottom up and doctors were free to decide on the treatment of patients. Moreover, the federal government was limited to setting (and altering) the framework in which the insurance funds and providers operated.

However, even social insurance schemes allow for some control of funding. In the Netherlands, for example, the (income-related) contribution rates for the two social insurance schemes are set by central government, and until the major changes in 2006 the yearly surveys on current and future expenditures published by the Department of Health had the status of spending ceilings (Loo *et al.*, 1999: 574). Interestingly, private health insurance has also been subject to extensive regulation such as pooling and a standard insurance package for high-risk employees. The recent reforms continued this trend and integrated the private insurance into a single, universal social insurance scheme. Japan is another example of successful public control of a social insurance system where insurance funds and providers are all strictly regulated by government. Importantly, all health care payments are made on the basis of a national fee schedule with implicit limits on the increase in overall expenditure. In Japan, all billing and payment is centralized through the payment fund of the National Health Insurance, which reviews all bills submitted and has the power to reduce payments to minimize fraud.

Systematic and effective public control of funding is weakest in health systems that rely on private insurance. The USA is a case in point. Rising health expenditure has been a major problem and the USA continues to be the most expensive health system of all industrialized countries. As seen earlier, the USA now spends over 15 per cent of its GDP on health care, almost double the average of industrialized nations. It is not only the predominance of private funding that makes public control of expenditure difficult, but also the fragmentation of insurance funds and provider organizations, together with the federalist structure in the USA. The US health system is an amalgamation of over 1,500 private insurance companies and managed care organizations; over 730,000 doctors, most of whom are specialists in private practice; over 5,800 acute care hospitals (with 5.1 million employees) and 15,000 long-term care facilities. Moreover, the public sector health system includes 3,141 counties that operate community hospitals and clinics; the 50 states which retain the primary constitutional roles of protecting the health of their respective residents and the training and licensing of medical personnel; and finally the federal government which funds Medicare and the joint federal–state Medicaid programme as well as specialized veterans' and research hospitals.

In the 1980s, the government attempted to control Medicare/ Medicaid spending by initiating diagnosis-related groups (DRGs), a system under which each category of treatment has a scheduled payment. Furthermore, in order to constrain private sector costs the government encouraged the creation of HMOs and other managed care systems. Other attempts to control cost growth have included a combination of selective provider contracting, discount price negotiations, utilization control practices, and risk-sharing payment methods. After the levelling-off of health care expenditures following the initiation of DRGs and managed care in the late 1980s to mid 1990s, costs have risen rapidly, again far exceeding general inflation rates. This is especially the case for Medicare/Medicaid where, despite DRGs, real growth is now approaching double figures annually.

Singapore is an exception to the rule. In 2000, the WHO ranked Singapore as the most effective health system in Asia and sixth in the world, despite spending only 3.1 per cent of its GDP on health care (*Straits Times*, 2000). This success has been attributed to: (1) the creation of the MSA system where individuals are encouraged to use their savings parsimoniously; (2) the government's success in dampening demand for health care through education programmes designed to keep health care expectations modest; and (3) the government's encouragement of family responsibilities for care of elderly and ill members (Duff, 2001: 147). The Medisave scheme emphasizes individual responsibility and family networks and gives the individuals control of their accounts but, crucially, this freedom is combined with strong government regulation. Participation is compulsory and caps on contribution rates, together with very high co-payments, have given government tight control of expenditure. The government also heavily subsidizes the primary care services and health promotion and disease prevention programmes, and emphasizes community health care over hospital care. The highly centralized political structure of Singapore and widespread regime approval ensures that government control is largely effective (Ham, 2001; Lim, 2004).

Health services and patient choice

Health services are first and foremost medical services, reflecting the prominence of doctors in the delivery of services and the allocation of health care resources. As Table 3.5 suggests, medical health services can be distinguished according to the specificity and the locality of care delivered (see also Chapter 1, p. 17). Primary care is typically less specialized

Table 3.5   *Types and settings of health services*

	Ambulatory settings	Hospital settings
Primary Care	Services provided by GPs working in their own practices or in health centres.	Services provided by GPs in long-term care nursing homes.
Acute Care	Services provided by specialists working in their own practices or health centres.	Services provided by specialists on wards or in outpatient departments in hospitals.

Table 3.6   *Expenditure on medical services as a percentage of health care expenditure, 2002*

	Inpatient care	*Outpatient care*	*Home health care services*
Australia	37.6	31.1	0
France	34.7	21.4	0.4
Germany	35.1	20.7	5.3
Japan	39.2	32.4	0.5
Netherlands	37.6	21.8	3.5
USA	27.6	43.5	2.2

Source: Data from OECD (2006).

than secondary care. This distinction corresponds to different localities of care delivery. Typically, primary care services are delivered in ambulatory settings (such as doctors' practices or health centres) whereas acute care services are delivered in (inpatient) hospital settings or in outpatient departments of hospitals. In contrast, chronic care services have traditionally been less medically oriented and are delivered in a range of settings, from people's homes to day centres and nursing homes.

As Table 3.6 suggests, in nearly all of these health systems inpatient care accounts for the single largest share of health care expenditure, more or less narrowly followed by outpatient care. Interestingly, the difference between expenditure on inpatient and outpatient expenditure varies considerably between countries. France and the Netherlands spend significantly more on inpatient care than on outpatient care, whereas in

Japan and Australia the difference in health care expenditure is less, about 7 per centage points. However, all countries are characterized by almost universal negligence of home health care services. This will be addressed in more detail in Chapter 6.

Patient access to different types of health care varies between countries, reflecting different levels of patient choice. Choice can mean different things, such as the ability to choose a generalist or a specialist doctor as the first point of contact or the ability to choose among different hospitals and ambulatory care settings. A broad distinction can be drawn among complete choice, extensive choice, and the GP model where choice is restricted. The level of patient choice reflects the way health services are organized, but also explicit decisions about the appropriate level of patient choice.

Singapore is the only country that offers complete choice, but only as long as an individual's MSA is active. Patients with an active account are free to go directly to the hospital (private or public) of their choice and choose the level of subsidy they receive in public hospitals. In relation to primary care services, patients are free to choose between private practices and government-subsidized health centres. MSAs can also be used to buy private insurance or MediShield coverage. The high level of patient choice coincides with the principle of individual responsibility, which is central to the health system in Singapore. Paradoxically, the high level of individual responsibility also limits choice when it comes to expensive or long-term care, because few patients are wealthy enough to afford such care and exercise free choice. Also, once a person's or family's MSA is exhausted, he or she must depend on the Medifund under which choice as to both providers and class of hospital care is limited (Massaro and Wong, 1996). Although the total amount in Medisave accounts is now S\$32 billion, 17 per cent of account holders have less than S\$1,000 in their accounts, an amount which could be depleted by a single hospital stay (see Box 3.2). Moreover, even those who accumulate the required minimum sum of S\$30,000 in their MSA upon retirement at age 55 are likely to find it insufficient to meet their hospitalization bills. Thus, in the end, the high level of individual responsibility constrains the choice of those persons who are most dependent on the health system and who have depleted their MSA. Although Medisave contributes to the 'cultural rhetoric' of personal responsibility for health care, Barr (2001) argues that at its core the Singapore system of health funding represents a 'strict rationing of health services according to wealth'.

The health systems in Germany and, to a lesser extent, Sweden offer extensive individual choice. In Germany, patients are free to choose any doctor working in ambulatory care, but require referral for hospital care. This leads to extensive choice as both generalists and specialists work in office-based settings. In Sweden, patients can choose between using a

Box 3.2   Liberalization of Medisave use

Although the Medisave scheme was originally designed to fund inpatient care, as of 2006 patients suffering from specific chronic conditions can pay their outpatient bills using MSA. This major departure for Singapore's health care financing system reflects the government's acknowledgement that outpatient costs, especially for patients with chronic diseases, can be very high and pose a financial problem to many patients. Patients are now allowed to use up to S$300 of their MSA a year or draw on any or all of their family members' MSAs to a maximum of S$300 for each account for approved outpatient treatment. The four conditions, diabetes, hypertension, high cholesterol levels and stroke, were selected because there are well-established, evidence-based protocols to treat them, and they can also be audited for treatment outcomes. In addition to the annual withdrawal limit of S$300, the use of MSAs under this scheme is subject to a deductible of S$30 on each outpatient bill with bills below S$30 to be paid in cash. Furthermore, a cash co-payment of 15 per cent on each outpatient bill in excess of the deductible is set. The government is concerned that the policy will create a future problem by allowing MSAs to become prematurely depleted. Patients, on the other hand, do not see the logic of saving for future needs when their current needs are not adequately met. Hence, the government was under pressure to explain to the public why saving for future (inpatient) health care needs was more important than meeting current outpatient needs.

Source: Bertelsmann Foundation (2006).

health centre or going directly to a specialist outpatient department in a hospital. However, in the case of the latter waiting times tend to be longer and co-payments are higher. Interestingly, patient choice was extended in the 1990s: patients can now choose between public and private health centres; they can seek a second opinion or treatment from alternative hospitals if the care offered is not appropriate; in some counties, patients have free choice where they seek medical treatment. This reflects a strong commitment to equity and quality and contrasts with Britain and the Netherlands, where patients' choice has been curtailed in the name of efficiency (Saltman, 1998: 164).

The health systems in Australia, Britain, the Netherlands and New Zealand have adopted a GP model, which offers the lowest level of patient choice. Patients have to register with a general practitioner (sometimes in their area) and it is the GP who refers patients to specialist out- and inpatient services in hospitals. This gives GPs a strong gate-keeping function. The predominance of the GP model is surprising. With the exception of Britain, the health systems in these countries share a commitment to individualism, as reflected in significant components of private funding. A possible explanation is that patient choice is expensive and therefore likely to be restricted, especially in times of cost containment. This can also account for the fact that in the USA one of the main characteristics of HMOs was to introduce a gate-keeping role for GPs, thus limiting the wide choices of specialists inherent in the traditional insurance system. As noted earlier, not surprisingly, this led to widespread condemnation of HMOs by US patients and doctors.

Welfare mixes in the provision of health care

Health systems allow for different levels of patient choice, reflecting the ways in which heath services are organized as well as specific decisions about the appropriate level of patient choice. This partly corresponds to the principles underpinning different types of health systems. The principles of equity, social solidarity and individual responsibility also inform the welfare mix in the provision of health care: that is, who the providers of health care are (see Box 3.3).

The differences in welfare mix apply primarily to hospitals, whereas the situation in ambulatory care is more uniform. In most countries, doctors working in ambulatory care are independent practitioners, who

---

Box 3.3   Welfare mix: mixed meanings and policies

As a *concept* welfare mix refers to the diverse ways in which health services can be provided. Welfare mix is concerned with the division of labour between the public, private, voluntary and informal sector. Inasmuch as the provision of health care is always mixed to a greater or lesser extent, welfare mix is also a *descriptor* of how services are delivered in individual health systems. Finally, as a *political programme* welfare mix challenges the notion that public provision is always best (Evers and Svetlik, 1993). By some, welfare mix is seen to serve better the needs of increasingly diverse societies. Others argue that a more mixed provision of health services is more cost efficient. Different health systems typically have different welfare mixes. Public funding through taxes often accompanies public ownership, leading to a highly publicly integrated provision of health services. Social insurance combines social solidarity with a commitment to individualism/subsidiarity. Public and private providers tend to exist side-by-side, creating complex and less well-integrated structures of health provision. The same is often true for health systems that predominantly rely on private insurance. In both social and private insurance systems, the welfare mix in health care provision comes naturally, whereas in national health services the welfare mix has been closely associated with market-oriented reforms.

either practise privately or who are contracted to provide publicly funded medical services. Reflecting their independent status, doctors are typically paid on a capitation or a fee-for-service basis (see Chapter 5, pp. 147ff, for details). The only exception is Sweden, where doctors in ambulatory care are salaried employees. This is a powerful indication of the high public integration of health care in Sweden.

The health systems in Britain, New Zealand and Sweden are typical examples of national health services, where public hospitals provide the majority of beds and where private hospitals are few. In New Zealand, for example, there are about 80 public hospital facilities, which operate under the direction of 21 community-focused District Health Boards, the regional administrative tier of the Department of Health (New Zealand Ministry of Health, 2001). Public hospitals derive their entire income from government funding agencies. A few private hospitals provide acute health care services and costs are met by individuals or by private insurance. Significantly, only a few District Health Boards have contracted with private hospitals to provide services. In comparison, the boundary between public and private provision is more blurred in Britain. Consultants are allowed to practise privately and the NHS has the largest number of private beds, which offer a lucrative source of income (Baggott, 2004). The Private Finance Initiative that uses private money and expertise as part of funding public sector projects has been extended to major hospital projects and there is now also a corresponding initiative in primary care (Ham, 2004). Australia is unusual in that it combines public funding through taxes with a strong element of private provision of services. In 2000, over 40 per cent of acute hospitals were in public hands, although the private hospitals tend to be smaller and less likely to provide complex, high-technology services. Nevertheless, the private hospital sector accounts for about 30 per cent of all admissions and 25 per cent of total hospital bed days (Hall, 1999: 98).

The provision of hospital care has traditionally been more mixed in social insurance systems. In Germany, for example just over 54 per cent of hospital beds are in public ownership, almost 37 per cent in private non-profit hospitals and the rest in private for-profit hospitals (Bundesministerium für Gesundheit, 2005). The high degree of welfare mix reflects the principle of subsidiarity, whereby public provision is a matter of last resort, as well as the fact that the present German health system was built around existing provision structures. The number of private non-profit hospitals is even higher in the Netherlands with over 90 per cent of hospitals in this category (Exter *et al.*, 2004). This echoes the traditional division of Dutch society into distinct religious and political segments, giving private initiative a prominent role in the delivery of health services (Maarse, 1997: 136). The situation in Japan is similar as the majority of hospitals are run on a private non-profit basis by doctors working in ambulatory care (Nakahara, 1997).

Market-based health systems are also characterized by high levels of welfare mixes and, compared to social insurance systems, private for-profit hospitals play a more prominent role. For instance, in the USA there are 245 federal government hospitals and 1,163 state and local government hospitals compared to 3,003 private non-profit hospitals and 749 for-profit hospitals (American Hospital Association, 2002). Singapore is unusual in that most beds are provided in publicly run hospitals. The eight public hospitals and five public speciality treatment centres constitute 84 per cent of available beds (Singapore Ministry of Health, 2002b). This reflects the unique combination of individual responsibility for funding and a strong role of government in regulation and the provision of hospital care in Singapore.

Models of contracting health services

Health systems are about funding and provision, and the two can be linked in different ways. In national health services, funding and provision have traditionally been integrated in public hands. In social insurance systems, by contrast, funding and provision are separate and contracts provide the key link between payers and providers. Private insurance systems operate in a similar way, although contracts are not subject to direct public regulation. The last two decades, however, have seen intriguing changes in many countries. National health services have experimented with the public contract model, often in an attempt to introduce market-style dynamics into their health service. Likewise, competition has been an important element of reform in social insurance systems, altering the nature of the more established public contract models. The public contract model, with its separation between public funding bodies and providers who relate to each other through contracts, is now the dominant model of organizing and reforming health services (OECD, 1992). Interesting variations exist in relation to the degree of government control of the contract process.

The Netherlands is a typical example of the social insurance variant of the public contract model that since 2006 includes strong market elements. Social health insurance is administered by private non-profit and for-profit insurance funds, which operate under public law. The insurance funds can choose which providers (i.e. hospitals and doctors working in ambulatory care) they contract with, although the government defines the statutory standard care package. The Statutory Health Insurance Board also has important supervisory functions especially concerning the management of the statutory standard care package

(Ministry for Health, Welfare and Sports, 2005). In short, there is some competition between providers and this is complemented by competition among purchasers, since patients have free choice of insurance funds and complementary health coverage.

The public contract model in Japan is even more state-centred. Providers are contracted under the uniform fee system, which the government's Central Social Medical Care Council negotiates with representatives of providers, payers and public interest groups (Ikegami and Campbell, 1999: 63). In contrast to the Netherlands and Japan, insurance funds and provider organizations enjoy more autonomy under the public contract model in Germany. As discussed in the next section, the public contract model is embedded in an extensive system of statutory joint self-administration, reflecting subsidarity at procedural level. This points to the incremental historical development of the health system (Bäringhausen and Sauerborn, 2003).

Among the national health services, Britain has gone furthest with the implementation of a public contract model. Primary Care Trusts are the purchasers of health care. They are corporate bodies that operate under the general direction of a chairperson appointed by the Secretary of State and receive funds from the Department of Health. In contrast to insurance funds, Primary Care Trusts enjoy less autonomy as they are in effect 'creatures of statute' (Paton, 1997: 23) The same applies to hospitals, which are non-profit trusts within the NHS. Their room for manoeuvre has been further curtailed by an extensive system of national priorities and tight performance management (Baggott, 2004). Primary Care Trusts negotiate and complete service agreements with other providers, but the contracts are not legally enforceable. In contrast to insurance funds, the role of Primary Care Trusts goes beyond paying for services since they, together with health authorities, are responsible for ensuring that the heath needs of the population are met. The public contract model was introduced in the early 1990s under the banner of an 'internal market', but has subsequently evolved into a system of managed competition with strong elements of planning and regulation (Harrison, 2004). Policy developments under New Labour have been ambivalent. Initially, the government emphasized collaboration, whereas recent years have been characterized by a return to stronger elements of competition, with an emphasis on patient choice and the development of greater plurality of provision coupled with payment by results (Crinson, 2005; Greener, 2004). The experience in New Zealand has been similar (see Blank, 1994). Cumming and Scott (1998) contend that the reforms in New Zealand were aimed at improving accountability and strengthening the purchasers' roles relative to providers. In the latest round of reforms, however, the Labour government consolidated the funding/provider roles in one agency, the District Health Boards, thus amalgamating the roles again (Ashton, 2005).

In contrast, Sweden is an example of a national health service where the purchaser–provider split was never introduced comprehensively. County councils are responsible for the funding and provision of health care and are also free to develop their own management systems (Rehnberg, 1997). In 1994, for example, only 14 out of 26 county councils had experimented with different models of the purchaser–provider split, a decision which reflected local traditions (Anell and Svarvar, 1999: 710). Also, the emerging market was very different from that in the UK and New Zealand because competition was combined with patient choice, thus limiting the extent to which purchasers could selectively contract with providers (Jacobs, 1998: 12f.). However, there has been a move away from the competition-based model and towards a model combining more long-term contracts with regional-based cooperation (Harrison, 2004; Harrison and Calltrop, 2000). This occurred against the background of problems with the implementation of the reforms, changing governing coalitions and new policy priorities that were less well served by market mechanisms. Here, regional autonomy also provided a strong catalyst for change.

Health governance between centre and locality

As we have seen, health systems are about the funding and provision of health care. Health systems are funded from a variety of sources that result in different levels of public control. Health systems consist of a range of services that are delivered by different providers to which patients have different levels of access. The diverse ways in which funding and provision are organized lead not only to different policies and pressures for reform, but also to different politics, different relationships between central and local government, among government and provider organizations/payers, and among payers and providers themselves.

Governance, for its part, does include the regulation of areas such as medical practice and pharmaceuticals, but it is broader than that. It is concerned with modes of coordinating health systems and their multiple actors (Freeman, 2000). Governance is underpinned by two sets of tensions: between public and private (i.e. between the state and the market); and between centre and locality. Government looms large in most health systems and governance can be thought of as government authority/capacity. Government authority/capacity is reflected in the degree of institutional integration in health systems: that is, in the power of the national government (executive integration), in the extent of government authority over private interests such as doctors, hospitals and insurers (public integration), and in the extent to which policy-making authority is concentrated at national rather than regional or local levels (central integration) (see Freeman, 2000). Executive and public integration are discussed in the next section. This section focuses on central integration that concerns the relationship among the different levels of governance.

Some health systems are more decentralized than others, reflecting the respective political systems in which they are embedded. However, over the last two decades many health systems have attempted to decentralize governance. This is about convergence, but offers equally strong indications of persistent differences, not least in terms of dissimilar types of decentralization. Here, Saltman and Bankauskaite (2006) distinguish between fiscal, administrative and political decentralization. The health systems in Sweden, Britain and New Zealand illustrate this point. In all three countries, health care is publicly funded and provided, resulting in health systems that are characterized by a high degree of public integration and control. At the same time, important differences exist in relation to the levels of governance.

In Sweden, responsibility for funding and provision rests with the county councils, leading to decentralized health governance. Sweden has a strong tradition of sub-central government and, importantly, a type of sub-central government that defines itself by democratic decision making (Håkansson and Nordling, 1997: 194). In addition, health reforms since the 1950s have systematically decentralized responsibility for health care to the regional level of counties (Saltman and Bergman, 2005). This contrasts with Britain where the publicly funded and provided health service is embedded in a highly centralized political system. The centrality of central government is compounded by a tradition that sees local government first and foremost as a provider of services. Not surprisingly, the NHS has been described as a 'command and control system' (Moran, 1999). In many ways New Zealand resembles Britain. The unitary political system of New Zealand ensures that a relatively high degree of control over the health system is centralized in the Ministry of Health, although this has varied considerably from one government to the next with the most current shift towards more central control (Ashton, 2005).

The differences in the degree of central integration can also help to explain differences in moves towards decentralization. In Britain, decentralization occurred as part of the introduction of a quasi-market in health care that was inspired by the new public management paradigm. The actors at local level are Primary Care Trusts and hospital trusts and, at regional level, health authorities which are not only creatures of central government, but also continue to operate within a highly hierarchical system of health governance. Indeed, central control has increased following the introduction of the internal market and most prominently the management of performance has become tighter as part of a more explicit 'quality turn' (Harrison, 2004). Not surprisingly, the autonomy of trusts and health authorities is confined to managerial responsibility. The complex division of labour among different levels of governance has highlighted problems of accountability (Iliffe and Munro, 2000: 322).

This contrasts with Sweden, where in the early 1980s county councils were given complete control over funding and delivery of services. Here, decentralization was a genuine devolution of power that built on traditions of sub-central government, and not simply a refocusing of central control as in the case of Britain. This further strengthened the directly democratic character of managerial decision making (Saltman, 1998: 164). However, there are limits to sub-central autonomy and the central level has become increasingly involved. At policy level, specific action programmes result in more direct intervention in service delivery and at the level of supervision the National Board of Welfare has now more extensive powers to regulate provider organizations based on national priorities and quality standards (Saltman and Bergman, 2005).

Funding from social insurance results in institutional complexity and often limits the degree of central integration of health systems. For example, in Germany a statutory, joint self-administration of insurance funds and providers is at the centre of health governance and this form of corporatism operates at different levels. At the local level, providers and insurance funds relate to each other through contracts, which specify the services to be provided and the prices to be paid, including the financing mechanisms. However, local contracts are embedded in a complex system of framework agreements at state and federal level (again between providers and insurance funds) and these, in turn, are embedded in federal legislation, the Social Code Book.

Corporatism is a particular approach to policy making and has several aspects to it (Schwartz and Busse, 1997: 104). Corporatism hands over certain rights of the state to corporatist self-governing institutions, including the insurance funds and provider organizations. As corporatist institutions, they have mandatory membership and enjoy the right to raise their own financial resources as well as the right to negotiate and sign contracts with other corporatist institutions. In Germany, institutional complexity is underpinned by corporatism as a form of procedural subsidiarity and is compounded by federalism, which taken together results in decentralized health governance, that in many ways also limits the capacity for radical policy change (Altenstetter and Busse, 2005).

However, as the Netherlands and Japan illustrate, decentralized health governance can coexist with strong elements of centralism. In the Netherlands, the central government enjoys extensive powers, for example in relation to the determination of (income-related) contribution rates and the setting of hospital budgets. And crucially, corporatism is also confined to the national level (Lieverdink and Made, 1997: 132). This more centralized form of corporatism is underpinned by a decentralized, yet unitary political system, where municipalities and provinces often act as implementation agencies of national policy programmes. Similarly, Japan combines central government control with strong elements of decentralization. Health governance is highly decentralized across 47 regional prefectures and thousands of municipalities, and provides a mixture of delivery levels reflecting a basic principle underlying national policies (Nakahara, 1997: 107). Despite this, the central government maintains strong control over all aspects of health care through the rigid and centrally controlled fee structure.

In contrast to Germany, the role of federalism in health governance is ambivalent in Australia and the USA, and the two countries illustrate how modes of governance can vary between sub-systems of health care. In Australia control over health funding is more highly centralized than in the USA where only the elderly and very poor are covered by federal programmes. Over the past two decades, Australia has moved to centralize effective control (Duckett, 2004; Rix *et al.*, 2005) and this has reduced substantially the proportion of funding derived from private sources. Moreover, there has been a 'strong centralising tendency' within each of the Australian States and Territories in recent years (Dwyer, 2004). Contrarily, the US system of finance continues to be highly fragmented. Both countries, however, have strong traditions of decentralization and individual state autonomy in the provision of health care services and of robust and powerful private sectors. Although the central governments in both the USA and Australia by necessity have substantial and growing roles in funding, governance of provision remains highly decentralized, distributed among myriad state, local and private sectors.

The authority of governments in health policy

Looking at the roles of centre and locality in health governance provides a powerful indication of the complexity of health systems and the importance of political contexts for shaping health systems. Ultimately, health governance always happens at different levels: health systems as *systems* require direction from the centre while the provision of health care inevitably involves localities. However, the relative importance of different levels varies among health systems as well as among different sub-systems within the same health system. The variation among and within systems reflects how health care is provided as well as specific political contexts. For example, health governance is highly centralized in Britain, whereas it is more decentralized in the USA. This reflects the fact that the British central government is key to the public funding and provision of health care, whereas in the USA mixed funding and provision naturally decentralizes governance. The differences between the two countries also point to the importance of political contexts. As the comparison with Sweden shows, however, public funding and provision alone do not make for centralized governance, but a unitary, centralized political system plays an important role. Similarly, decentralized health governance in the USA is underpinned by federalism. Differences among systems coexist with differences within the same health system. Japan and the Netherlands are a case in point: both countries combine centralized governance of funding with decentralized governance of provision.

Executive and public integration provide further evidence of the complexity of health systems. The power of national governments and the power of governments over private interests are closely related and offer key indications of the relative authority of governments in health policy. This issue has been implicit throughout the chapter when discussing the sub-systems of funding and provision. The basic assumption is that public funding and provision result in public control – that is, government authority – because the government is the principal public actor in health policy. Public control of funding can be measured in terms of the extent of public funding, the relative importance of taxes and social security as different types of public funding, and the power of government to control funding. Public control of provision can be measured in terms of the share of public provision of health care. On this basis, Figure 3.2 characterizes the health systems in different countries.

The summary of the modes of governance and the extent of government authority in different countries demonstrates the sheer diversity of health systems. Health systems are all confronted with pressures from

		Public Control of Provision		
		High	**Middle**	**Low**
Public Control of Funding	**High**	Britain Sweden		Japan Netherlands
	Middle	Australia New Zealand	Germany	
	Low	Singapore		United States

Figure 3.2   *Public control of funding and provision of health care*

ageing populations, advances in medical technology and periodic economic down turns, and these pressures often manifest themselves in pressures to control and contain costs. However, the institutional contexts of health systems and the capacity of governments to address these pressures continue to vary considerably between countries. For example, public control of funding and provision is high in Britain and Sweden, whereas it is low in the USA.

Significantly, the picture is more complex than the typology of health systems introduced in Chapter 1 would suggest. The typology assumes that certain models of funding are directly associated with certain models of provision to the extent that high public control of funding goes hand in hand with high public control of provision and vice versa. This is true for the health systems in some countries such as Britain, Sweden, Germany and the USA, which are closest to the ideal types of national health service, social insurance system and private insurance system, respectively. In the health systems of the remaining countries, government authority differs between the sub-systems of funding and provision. For example, Japan and the Netherlands combine relatively strong (central) public control over funding with relatively low public control over provision, reflecting the predominance of non-public providers. This makes government authority over funding comparable to Britain and Sweden, but in relation to provision government authority is closer to the USA.

Differences and similarities are specific to individual sub-systems of health care and as such point to the importance of country-specific political contexts. Examples of country-specific political contexts include the semi-federal political system in the Netherlands that often helps to concentrate authority in the hands of central government, and the legacy of a private insurance system combined with federalism in Australia that weakens government authority over funding to some extent. However, acknowledging the uniqueness of individual health systems does not mean abandoning cross-country comparisons; instead, it requires removing the blinders of ideal types of health systems and exploring what Moran (1999) calls the 'political embeddedness' of health systems. Chapter 4 continues this quest by examining the implications of these health system characteristics in the actual allocation of health care resources in these countries.

Chapter 4

Setting Priorities and Allocating Resources

Chapter 3 demonstrated that health systems display variation in the sub-systems of funding, provision and governance that impact on health policy and health care. It also revealed that these sub-systems are dynamic and that many of them have undergone significant changes in recent decades. In order to better understand their impact on health care, it is important to go beneath the institutional and structural dimensions and examine the goals, objectives and priorities of each health system. This chapter examines the criteria that health care systems use to allocate medical resources and the ramifications of these policies for their respective populations.

The goals of health policy

Every policy is founded on goals and objectives which should be clarified early in the policy-making process. Two levels of goals are discernible. The first are broad stated goals that often function symbolically and are often more in the realm of political rhetoric than reality. The second are specific programmatic goals that frame a particular policy. Both are critical in evaluating the success or failure of a policy. Although some goals can be specified and measured with accuracy, others are more amorphous; generally, the broader the goal, the more difficult it is to measure. Analysis becomes even more problematic when the goals themselves conflict, when they are defined differently by the various participants, or when they shift over time. In spite of these problems, it is critical to examine the stated goals of health policy.

Ideally, a successful health policy in a democracy would provide high quality services for all citizens on an equal basis. Moreover, it would be an efficient system with little waste and duplication and high levels of performance in all sectors. In addition to the goals of universal access, quality and efficiency, other goals might include maximizing the choice of patients, ensuring high accountability of health care personnel, and guaranteeing rapid diffusion of the newest medical technologies. As will be discussed in Chapter 7, goals also might vary as to whether the health

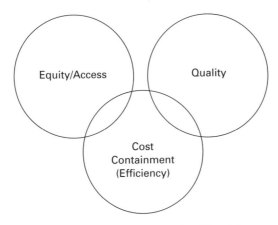

Figure 4.1   *Competing goals of health care*

of the population or the health of individual patients is primary. Although the goals of health care are many, Figure 4.1 displays the three that are at the core of health policy.

For the two decades following World War II, the predominant goals of health policy initiatives in all developed nations were *equity* or *access* and *quality* of health care. Even though the actual policies varied significantly, the goals of access and quality shaped health care priorities. In large part, the disparity among countries could be explained by how much emphasis each nation put on subsidiary competing goals of freedom of choice for consumers, autonomy of the health care providers and insurers, and assorted notions of common good or solidarity. The actual mix of these policy goals has been shaped by the distinctions in national cultures, politics and institutional structures discussed in Chapter 2. In the USA, for instance, with the strong weight put on individual freedom by both patients and the health care community, universal access and equity were never given the prominence they enjoyed in other countries. In contrast, New Zealand and the UK, with their stronger egalitarian roots and tradition of common good, enthusiastically embraced comprehensive national health services to deliver on the central goals of universal access and free care at the point of service.

Despite variation regarding universal coverage, health policy in all developed nations in the post-war period placed priority on ensuring all citizens had access to an expanding array of medical interventions. New hospitals were built and many beds were added to existing structures, significantly expanded investments were made in medical education and biomedical research, the supply of medical personnel was increased and the boundaries of medicine extended by the emergence of many new medical specialties. Furthermore, new institutional mechanisms were initiated to ensure access to these resources, thus issuing in the era of technological medicine as the new nucleus of health care. This post-war boom of medicine, in turn, was met by heightened expectations and demands from the public for greater access to an ever-expanding arsenal of often costly medical innovations.

Equity and access: continuing problems

Two types of access were addressed by health policies of this era: financial access and physical or geographical access. Financial access was met by restructuring health care funding and provision so as to provide universal access to at least a minimal level of health care for all citizens based on need. This entailed either creating systems of direct public financing and provision of services or governmental regulation and coordination of private sickness funds with guaranteed coverage for those patients who fell through the gaps in the private system. Some, such as Germany and the Netherlands, chose to strengthen health systems that pre-dated World War II while others, such as the UK and Sweden, set up new systems to meet these goals. Except for the USA, which chose not to establish a national system, all countries examined here were largely successful in achieving universal levels of access, despite major divergence in the means used to achieve that goal.

Many countries with universal coverage face a problem of equity of access related to the presence of a tiered system where persons with sufficient resources obtain services which are either unavailable or constrained in the public system. Ironically, there is greater public awareness of these discrepancies in the countries with national health services which have made the strongest claims for financial equity. For instance, while universality is at the centre of the British NHS, often it is up to health authorities to decide which services to fund, thus opening the way to local variation, also referred to as the 'postcode lottery'. Waiting lists also limit access to elective surgery and buttress the tiered system. An indication of the highly political nature of the issue is that one of the key pledges of the Labour party made before coming into office in 1997 was the reduction of waiting lists. Since then the government has added targets for waiting times for numerous specific treatments (Baggott, 2004: 197ff).

The second type of equity has proven increasingly problematic as health care became more specialized and capital intensive. Geographical inequities in health care, although initially reduced by regional reallocation schemes, remain troublesome. Isolated, rural communities consistently are undersupplied in terms of skilled medical personnel and facilities in health systems as diverse as New Zealand and the USA. The disproportionate number of physicians located in urban centres is reinforced by the insufficient number of patients in many rural areas to justify huge technological investment. The result is a concentration of health care facilities in core urban populations and inequities in access to specialized care (Stukel *et al.*, 2005).

Although most countries have created incentives to correct the geographical imbalances of physicians, financial inducements and other policies have not resolved the problem (this is discussed in more detail in Chapter 5). For instance, Germany has one of the highest numbers of doctors (see Table 5.1) but they tend to be concentrated in urban areas. In 1993 the freedom to set up practice anywhere was replaced by manpower planning based on needs, and the number of additional doctors per specialty and region was limited. Although the main aim of this policy was to limit the absolute number of doctors, one of its side effects was that rural regions became more attractive to new doctors (Burau, 2001).

An important barrier to establishing physical equity is the fact that the delivery of health care services to rural areas is significantly more expensive on a per-case basis, in part because of the high cost of capital equipment needed to supply state of the art medical care. As a result, many specialized services can be provided efficiently only in urban regional centres with a critical mass of population. This problem is especially acute in Australia, New Zealand and the USA where a significant minority of the populations live in remote rural areas. Even when patients from isolated geographical locations have equal financial access to the same level of medicine as their urban brethren, travel costs, relocation costs and costs in wasted time produce substantial inequities in effective access. Only in the highly concentrated population of Singapore is this not a problem.

Quality care: what is it?

The goal of high quality health care, a hallmark of the 1950s and 1960s, has also proved problematic. The main difficulty in defining 'quality' is that we lack an objective means of measuring what quality medicine is (Steinberg and Luce, 2005). International comparisons seldom address this factor because it is much easier to compare cost figures, usage figures and other readily quantifiable factors, although in 2001 the OECD Health Care Quality Indicator (HCQI) Project was initiated to collect internationally comparable data reflecting the health outcomes and health improvements attributable to medical care delivered in OECD countries (see Kelly and Hurst, 2006). The Project goal is to track health care quality by developing a set of indicators to provide international benchmarks of quality and give national policy makers an opportunity to compare the performance of their health care delivery systems against a peer group.

Even within individual countries, however, quality is rarely monitored systematically because there is little agreement on what criteria should be

Table 4.1   *MRI and CAT units per million population, 2004*

Country	MRI units	CAT units
Japan	35.3	92.6
USA	27.0	32.0
Italy	11.6	24.0
Sweden	7.9	14.2
Germany	6.0	14.2
New Zealand	n/a	12.1
France	3.2	8.4
UK	5.0	7.0
Australia	3.7	n/a

Source: Data from OECD (2006).

used. Unfortunately, quality is often equated with the latest diagnostic technologies, with curative medicine, and with specialist services. This emphasis can be deceptive in that it assumes that quality can be defined by the number of machines, medical specialists and intensive medical interventions performed (see McClellan and Kessler, 1999). Quality as defined by technology is also of dubious value when compared to health outcome. Table 4.1, for instance, compares countries by the number of CAT and MRI units per million people. Although the USA ranks high on 'quality' if measured solely by availability of this type of care, as noted in Chapter 1, it rates lower than other countries on many measures of health outcome. Also, when quality is defined this way it is likely to clash with the goal of access, which by necessity requires constraints on what levels of care are provided. While the goal of universal access presupposes some minimal level of care for persons in need, it cannot sustain unlimited amounts of resources expended on high-technology interventions for the few. Despite these dilemmas, quality, along with equity, were the most articulated goal of health policy until the mid to late 1970s.

Cost containment: strategies of constraint

In the 1970s escalating costs, in large part fuelled by the open-ended goals of access and quality, were aggravated by a global recession and oil crisis. One result was an unmistakable shift in emphasis from access and quality to cost containment in order to constrain unbridled health care spending. Ageing populations, boundless technological expansion and heightened public expectations solidified this goal in the 1990s. Moreover, its prominence was encouraged by the ideological shift towards neo-liberalism, which eschewed the welfare state and placed emphasis on efficiency of the market. No country escaped the conspicuous shifts towards improving productivity, maximizing efficiency and incorporating management procedures into health care. Moreover, to date, reform efforts in most Western countries, with the notable exception of the USA, have been effective to the extent that they have stopped or at least slowed the rate of increase of health care spending as a proportion of GDP (see Table 3.2).

Ironically, the emphasis on cost containment and system efficiency has forced evaluation of quality (an effort that was conspicuously absent when quality was a stated goal) by requiring that priorities be set in distributing health care resources in terms of value for money. Not surprisingly, this shift in goals has faced opposition from the health care industry, medical professionals and health care consumers who have 'grown accustomed to expensive care at low direct cost' (Harrop, 1992: 159).

Cost containment strategies differ significantly across health systems. Objectives can be to slow the rate of increase in costs, to stop costs from rising in real terms, or more rarely to actually reduce the costs of health care in real terms. The health care sectors to which a particular cost containment strategy is targeted vary depending on whether the health services are financed by the government on a direct budget basis, through public contracts with independent providers such as physicians paid on a fee-for-service basis or hospitals paid per item of service provided, or by the private marketplace. As seen in Chapter 3, countries with national health services, such as the UK and New Zealand, as well as several without, such as Singapore and Japan, exercise direct budgetary control, while countries such as Germany, France and the Netherlands rely more on the second, contractual-based approach. In contrast, the USA, and to a lesser extent Australia, depend upon a less effective mixture of approaches, including those based in the marketplace. The capacity for successful cost containment policies, therefore, fluctuates considerably from one country to the next.

Sweden is a good example of a country with a national health service that has effective controls and where the general rule of 'public funding makes for public control' applies. However, in contrast to Britain and New Zealand, the control over funding is decentralized, since health care is predominantly funded from taxes raised by the regional tier of government, the county councils (Glenngård *et al.*, 2005). 'Macrolevel' measures of cost containment vary, because county councils decide on the rate of regional taxation, the majority of which goes to health care. Besides this, global budgets play an important role and county councils may allocate funds to districts using needs-based global budgets. Similarly, county councils or districts may fund health centres and hospitals using global budgets in conjunction with other forms of payment. The only true 'macrolevel' measure of cost containment is when central government decides to control total expenditure by putting limits on taxation, as it did during the severe recession in the early 1990s (Harrison, 2004).

Cost containment strategies can operate on either the *demand* or the *supply* side of health care. Additionally, they can be carried out through a direct, regulatory edict (macro-management) or through indirect incentive systems aimed at providers and patients (micro-management). Furthermore, depending on the system, the major efforts can be initiated and implemented either by public agencies – national, state or local – or by the private sector. According to Reinhardt (1990: 107), European countries tend to emphasize macro-management strategies such as global budgets to control their health systems, while the USA, with its basic fear of centralized control, largely rejects regulatory macro-management opting instead to fine-tune financial incentives for health care. However, even in Europe this is changing with moves to micro-manage some aspects of medical care.

Demand-side cost containment relies primarily on strategies designed to reduce consumer demand by increasing patient consciousness of the costs of providing care. Usually this is accomplished by requiring some form of cost sharing by the users of health care, either through user charges as a flat rate per unit of service (e.g. $50 per hospital night, $20 per doctor visit, $20 per prescription), some proportion of the cost (e.g. 20 per cent of outpatient costs, 30 per cent of inpatient costs), or some combination of these. Out-of-pocket costs are normally applied at the time of use with the explicit goal of discouraging user demand and, by extension, acting indirectly on physicians to reduce services on the knowledge that the patient must share in the cost. Another approach is to require deductibles or excesses (e.g. the first $100 per condition) which the consumer must pay, thereby allegedly discouraging demand.

The form of demand-side strategies varies significantly across countries. In Germany, for instance, co-payments are the most common form of out-of-pocket payments and have a long tradition, particularly in relation to drugs. Since the early 1990s, however, they have increased considerably and in 2002 represented 12 per cent of total expenditure on health care (Busse and Riesberg, 2004: 73). With increasing cost pressures, co-payments in other areas have been added, including charges for inpatient days in hospitals, rehabilitative care facilities, ambulance transportation, and dental treatment. In 2003, Japan increased the co-payment rate of all care for patients insured by the Employees' Health Insurance from 20 to 30 per cent to put it in line with that of the National Health Insurance (Bertelsmann Foundation, 2003a).

In contrast, in the Netherlands out-of-pocket payments have traditionally played a marginal role and only co-payments for glasses have been a long established feature of the Dutch health system, reflecting entrenched expectations that all health care should be free at the point of use (Maarse and Paulus, 2003). However, this is different for the exceptional medical risks scheme that accounts for almost half of the total co-payments (Exter *et al.*, 2004: 48). Under the new unified social health insurance for acute risks people have to pay a flat-rate premium directly to their sickness fund. The flat-rate premiums are set by individual insurance funds and are the key component for insurance funds to compete for customers who have free choice of insurance fund. Significantly, with the introduction of the new unified insurance in 2006, the flat rate premium has risen, whereas the income-related contributions have been lowered (Bartholomée and Maarse, 2006).

Out-of-pocket payments in Sweden exist in form of direct, small patient fees that are paid for receipt of medical attention. The payments are a flat rate and are set by the county councils; however, the national Parliament sets ceilings on the total to be paid by patients annually (Burstrom, 2004). There are separate co-payments for drugs that are set by central government and are uniform across the country. In Britain, out-of-pocket payments take the form of co-payments. Prominent areas of cost sharing include: drugs, where co-payments have risen steeply over time; dental services, where patients have to cover 80 per cent of the costs up to a maximum; and ophthalmic services that have been widely de-regulated (Baggott, 2004; for a good European comparison of cost sharing arrangements, see Ros *et al.*, 2000).

The major assumption of demand-side cost containment measures is that use of services will decrease when market incentives are implemented making patients bear a significant part of the costs (see Box 4.1 for reverse situation). Studies have found that cost sharing through either supplementary insurance or deductibles does, indeed, reduce health spending. The European Observatory on Health Care Systems (1999: 41) cites a study in the UK showing that, despite the existence of wide-spread exemptions, changes in prescription charges can have a noticeable impact on the number of prescriptions dispensed. It estimated that even the modest increase in prescription charges from £3.75 to £4.25 per item in 1993 resulted in a reduction of 2.3 million prescriptions dispensed.

Similarly, the Rand Corporation Health Insurance Experiment found that outpatient spending was 46 per cent lower among individuals enrolled in health plans that required 5 per cent co-insurance compared with those in free care plans. The 25 per cent co-insurance plans produced even larger savings from the free care plan. Likewise, outpatient spending was 30 per cent lower and inpatient spending 10 per cent lower under individual deductible plans. Moreover, cost sharing reduces adult hospital admissions by up to 38 per cent as compared to free plans (Peterson, 2006; Thorpe, 1992).

Box 4.1   The politics of co-payments

Between 1996 and 2001 out-of-pocket payments in Australia increased by 52 per cent, the second highest among OECD countries. In the lead up to a Federal election where health care policy was perceived to be the Government's area of weakness, it introduced the Medicare Safety Net under which patients are eligible to claim 80 per cent of their out-of-pocket costs once they reach an annual threshold. The safety net is an uncapped programme financed out of general tax revenues. There is concern that this change will have an important bearing on provider incentives because they will now be able to set fees at their own discretion and be fully paid on a fee-for-service basis. Prior to the introduction of the safety net, competitive pressure among provider groups limited fee rises, but now these competitive pressures will ease as patients no longer face the full impact of above schedule fees once they reach their annual threshold. Moreover, while it is impossible to predict if the 20 per cent co-payment feature will be enough to prevent consumption of unneccesary medical care, as patients face lower out-of-pocket charges, they may consume additional health care services (Bertelsmann Foundation, 2004c).

Despite these findings of cost savings, there is some question as to how genuine the benefits of a demand-side approach are in the long run. An important question is whether the reduced use of medical resources leads to lowered levels of health for those individuals who do not seek treatment due to cost considerations. In the Rand study, access to more services did not result in better health among consumers who were young, middle income and in good health. In contrast, access to more services did result in better health outcomes among the poor and those persons with initial clinical indicators of poor health. In other words, while many healthy people can reduce care without adverse health consequences, when ill people forgo needed services, health outcomes suffer. Part of this difference might be explained by the fact that relatively young, healthy and affluent consumers are able to carry supplemental insurance to cover charges, thus undercutting the strategy of cost sharing. Unless prohibited from doing so, those using insurance resources will counteract the apparent cost savings.

Other demand-side approaches to cost containment include the exclusion of certain types of coverage or the reduction of reimbursement for specific services. Moreover, some systems such as Australia and the USA allow extra billing while others have either prohibited or strictly limited extra billing because of its impact on equity and its overall inflationary effect. While Germany, Japan, the Netherlands, Sweden and the UK allow no extra billing by office-based doctors working in ambulatory care, a clear example of extra billing is France. As in many other countries, doctors in ambulatory care are self-employed, independent practitioners, and they are paid on a fee-for-service basis. The majority of doctors contract with the social insurance system, but up to a quarter depart from the negotiated fee schedule in favour of extra billing, referred to as 'sector 2' (Freeman, 2000: 52). Patients are reimbursed by the statutory social insurance according to the national fee schedule, regardless of whether they choose a doctor who charges higher fees. Patients have to pay for the extra billing themselves, although over 90 per cent have additional non-statutory insurance to cover extra billing and other co-payments (Freeman, 2000).

Overall, demand-side approaches are inhibited by their adverse impact on access and their inequitable financial burden across groups in society. While the problems of inequity they raise hypothetically can be reduced by providing subsidies or a safety net for those unable to pay or by providing exemptions to the co-payments (e.g. New Zealand's policy on GPs), this entails a complicated administrative and monitoring system that in turn adds to costs. According to the OECD, 'it is doubtful whether anything other than modest charges (with exceptions for poor and high users) will be either equitable or efficient' (1992: 139).

Supply-side cost containment measures are generally more effective than demand-side measures, especially when they entail the imposition of direct, central controls on payments to providers. In commenting on seven European countries, for instance, the OECD concludes that there is a 'strong suggestion that any cost-containment that was achieved came through direct action on the supply side such as the introduction of global budgeting or central regulation of fees and charges' (1992: 148).

Other than the USA, most countries emphasize strategies that control the supply side by strengthening the hands of insurers and/or by imposing direct, central controls on payments to providers and on the capacities of their health systems (see Table 4.2). For instance, during the 1980s, France

Table 4.2   *Supply-side strategies*

Global budgeting	Centralized control	Move to ambulatory and home care
France	Germany	Germany
New Zealand	Japan	New Zealand
Netherlands	Netherlands	UK
Sweden	Singapore	Australia
UK	US (Medicare DRGs)	
Singapore		

and the Netherlands introduced systems of global budgeting to replace the daily rates paid to hospitals, thus joining the UK and New Zealand which already had mechanisms for capping hospital expenditures (Hurst and Poullier, 1993: 5). Similarly, in 2005 Singapore implemented a global budget policy for public sector hospitals and health care institutions (Bertelsmann Foundation, 2005a). Public health sector hospitals and health care institutions, including polyclinics which provide primary health care, are given a fixed budget regardless of the number of patients they treat.

Additional instruments of regulatory cost containment are fee and price controls, control over capacity of the system and control over wages and salaries. Table 4.3 illustrates the wide array of possible short to long-term supply-side controls available. The most direct supply-side strategy is to tighten controls over reimbursement or enforce payment schedules. This is easiest to accomplish in an integrated system where the government has the capacity to set global budgets. Sweden and the UK are classical examples of integrated health systems where government sets global budgets, in the former case at the regional level. In Britain, the total expenditure of the NHS is set by the Treasury and is part of the government's three-yearly general spending review. Once the overall spending has been set, the Department of Health determines the funds allocated to Primary Care Trusts. In contrast, hospitals are funded through contracts. Cost-volume contracts are predominant and increasingly include national tariffs for specific Health Care Resource Groups (Baggott, 2004: 177). As

Table 4.3   *The range of supply-side controls*

Short-term controls
  Budget ceilings for hospitals
  Controls on staff numbers in hospitals or clinics
  Controls on levels of remuneration
  Controls on prices or quantities

Medium-term controls and incentives
  Controls over construction or extension of hospitals
  Controls over the installation of expensive equipment
  Controls and incentives to develop substitutes to traditional
    hospital care

Long-term controls on manpower
  Controls over number of students entering medical school
  Controls over entry to specialist training

Source: Adapted from Abel-Smith (1984: 3–4).

such, the UK payment system can be described as a mix of global budgets with elements of cost-per-case payments.

The situation in Sweden is more complex as funding arrangements vary among county councils. Some county councils/districts use global budgets to pay hospitals and health centres, while others have introduced a purchaser–provider split. For example, contracts with hospitals are often based on fixed, prospective per-case payments that are combined with price/quality ceilings as well as quality components (Glenngård *et al.*, 2005).

Another approach is that of Germany where cost containment policy means limiting insurance funds' expenditure to a level where it matches income so that contribution rates remain stable. To achieve this, the 1990s have seen the introduction of sectoral budgets or spending caps based on historic spending patterns rather than any needs-based formula as in the UK. Some of the budgets limit the expenditure of individual funds while other budgets do not impose these kind of limits. At the level of the individual hospital, this has coincided with the abolition of the full-cost cover principle and, instead, fixed budgets are calculated for each hospital. These budgets are targets in relation to service number and per diems and are made up of prospective case and procedure fees, introduced in 1996, as well as the old, prospective per diem charges (European Observatory on Health Care Systems, 2000: 101f). Furthermore, since 1989 fixed regional budgets exist. This means that the fees for individual services are not fixed, but vary depending on the total budget negotiated with the insurance fund and the total volume of services delivered within the regional association of insurance fund doctors. There are also ceilings for the amount of refundable services per doctor that in effect functions as a budget.

Global budgets for hospitals are more effective than price or volume controls alone because they cannot be avoided by raising volume when prices are fixed or raising prices when volume is fixed. Usually, although not always, discretion is given to local managers to spend within the prospective budget. Budget caps work provided there is the political will to enforce them, but they can be politically risky because they make the central government responsible for the failure of micro-decisions. In other words, global budgets allow hospitals to blame the government policy makers for shortfalls in service due to lack of adequate funding levels. Because hospitals consume the majority of health spending, this single approach is effective; however, budget caps are less effective when the government grants additional funds to those hospitals that overspend and require supplements to their budgets in order to keep operating. According to the OECD, the analysis of per capita health expenditure across all OECD nations suggests that hospital global budgets reduce total national health expenditures by about 13 per cent (1992: 141).

One problem with global budgets is that they might effect cost containment by forcing hospitals to cut corners, thus providing a lower quality of care. Because they do not readily distinguish as to the quality or intensity of care, there are often no rewards for *good* economical treatment. Although this problem can be minimized by close auditing of quality, global budgets themselves are not sufficient to protect consumers because the focus is on lowering the costs per case. In terms of the goal of containing costs, however, any form of prospective payment will succeed by relating rewards to planned workload and encouraging awareness of cost per case. In contrast, any system with open-ended retrospective reimbursement for hospitals, such as traditional private insurance in the USA, will have higher expenditures per capita (Blank, 1997).

Although global budgets are more easily implemented if there is one central authority, single-source funding is not essential. Germany and the Netherlands, for example, have been successful in securing cost control in systems composed of many payers. Germany has accomplished this by the combination of changing the payment to providers and centralizing control of funding. The 1990s saw the partial introduction of a system of prospective payments in hospitals that in 2000 culminated in the gradual introduction of a comprehensive system of DRGs. In ambulatory care, a maximum ceiling for fees per doctor was introduced, coexisting with fixed sectoral budgets. At the same time, the autonomy of insurance funds in raising and allocating funds has been curtailed, with contribution rates now linked to the income of insurance funds rather than expenditure. The federal government also has become more interventionist and in 1997, for example, mandated that contributed rates had to be reduced by 0.4 percentage points.

In the Netherlands, cost containment has been achieved by a combination of integrated control over funding and measures of spending control. The income-related contribution rates for the two social insurance schemes are set by central government. The central government also sets the overall budget for the social health insurance and sets rules about how funds are to be allocated to individual insurance funds (Exter *et al.*, 2004). This has been complemented by regulated competition both among insurance funds for employees and providers for selective contracting with insurance funds as well as by micro-level measures to increase efficiency.

Similarly, Japan has been quite successful in controlling a vast network of private insurance funds and local providers by instituting a strict uniform fee structure and prohibiting extra billing. In 2003 Japan began to introduce a diagnosis-based hospital reimbursement system as a financial incentive for university hospitals to decrease inpatient costs by capping the cost per day for each inpatient by disease category (Bertelsmann Foundation, 2003a). The disparate policies of these countries show that control over medical spending can be accomplished without centralized global budgeting. Although direct price and quantity controls may be less effective than global budgets or direct caps, they can be applicable to all segments of health care, including pharmaceuticals, and thus are potentially more comprehensive.

Lacking the centralized regulatory control over health care found in other countries, the USA implemented a prospective payment system in the mid 1980s in the one area it could control, the Medicare programme. As noted in Chapter 3 (p. 78), DRGs were introduced to constrain costs of Medicare spending by setting prospective limits per diagnostic category on a fixed schedule. It was hoped that the private sector would follow its lead to reduce overall costs, but this did not happen. There is evidence, however, that this approach alone cannot constrain costs in the long run even for Medicare and that it has resulted in a 'revolving door' through which patients are simply readmitted for a new DRG when the previous one runs its course (Blank, 1997: 142). For instance, while hospitals under the DRG system initially were found to have reduced costs per day by 9.8 per cent and average length of stay by 6.5 per cent, the effect on total costs was offset by an 11.7 per cent increase in admission rates (Culyer *et al.*, 1988). In the late 1990s after the one-time savings from managed care began to dissipate, health care costs in the USA resumed their escalation, surging to nearly 15 per cent.

Other supply-side approaches include controls over construction of hospitals, the purchase of expensive equipment, and the numbers of medical students entering particular specialties. Encouragement of outpatient over inpatient facilities and a reduction in the oversupply of acute hospital beds are likely to reduce costs, as is the shift from more expensive hospital beds to nursing homes or home care (see Chapter 6). The changes in Germany are an example of a move towards this strategy. Traditionally, the monopoly of office-based doctors over the delivery of ambulatory care has hindered the development of outpatient facilities. However, in the face of cost pressures, hospitals are now allowed to offer day surgery, pre-admission diagnostic procedures, and post-discharge treatment. Furthermore, the role of the outpatient departments of university hospitals in the provision of highly specialized care has been recognized through special contracts with insurance funds. Despite these changes the position of specialists in ambulatory care remains strong.

Meanwhile, in the Netherlands there has been a reduction in the capacity for inpatient care and day surgery has expanded (Exter *et al.*, 2004). This has gone hand in hand with increasingly tight government regulation of hospitals. For example, the Hospitals Facilities Act regulates the number of hospital beds and specialist units. Moreover, all major investments in hospitals need the formal approval of the Minister of Health if any added facility is to be reimbursed through social health insurance (Maarse, 1997).

Throughout the 1990s, Sweden saw a substantial decline in the number of hospital beds that was more drastic than in other countries (European Observatory on Health Care Systems, 2001: 49). At the same time, the position of ambulatory care was strengthened. The 1995 Primary Care Act acknowledged primary care as a separate level of care and defined it as the basis of health care. This is significant, because compared to other European countries primary care in Sweden has traditionally been less developed.

As in other countries, at least at a rhetorical level, there has been a movement away from hospitals in the UK. Instead, ambulatory care settings seem to hold the promise of both tailored and cost-effective care (Saltman *et al.*, 2006). Both points are particularly relevant in the context of the British NHS where patient demand often remains unmet and where successive governments have been interested in making existing funds go further. This is epitomized in the vision of a 'primary care-led' health service where GPs have become key players, not only in the provision, but also in the organization of health services. Following the purchaser–provider split in the early 1990s, GPs were given the option of becoming 'fund holders' and receiving funds to purchase a range of diagnostic and elective procedures. The health reforms under the New Labour government in 1997 built on these developments and GP practices became so-called 'Primary Care Trusts'. As part of these trusts, GPs are responsible for the commissioning of all health care services in their areas while remaining responsible for the provision of ambulatory health care services.

A final supply-side strategy to cost containment is the creation of competitive market conditions under which the more efficient providers thrive and the relatively more costly ones are driven out of existence. One such approach entails separating the funding and provision functions and thus, it is assumed, opening up competition among providers. In the UK internal market, introduced in the early 1990s, for instance, self-governing public hospitals, together with private-sector hospitals, were envisaged as competing for contracts with the health authorities that funded secondary health. Because of the heated controversy surrounding moves to incorporate marketplace mechanisms, it is important to look at role of market in health care in more depth.

The government and the marketplace

Fuelled by ideological shifts towards neo-liberalism, one trend over the last few decades across Western democracies is the inclusion of market or quasi-market mechanisms in public health systems in order to provide incentives to improve efficiency (Ranade, 1998). According to neo-liberalism, public sector monopolies provide few incentives for system efficiency and in fact are likely to contain perverse incentives which in effect punish efficiency (see Heywood, 2002). Despite this paradigm shift, however, evidence suggests that a totally free market in health insurance can produce neither equity nor efficiency. Even in the USA, clearly the most market-oriented system, the government exerts considerable regulatory influence over the workings of the market though, despite this effort, it remains the least successful effort in controlling costs.

Generally, governments can take one of two main routes in regulating health care systems, although as Saltman (2002) suggests the two approaches often exist side by side. The first approach involves regulation in the more conventional sense of setting constraints on the non-public sector. This detailed command-and-control type of activity is generally designed to supplant and override market forces and institutions. This can be effected by specifying coverage of insurance policies, regulating membership and premiums, controlling the quantity and quality of prices, mandating set fee structures and schedules, fixing wage rates, and controlling planning capacity. For example, although the Japanese health system is largely non-public, over 5,000 independent insurance plans and the largely private providers are highly regulated by the government through the universal fee structure, centralized billing and payment, standard co-payments, and prohibition of extra billing.

The second approach, generally termed pro-market or pro-competitive, places more emphasis on the promotion of self-regulation by the health care community. The goal here is to maximize autonomy for insurers, providers and consumers through the operation of traditional marketplace principles. The government's role is to provide a balance among the various stakeholders as it would in other areas of the economy. Under a pure market model, the health care system is, in effect, a large business that, if left alone to operate according to the principles of supply and demand, will best serve the consumer public. For reasons discussed below, no system embodies the pure model, and even in the USA, providers, especially hospitals, face severe constraints as a result of regulation by local, state and national government. Some observers argue that the major US problem is overregulation and contend that if the competitive marketplace were left to operate on its own, health care dilemmas would dissipate (Califano, 1992).

The reason why a pure market approach cannot work is that health care contains none of the self-selecting mechanisms that work to check market excesses. In order for an efficient, market-based health care system to work, several conditions are essential. First, all decisions must be that of the consumer. Second, consumers must know the value and costs of the goods they are contemplating purchasing. Third, consumers must pay the full cost and receive the full value of the goods they choose to buy.

Importantly, not one of these conditions is present in the market for health care services. First, no medical decision is solely that of the patient. Although some discretion is possible, ultimately the individual patient's choice is heavily conditioned and constrained by the providers of health care. Second, most patients have a difficult time judging the value of the care they get. As a result, health care providers have enormous sway in deciding both the type and cost of care provided. The specialized knowledge required for the dispensation of health care, in conjunction with the emotional and often urgent nature of medical decisions, undercuts the patient's ability to be a rational shopper. Furthermore, it does not follow that more informed consumers of health care will shop for lower cost. In fact, evidence suggests that more information often leads to higher costs because patients with more knowledge tend to be more demanding in terms of the drugs, tests and treatments (Ubel, 2001).

The major reason that patients are unlikely to be frugal consumers as assumed by marketplace models, however, is the failure to meet the third condition. Third-party payment, whether public or private, ensures that the potential consumer who receives the value pays only a fraction, if any, of the costs. Under this incentive structure, it is well recognized that people consume more when they do not pay the full cost of something than they would if they had to pay (Ubel, 2001: 32). Also, while health economists might put cost containment first, politicians are likely to emphasize access and thus drive up the expectations of the public for an ever-expanding array of services.

Health insurance, either social or private, is accompanied by over-consumption because neither the patient nor the physician has an incentive to economize when an amorphous third party is paying the bill. *Moral hazard* (see Box 4.2) is the term used by economists when referring to the behavioural changes that occur when people are put in a position to spend or risk the funds of others (Havighurst, 2000). The bottom line is that unless there are strong incentives not to do so, people will generally want more when someone else is paying for the service.

The moral hazard problem is by no means unique to private insurance, and in fact is inherent in any third-party payment system. However, without strict controls and a restructuring of the traditional market functioning, both equity and efficiency are lacking. Pure market solutions are bound to fail in the long run because they serve to reaffirm claims to unlimited resources by those persons who can afford it or have coverage. Although there are steps that can be taken by governments to modify the marketplace (e.g. move from retrospective to prospective payment systems), adequate regulation requires inclusion of bureaucratic controls

Box 4.2   What is moral hazard?

You have just finished a meal with a group of five of your friends at a fancy restaurant, and the waiter rolls by with a cart of desserts at a price of £6 each. You are hesitant to order because you are full and do not chink you can get £6's worth of pleasure from the dessert. Then in a flash of brilliance, you remember that you are splitting the bill six ways, meaning the cost of the dessert to you will be only £1. Surely you will be able to get a pound's worth of pleasure? So you go ahead and order. Unfortunately, your friends, reasoning the same as you, all order a dessert too. As a result, each of you pays the full price for a dessert that none of you would have spent £6 on. 'Health care insurance, like the single check in a restaurant, distributes expenses across many people, creating an incentive to buy health care services that cost more than they are worth, a phenomenon health economists refer to as moral hazard' (Ubel, 2001: 31).

in order to shape the diverse demands of the health care marketplace. While this does not negate a role for the market, alone it is insufficient to deal with the peculiarities of health care. A major objective of moves towards managed care in the USA and elsewhere is to curb this moral hazard by limiting services that the insured can use at the plan's expense. Other mechanisms designed to rein in moral hazard are co-payments, the medical-necessity test, and medical savings accounts as found in Singapore.

In addition to the asymmetry of knowledge and power between patients and health care professionals, the inability of health care consumers to judge the value of the services they receive, and the general failure of marketplace mechanisms to produce efficiency, risk spreading through insurance is essential but also highly problematic. Although private insurance can spread the risk and the burden of payment, private insurers have an incentive to exclude, or at least raise the premiums of, high-risk individuals. Typically, private health insurance is most economical to people who are healthy while most health care is consumed by sick people unable to obtain affordable private insurance. Income redistribution based on market principles thus is not possible without intervention that negates those very principles of supply and demand. To some extent, then, a social insurance mechanism is needed to resolve this problem.

There are ways of controlling the non-public sector, however. As noted earlier, although Japan's health care system is dominated by the private insurance sector and providers compete for patients, all sectors are strictly regulated through a centralized national fee schedule. While universal coverage guarantees access to available health care, in large part the uniform fee schedule has been successful in restraining total health care expenditures and has a critical role in setting allocation priorities. It serves as an allocation mechanism by providing a financial incentive structure for the provision of selected services (i.e. primary care) by setting the fee allowed higher than the actual costs. In contrast, it can discourage medical applications deemed unwelcome by setting the allowable fees lower than the actual costs. For Ikegami (1992: 691) the schedule is a 'powerful tool' for promoting certain services and thus shaping the distribution of health care resources.

In addition to Japan, other countries actively intervene in private health care markets with detailed regulations of the command-and-control type. In the Netherlands, for instance, private insurers are mandated to provide basic insurance at set premiums for certain high risk individuals who are not eligible for public insurance. In contrast, in the UK, where private insurance plays only a supplementary role, there is little regulation of the private insurance market, while in the USA regulation is widespread but largely uncoordinated, confusing and often counterproductive.

Although many traditionally public health systems have undergone reforms aimed at increased reliance on market or quasi-market mechanisms, in all cases the governments have maintained firm control. Germany, the Netherlands, New Zealand, Sweden and the UK have introduced or strengthened competition among the providers in their health systems without sacrificing cost control and universal coverage.

In Sweden, New Zealand and the UK, the so-called 'purchaser–provider split' was introduced in an attempt to mimic market mechanisms and to stimulate competition among providers. In the UK, the initial internal market with its emphasis on regulated competition has been replaced by a public contract model, which aims to build on long-term cooperation (Ham, 2004). For example, contracts have been replaced by long-term service level agreements and purchasers have become commissioners, that is, organizations that are concerned not only with paying for services but also with planning. In contrast to the UK, the introduction of the purchaser–provider split has been much less widespread in Sweden, reflecting the high degree of decentralization in the health system.

Meanwhile, in Germany and the Netherlands, the introduction of market mechanisms has mainly focused on competition among purchasers rather than providers: that is, the insurance funds (Greß et al., 2002; Lieverdink and Made, 1997). This was brought about by allowing employees a free choice of insurance fund, thus breaking with the tradition of occupation-based health insurance. In Germany, the insurance funds compete for employees on the basis of the contribution rate. To mitigate the unequal distribution of health risks, a risk adjustment mechanism has been established so that in theory at least differences in contribution rates reflect the efficiency with which insurance funds manage their finances.

Ironically, Australia has taken measures to bolster private insurance in light of the steady decline in the proportion of the population with insurance for private hospital treatment since the 1980s. In order to increase the population coverage of private health insurance (PHI), reduce pressure on public hospital waiting lists and services, and support and improve the viability of the PHI industry, Australia introduced a series of measures under the PHI Incentive Scheme. In 1999, anyone purchasing private insurance received a 30 per cent subsidy, paid either as a tax rebate or as a reduced purchase price of insurance. Then, in 2000, the Lifetime Health Cover was introduced which applied a base premium to those purchasing insurance up until the age of 30. Those who have continuous private health insurance cover from age 30 continue to pay the base rate. Those joining after 30 pay an age related premium calculated at 2 per cent on top of the base premium for every year of age, up to the age of 65. Thus the government's solution to the private health insurance problem was to secure a reduction in the costs of premiums (the 30 per cent rebate), limit the out-of-pocket costs faced by the insured patient (the introduction of no-gap policies), and encourage younger people to join and maintain their fund membership through the Lifetime Health Cover (Bertelsmann Foundation, 2003b).

Although cost containment, accompanied by market mechanisms, became a central tenet of health policy reforms of the 1980s and 1990s, by itself it has not proved to be a sensible objective as evidenced by the USA. The major goal of health policy should not be to save money, but rather to promote the health and welfare of the population. To the extent that these cost-containment measures undermine this broader goal, they invite condemnation. On the other hand, it is evident that without successful initiatives to constrain costs, health care systems face severe funding crises, and perhaps breakdown, in the not too distant future. Because of these counter-pressures, the problem of priority setting in health care will become an even more incendiary an issue than it now is. Central to this is the issue of rationing medicine.

Allocation and rationing: the need to set priorities

As pressures emerge to expand basic care coverage to include access to intensive curative regimes, the goal of universal coverage is threatened. The fundamental problem facing all countries, then, is how to accommodate these important, but often conflicting goals. Weale (1998) likens this dilemma to what logicians call an inconsistent triad: a collection of propositions, any two of which are compatible with each other but which, when viewed together as a threesome, form a contradiction. 'Perhaps we can have only a comprehensive service of high quality, but not one available to all. Or a comprehensive service freely available to all, but not of high quality. Or a high quality service freely available to all, but not comprehensive. Each of these three possibilities defines a characteristic position in the modern debate about healthcare costs and organisation' (Weale, 1998).

While most Western countries have opted to ensure universal coverage but limit the range of health care services, the USA has a system that offers high-technology, comprehensive care, but care not guaranteed to all. Those who have first-rate insurance coverage have ready access to high quality medicine with considerable freedom of choice, but at the cost of equity in the health system. Critics of national health systems argue that free availability comes only at the cost of quality, choice and rapid technological diffusion. Weale (1998) suggests that while the third option – sacrificing some comprehensiveness in order to achieve at least a core range of high quality services available to all – was a possibility when drugs were few and treatments simple, that is no longer so. It is simply not possible to meet the needs of all citizens without compromising goals. To some extent, that is what allocation and priority setting are all about – balancing competing goals and demands facing the health system. In the end, this entails making hard choices among equally admirable goals.

Allocation decisions are necessary at three levels: allocation to health care; allocation within health care; and rationing at the individual level. The first level, macro-allocation, requires a decision as to how much of its resources society is willing to devote to health care: 5 per cent of GDP, 10 per cent, 15 per cent? More? What priority does society place on spending for medical care as compared to education, housing, social welfare, national security or recreation? Also, does increased allocation to medical care improve the health of the population if the funding comes at the expense of these other areas? In other words, what are the opportunity costs of putting more into health care? (See Chapter 7 for expanded discussion of this issue.)

Once society makes this decision, it must decide how these resources are to be allocated among the myriad competing categories of spending within health care, to particular forms of treatment, and to specific disease categories. Should priority be placed on preventive medicine, health promotion and primary care, or on more intensive high-technology medicine? Should treatment of diseases of the elderly or care of young mothers and children be given higher priority? Similarly, should priority be put on extending life or improving quality of life; the marginally ill or the severely ill; high-incidence diseases or rare diseases; AIDS or cancer or heart disease? At some stage, allocation within health care requires consideration of tradeoffs that can be more or less transparent, centralized or decentralized, fair or unfair, but always controversial.

Finally, assuming that we are unable and unwilling through our allocation policies to meet the health care needs of all persons due to limited resources, rationing decisions at the individual level are unavoidable (Lamm and Blank, 2007). The ubiquitous nature of scarcity driven by the trends discussed in Chapter 1 makes it certain that the demands of individuals and groups will exceed the available resources, thus requiring the rationing of these resources (see Box 4.3). Collectively, it is impossible for doctors to offer all technologically feasible and clinically beneficial medicine to all patients (Weinstein, 2001). As noted by Fleck (2002) there can be no health reform without health care rationing and no fair health reform without health care rationing for all.

Rationing is generally defined as the denial of a treatment to an identifiable patient who would benefit from it. This could be any type of treatment, but most often it is an expensive procedure or drug. Whatever specific form it takes, rationing always results in the situation where potentially beneficial treatment is denied on cost grounds. Given that rationing is necessary, the question becomes one of how to implement it. How do we assure legitimacy and impartiality without compromising success? Furthermore, if resources are to be focused on the provision of 'appropriate' health care, who defines it and how is it defined? And what

Box 4.3   Rationing is essential in tax-funded health systems

It has become commonplace for decisions made by the UK's National Institute for Health and Clinical Excellence (NICE) to be greeted with public outrage. It comes as little surprise that the Institute's rejection of five appeals against its guidance restricting the use of four drugs for Alzheimer's disease has been branded 'blatant cost cutting' by the Alzheimer's Society. But this reaction says less about NICE's decision-making process than it does about the gulf between patient expectations of the health system and understanding about the necessity for rational spending. Public-opinion surveys in the UK repeatedly show overwhelming support for a universal health system, but it is clear from reactions to decisions such as that of NICE that individuals do not connect the NHS ideal with the necessity for some form of rationing to make the best use of limited funds. A simple case of misunderstanding? Not quite. One big barrier to resolving this communication problem is the Government's unbending commitment to the mantra of patient choice. By urging patients to demand more from health services, the Government effectively ignores the fact that a tax-based system means some kind of rationing is essential (*The Lancet*, 2006).

are the criteria for rationing – total lives saved, life-years saved, or qual-ity-of-life years saved? Because there are no unequivocal answers and because rationing is so entangled with problems of cost containment and efficiency, its implementation is always very divisive.

Although the term rationing provokes strong emotions, all health systems ration medicine because none can provide unrestricted health care resources for all its citizens (Ham and Robert, 2003; Maynard and Bloor, 2001). Furthermore, despite intensified pressures on health care systems today, rationing has always been a part of medical decision making. Table 4.4 illustrates the range of ways in which health care can be rationed. Whether imposed by a market system where price deter-mines access, a triage system (see Box 4.4) where care is distributed on the basis of benefit as defined by the medical community, or a queue system where time and the waiting process become the major rationing

Table 4.4   *Forms of rationing medicine*

Form	Criteria used
Physician discretion	Medical benefit to patient
	Medical risk to patient
	Social class or mental capacity
Competitive marketplace	Ability to pay
Private insurance	Ability to pay for insurance
	Group membership
	Employment
Social insurance	Entitlement
	Means test
Legal	Litigation to gain access and treatment
Personal fundraising	Support of social organizations
	Skill in public relations
	Willingness to appeal to public
Implicit rationing	Queuing
	Limited manpower and facilities
	Medical benefits to patient with consideration of social costs
Explicit rationing	Triage
	Medical benefits to patient with emphasis on social costs and benefits
Controlled rationing	Social benefit over specific patient benefits
	Cost to society is main criterion

Source: Adapted from Blank (1997: 93).

> ## Box 4.4   Medical triage
>
> Triage, meaning 'choice' or 'selection', is used when many patients simultaneously need medical attention and medical personnel cannot attend to all. The rule is to first treat persons whose condition requires immediate attention without which they will progress to a more serious state. Others, whose condition is not as serious and who are stable, are deferred. This sort of triage is often necessary in busy emergency departments. A second sort of triage is indicated in disasters where the most seriously injured may be left untreated even at risk of death if their care would absorb so much time and attention that the work of rescue would be compromised. As applied to rationing, triage means that some patients will not be treated if the use of resources on them would be futile and would divert resources from those patients who would benefit more.

mechanisms, medical resources have always been distributed according to sets of criteria that inherently contain varying degrees of subjectivity. In almost all instances, rationing criteria are grounded in a particular value context that results in an inequitable distribution of resources based on social as well as strictly medical considerations.

Although a combination of these types of rationing is present in every country, different health care systems place emphasis on particular forms. Countries with national health systems have an easier time using more explicit rationing mechanisms through their control of the supply of resources. This is because they usually have not explicitly defined their services, as is common in social and private insurance systems where the member has, in effect, a contract for specific services. In national health systems, the services are purposely kept vague by the government so as to provide more room for manoeuvre. Also, in countries with socially determined health budgets, constraints in one area can be justified on grounds that the money will be spent on higher-priority services in another area. According to Wiener (1992: 15), this closed system of funding provides a 'moral underpinning for resource allocation across a range of potentially unlimited demands'. By contrast, in the fragmented US system or Singapore's individual responsibility system funded by personal savings accounts it is considerably more difficult to refuse any services for specific patients because there is no certainty the funds will be put to better use elsewhere. The lack of a fixed budget, either for government funding or overall national health care spending, makes it impossible to say where money 'saved' from rationing will go.

Not surprisingly rationing is both easier and more difficult in social insurance systems where legislation and/or contracts explicitly spell out the coverage. In principle, this makes rationing easier as it merely involves excluding certain treatments and procedures from the list of reimbursable services. An obvious leverage is the assessment of medical technology discussed below. In the Netherlands, for example, the coverage of social health insurance has come under scrutiny and homoeopathic drugs have been excluded, while the standard dental package has been considerably reduced. However, the explicit way in which coverage is defined also makes rationing more difficult because it makes any exclusion of services highly visible and therefore potentially very costly in political terms.

Supply-side rationing is traditionally practised by national health services and depends upon setting strict limits on medical facilities, equipment and personnel. Rationing in both the Netherlands and Germany has focused on measures such as reducing the number of hospital beds, setting sectoral budgets and contribution rates, and restricting the increase in the number of doctors. In these systems the availability of resources inevitably affects clinical decisions, with, as noted in Chapter 3, GPs often serving as gatekeepers and deflecting patients from overloading the system.

In contrast, market-oriented systems must depend on some form of *demand-side* rationing which is even more contentious. The USA, for instance, begins with excess hospital capacity and an oversupply of accessible specialists. As a result, the system has the capacity to perform any available procedure, including those that the public system does not cover. Persons with adequate insurance or resources, therefore, are unlikely to accept artificially imposed constraints on their access to medical specialists. Moreover, demand-side rationing in this environment is susceptible to constant personal appeals for coverage and is difficult to sustain politically.

A further distinction is between *price* and *non-price* rationing (see Figure 4.2). Price rationing is commonplace in the USA where health care resources are denied only to persons who cannot afford them or who have inadequate third-party coverage. In contrast, non-price rationing, which is characteristic in public health systems, depends on limiting the availability of certain health services, and thus denies medical resources even to persons who have the means to afford them. Of course, one option open to patients in countries with strict non-price rationing is to go elsewhere for treatment and pay for it out-of-pocket.

	UK	NZ	Germany	Japan			Australia		USA
Sweden				France		Italy		Singapore	

No Price Rationing   **High Price Rationing**

Figure 4.2   *Degree of price rationing*

Another aspect of rationing is that some forms can be carried out only by government action while others fail to distinguish clearly between public and private sector choices. As one moves to the more explicit forms of rationing at the bottom of Table 4.4, a more systematic government role is required and thus it is no surprise that these types are found primarily in national health systems. Other forms of rationing, such as public relations and market, often occur outside the public sphere. A related question regarding the government role in rationing centres on where they are carried out: are these decisions made by government, by a department or ministry, by regional health boards, or by individual hospitals? Are these decisions highly centralized or decentralized, bureaucratized or ad hoc?

Rationing also has been proposed as a means of guaranteeing every citizen a basic level of health care and excluding from coverage treatments outside this package. The explicit trade-off here is between universal access to those services deemed basic on the one hand and unequal access to the full range of technically feasible services on the other. In many countries, a *basic* level of health care focuses on primary care and excludes high-technology services such as organ transplants, fertility treatments and cosmetic surgery. However, when basic care is broadened to include unlimited access to intensive and expensive curative regimes, it undermines the goal of universal coverage. Health systems such as Britain, New Zealand and Japan are more successful in providing universal coverage and in maintaining lower per capita costs than the wide-open US system, but only so long as they limit the availability of high-technology medicine. Once they try to provide levels of medical care similar to the USA, they lose this advantage.

One approach to rationing, then, is to define a set of funding priorities or list of core services to be funded. In 1992, New Zealand set up the Core Services Committee with the objective of implementing a comprehensive core services strategy to ration health services. The Committee promulgated four principles for assessing a service: benefit; value for money; fairness; and consistency with the community's values and priorities (New Zealand Core Services Committee, 1992). After extensive public consultation and research on a range of specific treatment regimes, however, the Committee concluded that a specific list of funding priorities with exclusion of specific treatment categories was untenable and opted instead to continue services already funded. Exclusion of treatment categories was not only politically explosive, but also raised questions of fairness and did not account for variation among specific patients within a category.

Another approach was offered in the 1991 Dunning Committee report advising the Dutch government on priorities in the social health insurance (Ham, 1997b: 51). Similar to New Zealand, the Committee proposed a comprehensive approach that would include health technology assessment, the use of guidelines for the adequate provision of care, and the identification of criteria for prioritizing patients on waiting lists. The aim was to provide politicians with tools to decide on a basic health care package. Such explicit priority setting was considered necessary in order to continue guaranteeing access to essential care for all. Interestingly, however, since the publication of the Committee's report, initiatives have focused on assessing the cost-effectiveness of health technologies (and developing guidelines) rather than on choices between services (Ham, 1997b: 54). Again, this reflects professional and public resistance to the removal of certain services, such as contraceptives, from public funding.

The Swedish Parliamentary Priorities Commission, which reported in 1995, was distinctive not only in its cross-party membership but also in its emphasis on ethical considerations of priority setting (Ham, 1997b: 51). As such, the Commission offered different ways of thinking about priority setting to front-line practitioners and decision makers. The primacy of ethical considerations meant that human dignity was more important than the principle of need or solidarity, whereas cost efficiency was subordinate to all three principles. In contrast to the Netherlands and the UK, in Sweden human dignity and the rights of the individual were central. 'Applying this approach meant that discrimination based on age, birth weight, lifestyle and whether illnesses were self-inflicted would not normally be allowed' (Ham, 1997b: 59).

Unlike the Netherlands and Sweden, the UK has not conducted a national inquiry into priority setting. This reflects the fact that in the UK priority setting happens at the local level of the health authority (Locock, 2000). In response to a comprehensive review by a parliamentary committee, however, the government articulated its view on the issue. While explicitly excluding services from the NHS was seen as unnecessary, it was felt that resources should be concentrated on the most effective type of treatments. This plea for evidence-based medicine has been echoed by developments in health technology assessment, particularly the creation of the National Institute for Clinical Excellence (NICE) in 1999 which, interestingly, is perceived to constitute explicit, national rationing (Syrett, 2003).

Perhaps the most detailed prioritization system was adopted in the State of Oregon in the 1990s (Box 4.5). Oregon generated a list of prioritized health care services in order to extend Medicaid services to all persons on public support. The criteria used to rank over 700 diagnostic and treatment categories included the cost of the procedure, its potential to improve quality of life and the number of years the improvement is expected to last. In order to measure cost-effectiveness of treatments, a Quality of Well Being (QWB) scale defined 24 distinct

> ## Box 4.5   The Oregon Health Plan (OHP)
>
> Under Oregon's plan, the state created a list of disorders ranked in descending order from those most to least economically worthwhile. Thus, instead of excluding certain members of the population from having any access, Oregon attempted to ration care according to a priority list of services. The plan worked well at first, but by the late 1990s rising costs and a falling economy made it harder for the state to maintain uniform universal coverage. In 2004, when the state's budget crisis threatened all state programs, the Oregon legislature attempted to preserve OHP coverage by proposing additional funding sources and establishing priorities with regards to populations and services to be covered. However, voters were able to block the most important source of additional funding and the Department of Human Services was forced to use the coverage priorities articulated to create a budget cuts plan that called for the elimination of coverage for the working poor. The savings from this cancellation of coverage was used to 'buy back' services not federally mandated but prioritized by the state for those recipients remaining on the plan. Whatever happens in the future, these cuts signal the demise of Oregon's experiment with state insurance coverage for the working poor (Bertelsmann Foundation, 2004b).

states of health. One thousand individuals were surveyed and asked to assign a numerical score to each of these states of health, from a scale of zero (as good as dead) to 100 (perfect health), and each of these states of health was assigned an overall numerical weight. These QWB scores were used to calculate the cost-effectiveness, and thus the priority ranking, of the condition-treatment pairs (Mendelson *et al.*, 1995). The result of this process was a series of 'league tables' of condition–treatment pairs ranked in descending order of priority. Under the implementation of the Oregon Plan, the procedures to be funded in a given year depend on the total amount budgeted by the state legislature, thus explicitly tying specific treatment to level of health care funding.

Rationing by exclusion has been criticized as price rationing because those patients with the ability to pay can obtain the services in the private market or elsewhere while those who do not must do without. Other problems include 'co-morbidity inconsistencies' when one condition is included and the other not and 'diagnostic creep' where doctors manipulate diagnoses to ensure they fall within the funded list (see Mullen, 1998). Core service or other prioritizing schemes also can lead to political pressures to add dramatic, often lifesaving, interventions for specific individuals when services that have traditionally been supported are eliminated from the list.

Although not as transparent as these attempts to prioritize health care services, the universal fee structure of Japan has a clear prioritizing function through its control over the diffusion of new technologies. More expensive innovations are discouraged because the charge allowed for a new treatment is computed by comparing it to the cost of the nearest existing treatment. Therefore, while one might explain the low rate of organ transplantation in Japan by cultural veneration of the dead and dislike of invasive technologies (Miller and Hagihara, 1997), expensive medical interventions are discouraged by the government's strong role in fixing prices. Rationing decisions are made through the incentive structure determined by societal priorities as reflected in the fee levels. Moreover, the government ensures equity in financing among the multitude of private and public plans and equality of service since providers are always paid the same amount for a service no matter what insurance plan the patient has, even if on public assistance. Although the system has problems with multiple diagnoses and increased volume to make up for fee constraints, overall Japan has created an effective system for eliminating the necessity of making patient-specific rationing decisions at the individual level.

In Germany, priority setting is both implicit and explicit (R. Busse, 1999). In comparison to the Netherlands and Sweden it is implicit, in that there has been no formal review of the issue. At the same time, priority setting is quite explicit in that it is part of the contractual and fee negotiations between providers and insurance funds. For example, broad priorities can be expressed by defining the coverage of the social health insurance through a positive list (as in the case of care by non-physicians) or through evaluating the effectiveness of new as well as existing diagnostic and therapeutic methods. Fine-tuning of priorities is also possible through defining the relative value of an individual treatment as part of the fee schedule. For example, changes in the fee schedule in ambulatory care have reduced reimbursements for the more technically oriented specialists and rewarded generalist office-based doctors (Rosenbrock and Gerlinger, 2004).

These diverse efforts at rationing represent rather primitive initial attempts to face systematically the problems of setting health care priorities within the context of scarce resources. Although none of these efforts has been fully successful, they have helped lay the groundwork for fair and workable rationing approaches. Explicit priority-setting efforts will have to withstand pressures for dramatic, often lifesaving, interventions for specific individuals identified as needing them and face claims that a narrowed core services agenda will magnify the inequities between those with private insurance and those without. According to Klein (2005), the legitimacy of any rationing scheme depends on better, more evidence-based methods of analysis. Moreover,

Given conflicting values, the process of setting priorities for health care must inevitably be a process of debate . . . which cannot be resolved by an appeal to science and where the search for some formula or set of principles designed to provide decision-making rules will always prove elusive. Hence the crucial importance of getting the institutional setting of the debate right . . . the right process will produce socially acceptable answers – and this is the best we can hope for. (Klein and Williams, 2000: 25)

In order to attain legitimacy, rationing processes need to command the confidence of a public who do not know, or care, about the technical aspects but want assurance that decisions reflect social values and are taken in ways that are transparent.

Rationing and the individual

Any rationing of health care resources is complicated because, as noted in Chapter 1, the distribution is skewed towards a very small proportion of the population. With the shift towards sophisticated curative care, health care spending has become concentrated in a relatively small number of patients in acute care settings. Typically, high users are more likely to be persons with chronic medical problems who are repeatedly admitted to the hospital than persons with a single cost-intensive stay. This small fraction of patients exerts disproportionate leverage on medical resources by repeated use of hospital facilities. In addition to the elderly, high users of health care predominantly are identified as persistently ill individuals many of whom have unhealthy lifestyles and are non-compliant. A few risk factors, including alcohol and drug abuse, cigarette smoking, obesity, sedentary lifestyles and unhealthy diets, are particularly evident among high users of medical care (see Table 4.5). In addition to having more frequent episodes of ill health, patients with these behaviours require greater repeated hospitalizations for each episode, thus increasing the 'limit cost' of the illness.

Data on the major causes of mortality reflect a shift from infectious diseases to degenerative chronic diseases linked to individual behaviour over the last half century. Today, it is estimated that 50 per cent of all premature deaths are associated with choices individuals make (U.S. Public Health Service, 1995:3). As illustrated in Table 4.6, two factors, smoking and obesity, alone account for 35 per cent of the 2.4 million deaths in the USA. Moreover, it has been estimated that 50 to 90 per cent of all cancers are promoted or caused by various personal and environmental factors (Cundiff and McCarthy, 1994: 33). 'Better control of fewer than ten risk factors . . . could prevent between 40 and 70 percent

Table 4.5   *Lifestyle and self-inflicted diseases*

Lifestyle	Self-inflicted diseases
Alcohol abuse	Cirrhosis of the liver, encephalopathy, foetal alcohol syndrome
Cigarette smoking	Emphysema, chronic bronchitis, lung cancer, coronary artery disease
Drug abuse	Suicide, overdose, malnutrition, infectious diseases
Overeating	Obesity, hypertension, diabetes, heart disease, varicose veins
High fat intake	Arteriosclerosis, diabetes, coronary artery disease
Low-fibre diet	Colorectal cancer
Lack of exercise	Coronary artery disease, hypertension
Sexual promiscuity	Sexually transmitted diseases, AIDS, cervical cancer

Source: Adapted from Leichter (1991: 77).

Table 4.6   *Causes of death in the USA, 2000*

Cause	Estimated number of deaths	Percentage of total deaths
Tobacco	435,000	18.1
Diet/activity patterns	400,000	16.6
Alcohol	85,000	3.5
Microbial agents	75,000	3.1
Toxic agents	55,000	2.3
Motor vehicles	43,000	1.8
Firearms	29,000	1.2
Sexual Behaviour	20,000	0.9
Illicit use of drugs	17,000	0.7
Total	1,159,000	48.2

Source: Adapted from Mokdad *et al.* (2004).

of all premature deaths, a third of all cases of acute disability, and two-thirds of all cases of chronic disability' (Sullivan, 1990: 1066). Although there are no accurate estimates of the health costs of premature mortality or preventable morbidity caused by imprudent behaviour, it runs into the hundreds of billions of dollars annually. Likewise, as will be discussed in

Chapter 7, the impact of obesity on health care spending is substantial and growing rapidly (Thorpe *et al.*, 2004a).

These data raise serious implications for rationing. First, they suggest that any efforts to reduce health care costs must be directed at high users simply because they collectively consume such a high proportion of the funds. 'There are serious limitations to the effectiveness of any cost containment strategies that focus on the 90 percent of the population that collectively accounts for only one-third of the total U.S. health care spending' (Berk and Monheit, 2001: 17). Second, they demonstrate that considerable redistribution of societal resources is necessary if these individuals, many of whom are poor and/or on benefits, are to obtain the health services they need. Third, they raise vital questions concerning the extent to which society can afford to support individuals who knowingly engage in high risk behaviour. This is a particularly salient issue when these services include long-term, expensive interventions such as intensive care and organ transplantation. A peripheral issue centres on the fact that with this knowledge, private insurers are able to selectively exclude from coverage groups and individuals who are likely to be in these high-risk categories based on their lifestyles. Without government regulations prohibiting this pattern, the low-risk, healthy groups become concentrated in the private sector while actual and potential high users are reliant on the public sector.

Due to the high costs risky behaviours generate, health systems are under heightened pressure to become more actively involved in personal lifestyle choices. Whether out of concern for fairness, paternalism, strict economics or a blame-the-victim mentality, momentum has increased for aggressive efforts to effect changes in individual behaviour deemed dangerous for health. This is clearly evident for smoking and drinking. Attempts to prohibit smoking in public places and discourage its use through high taxes and to remove the drinker from the highways are being approached with near missionary zeal in many countries. Anti-obesity programmes are likely to follow (see Chapter 7).

What should be done, however, when efforts to change behaviour fail and we are faced with patients who need treatment for self-imposed illness? Should smokers get heart transplants or by-pass surgeries? Should alcoholics who drink themselves into liver failure be candidates for liver transplants? If so, should they go to the top of the organ waiting lists if they are the most urgent cases? Is it fair for those who try to live healthy lives to pay the enormous costs of those who do not? In other words, can it ever be fair to ration medical resources away from those individuals who cause or contribute to their own ill health? The answers to these questions, of course, are in part to be found in the cultural frameworks discussed in Chapter 2, but they also reflect the economic realities of limits.

Box 4.6　How much is too much?

Gregory 'X' is a 'frequent flyer', a label that many emergency rooms give to their regular visitors. Developmentally disabled and unwell in large part because he refuses to take his blood pressure medicine, between 1996 and 2001 he called '911' and was taken to the emergency room by ambulance over 1200 times. His emergency room visits, ambulance rides and hospital stays have cost the taxpayers over $900,000, with no end in sight. According to the staff, Mr. X enjoys his notoriety and the treatment he receives which he takes for, granted – 'last year they told me my bill was a quarter-million dollars. I said so what? I'm sick. Take care of me.' Is there a moral obligation to treat such patients indefinitely or should society set limits? If so who should implement these limits?

Source: Extracted from Foster (2001).

In an age of scarce resources in which medical goods and services are rationed, the debate over lifestyle choice increasingly will focus on the extent to which lifestyle ought to influence rationing decisions. More than any other issue surrounding the rationing of medical resources, this aspect of lifestyle promises to be the most poignant. When should lifestyle criteria be expressly entered into the rationing equation? Who is responsible for establishing the criteria? What impact will this selection process have on the practice of medicine? What limits, if any, are there on the care of persons who continually harm themselves? (See Box 4.6 and consider what decision you would make in this case).

Another highly controversial aspect of rationing centres on the disproportionate use of health care resources by the elderly, especially those over age 80. With the ageing of the baby boomers, unless something is done to change this skewed spending pattern, this burgeoning cohort will consume an inordinate proportion of health care resources. Simply put, health care costs cannot be controlled without using age as a criterion in rationing simply because the elderly are the prime users of technologies that increase the costs of medicine. Although logically the elderly offer a prime target for rationing and some authors (see Callahan, 1987) have suggested this, any attempts to explicitly ration medical care on grounds of age alone is improbable in many countries given the political influence of the elderly. Not surprisingly, using age as a factor in rationing has been most widely condemned in the USA although in other countries such as the UK old age 'is a criterion for rationing health resources and it occurs at all levels of the National Health Service' (Williams, 2000). Whether countries choose explicity to use age as a factor in rationing or not, the end result will be the same if social priorities allocate resources away from high-technology medicine and towards prevention and health promotion since the elderly are the prime beneficiaries of the former.

Efforts to control new technologies

As noted in Chapter 1, the proliferation of biomedical technologies is a major force pushing up health care costs in all countries. Although the patterns of introduction, diffusion and rationing of new technologies vary across countries, generally those with centralized funding and controls require that new technologies be accommodated within the existing systems of resource allocation. Because tradeoffs must be made between the innovation and current treatment for that particular condition as well as other existing conditions, there is an evident need to establish priorities. Analysis of the marginal costs and benefits and comparison with existing treatments is critical, and a new procedure or drug rejected unless there is evidence it will have a major positive impact on health outcomes and/or reduce costs.

In contrast, in market-oriented systems new technologies are seldom rejected even when found to be ineffective and less so if they are efficacious and safe, but unaffordable. Since elimination of ineffective technologies alone is unlikely to constrain costs, countries face difficult decisions that involve sacrificing clinically useful technologies that might work but that collectively could bankrupt the system while contributing very little to the health of the population. In any case, mechanisms are needed to engage in prospective assessment of technologies before they are diffused as well as compel discontinuation of those technologies that are ineffective, only marginally effective, or effective but too expensive to find social justification.

Bodenheimer and Fernandez (2005) suggest that controlling costs while preserving quality requires a multi-faceted approach. In addition to strengthening primary care and disease management programmes and reducing inappropriate care, medical errors, and the use of hospital and emergency departments by high-cost patients, we need the diffusion of effective technology assessment mechanisms. Yet, in most countries, the history of health technology assessment (HTA) has been inconsistent and controversial. It has been characterized by strong opposition from interests which see it as a threat to their autonomy and by criticism from others who feel it has failed to provide critical assessment and thus stem the dissemination of questionable technologies and procedures.

HTA has been well established in Australia, Britain, Sweden, the Netherlands and the USA, whereas in other countries it is still in its infancy (Banta, 2002). MacDaid (2001) offers possible explanations for this. In Germany and Italy biomedical and clinical research has been dominant, whereas the status of health services research and economic evaluation has been low. In the case of Germany this is exacerbated by reliance on decisions obtained through consensus and expert opinion. The importance of economic evaluation also seems to be related to the strength of health economics training, which has a long tradition in France, the Netherlands, Sweden and the UK.

In the Netherlands, when the implementation of the Dunning Report guidelines for the exclusion of some medical services from social insurance coverage proved too controversial, attention turned to health technology assessment. The initial evaluation of the effectiveness of 126 existing technologies was undertaken as part of the investigative medicine programme run by the Health Insurance Funds Council (Ham, 1997b: 62). In this shift towards evidence-based medicine, emphasis has been placed on the role of professional bodies and specialist associations. Interestingly, as Exter *et al.* observe, 'since the 1990s, such systematic evaluations . . . are used as an important tool to assist policy-making, including priority setting' (2004: 99).

In 1987, Sweden established a public agency, the Swedish Council on Technology Assessment in Health Care, which is responsible for promoting the cost-effective use of health care technologies. The Council reviews and evaluates the social, ethical and medical impact of health technologies and then distributes the information to front-line decision makers, including officials in the central government and county councils as well as doctors (Werkö *et al.*, 2001). In addition, the National Board for Health and Welfare is now commissioned to develop evidence-based guidelines for the treatment of selected chronic illnesses. Interestingly, the guidelines come in versions not only for health personnel and patients, but also for policy makers and include guidance in priority setting (Glenngård *et al.*, 2005).

Similarly, in recent years, health technology assessment in Britain has received high public attention with the creation of NICE (Butler, 2002). The Institute is responsible for evaluating, at the request of the Department of Health, new technologies and care guidelines with regard to their clinical and cost-effectiveness. The Institute's guidance on the effectiveness of specific drugs has attracted particular public attention, among them Beta Interferon for multiple sclerosis sufferers, the flu drug Relenza, and new types of drugs for breast cancer patients. The establishment of NICE accompanied the development of the National Service Framework, which set out patterns of care for specific diseases, disabilities and patient groups and the establishment of the Commission for Health Improvement which, in turn, is responsible for monitoring and improving standards at the local level (Dillon, 2001).

The Australian Health Technology Advisory Committee advises the government on the costs and effectiveness of targeted medical technologies. The Committee has representatives from the Commonwealth, the

Box 4.7   Evidence-based medicine in Australia

In 1998 a formal process using the criteria of safety, effectiveness and cost-effectiveness (evidence based medicine) on the introduction and use of new medical procedures was implemented in Australia. As part of this process an expert panel, the Medical Services Advisory Committee (MSAC) was created. The MSAC makes recommendations to the Minister of Health as to which new medical services and technologies should be included on the Medicare Benefits Schedule (MBS). The MBS sets a schedule fee for medical services for which the Commonwealth government will pay medical benefits. Only medical procedures and new technologies which are deemed safe, cost-effective and of real benefit to patients are funded through Medicare. In order for a medical procedure to attract funding to cover the fee for the medical practitioner the procedure must have a MBS Item Number. Applications to the MSAC are evaluated by contractors employed by the Medicare Benefits Branch. Additionally, this process has a reasonably high level of transparency with publication on a Web site of the receipt of the application, its progress, and a detailed written report of the outcome (O'Malley, 2006).

state governments and representatives of the medical profession, insurance funds, hospitals and consumers. The Australian Institute of Health and Welfare has also established a health technology division to monitor technological developments and advise the government on whether and under what conditions technologies should be used in Australia. Of the specific major areas studied, including MRIs, organ transplant procedures and laparoscopic surgery, the recommendations have led to introduction of these new techniques on a controlled basis (Palmer and Short, 2000: 207–8). Additionally, in 1998 the Medical Services Advisory Committee was established to screen new medical procedures and services (see Box 4.7)

In the USA, assessment of medical technology has been widespread in both the private and public sectors, but there has been little cooperation, coordination or even exchange of data among the many assessment efforts. In 1984, Congress passed legislation that extended the mandate of the then National Center for Health Services Research to include not only considerations of safety and efficacy, but also cost-effectiveness, and changed its name to the National Center for Health Services Research Assessment/Health Care Technology Assessment (NCHSR/HCTA). The law also instituted a Council on Health Care Technology under the sponsorship of the National Academy of Sciences, with partial governmental support. After considerable problems in soliciting long-term private support to match federal grant monies and in gaining cooperation from groups in the private sector, the Council was ultimately abandoned. Its demise again reflected the uncertain attitudes both in the private and public sectors regarding limiting the diffusion of medical technology in the USA.

In part because of a lack of effective national guidance in the USA and largely driven by rapidly expanding Medicaid costs, individual states have begun to 'reevaluate their once-limited role in the assessment of medical technology' (Mendelson *et al.*, 1995: 84). In a few states, detailed assessments are being conducted on selected technologies. Leading the way are Minnesota's Health Technology Advisory Committee, Washington State's Health Services Effectiveness Advisory Committee, and the Oregon Medical Technology Assessment Program.

Medical technology assessment in Germany has tended to lag behind other countries and until recently was focused on the licensing of pharmaceuticals and medical devices (Perleth *et al.*, 1999). Beyond that, the assessment of medical technology is linked to the coverage specified in contracts with health care providers. In the case of ambulatory care, where regulation has developed furthest, the federal committee of doctors and insurance funds decides on the effectiveness of new technologies to be covered by health insurance as well as re-evaluate existing technologies based on the criteria of benefit, medical necessity and efficiency. As assessments are sector-specific, overall the system of medical technology assessment is fragmented (R. Busse, 1999), although developments in recent years mark a more systematic approach (Burau, 2005). Examples are the Disease Management Programmes for selected chronic illnesses, which are based on evidence-based clinical guidelines and the new Institute for Quality and Efficiency.

In summary, HTA will become increasingly critical in priority setting as the scarcity of resources comes into conflict with the intensified demands and pressures for the diffusion of innovative techniques. Evidence-based medicine currently is the catch phrase for efforts to resolve the health care dilemmas and the foundation for the allocation and rationing of health care resources.

Trends in priority setting

National policies on priority setting are a pertinent area to test the concept of convergence (discussed in Chapter 1) since the predominance of public funding means that resources are limited, thus, making priority setting inevitable. Table 4.7 summarizes our findings that reconfirm the interrelationship between convergence and embeddedness suggested by Saltman (1997). Using Bennett's (1991) distinctions of convergence by policy goals, policy content and instruments, our analysis shows that there is some convergence, but it is restricted largely to the procedural

Table 4.7   *Substantive and procedural aspects of health policy convergence*

	Procedural aspects of health policy convergence		
Substantive aspects of health policy convergence	*Policy goals*	*Policy content*	*Policy instruments*
Rationing/ priority setting	An issue in all countries, but limited agreement on its meaning.	Much variation. Demand vs supply, price vs non-price rationing.	Wide variation though some moves towards more centrally controlled instruments.
Increased dependence on marketplace	An issue in all countries, highly controversial in many countries.	Most countries have adopted some market features, often limited, but no clear convergence.	Wide variation even among national health and social insurance systems.
Cost containment strategies	An important objective in all countries, but even at this level its importance relative to universal access and equity varies.	Some moves to co-payment, provider-payment mechanisms, etc., but persistent differences in weight given to demand vs supply.	Considerable variation and mixes of policy instruments used to contain costs.

Source: Adapted from Blank and Burau (2006).

aspect of policy goals and does not appear to extend to content and instruments. Despite signs of a convergence at the ideational level, policy content and the preferred policy instruments for implementing such policy continue to vary widely across these countries. By and large, countries continue to adopt different strategies to deal with similar problems.

For instance, while there has been a shift in goals in all countries towards cost containment, the varied emphases on an array of demand- and supply-side approaches displays considerable diversity across these countries. Also, while the inclusion of efficiency or cost containment as a goal appears universal, there remain wide disparities among the countries as to the degree of access and equity in their respective health care systems. Similarly, although all countries have integrated some aspects of the market into their systems through recent reforms, the wide variation in both form and degree argues against the conclusion that they are converging to a market-driven health system. Far from it! Unlike the USA, other countries continue to maintain relatively robust regulatory controls over market forces.

Regarding the allocation and rationing of health care resources, about the only perceivable convergence is that it is increasingly clear in all countries that medicine must be rationed because, in the light of endless technological possibilities, no country can serve all the health needs of their population to the fullest. Countries with global budgets or other supply-side controls are likely to depend on non-price rationing mechanisms and make harder choices at the macro-allocation level. In contrast, countries that rely more heavily on price rationing forgo setting broad limits, thus losing any semblance of equity or systematic rationing policy. The result is that rationing in national health systems differs greatly from that in social insurance systems and, especially, market-dominated systems.

It should also be noted that health policy is not static and that movement in one direction is often followed by a move in the opposite direction as political fortunes change or the public responds negatively to a change. Any discussion of convergence risks underestimating the political dynamics inherent in health policy. For instance, New Zealand was widely cited as an example of convergence towards a market system in the early 1990s when it initiated strong market reforms, but most of these were withdrawn by succeeding governments.

In the end though, all countries must face the issue of rationing of health resources for the high users of medicine, including the elderly and individuals who engage in multiple high-risk behaviours. Evidence suggests that there is little consensus in these countries as to whether or how to do this. Finally, because the diffusion of new medical technologies is such a critical factor in cost containment and central to any debate over rationing since it is generally expensive technologies or drugs being rationed, the preliminary efforts at technology assessment outlined here must be strengthened. The process must be made more transparent to the explicit tradeoffs required when a decision is made to fund expensive new technologies: where specifically will the money come from, and what other programmes might be cut? This leads us back to medical professionals who, as we shall see in the next chapter, continue to wield considerable power and have a substantial stake and interest in cost containment, rationing and health policy in general.

Chapter 5

The Medical Profession

The power of the medical profession stems from the fact that health care is largely defined as medical care. Doctors are responsible for diagnosis and as such define patients' health care needs. Doctors also provide treatment, but more often than not this involves (either directly or by referral) other health practitioners, such as medical specialists, nurses, physiotherapists, laboratory technicians or dieticians. This puts doctors in a key position regarding the allocation of health care resources. Health systems, health policy and politics cannot be understood without doctors and vice versa. Doctors often enjoy considerable power and are seen as the archetypal example of a profession. Autonomy and dominance are at the heart of medical power and refer to the ability of doctors to make autonomous decisions concerning the contents and the conditions of medical work (see also Box 5.1).

Inasmuch as doctors are embedded in specific sub-systems of funding, provision and governance, professional autonomy will always be contingent and relative, and this also points to the complex relationship between doctors and the state. Significantly, professional autonomy and power are part of the implicit contract between doctors and the state. The state grants professional autonomy in return for doctors providing services that are central to the legitimacy of modern states. Medical practice, by virtue of the specialized knowledge on which it is based, also gives legitimacy to the (potentially problematic) allocation of health care resources. However, inherent in this interdependent relationship between doctors and the state is conflict, such as that between medically defined need and the finitude of financial resources. For the medical profession, the challenge is 'to manage the relationship with the state so as simultaneously to appropriate public authority without surrendering to public control' (Moran, 1999: 99).

What are the implications for understanding doctors in the context of health systems and policy? Power emerges as a central theme, as does the complex nature of medical power. Far from being absolute, the power of doctors is relative and varies between different specialties, points in time and countries. This comparative analysis highlights how medical power is contingent upon the specific sub-systems of funding, provision and governance. At the same time, the power of doctors is intrinsically changeable as it is linked with states and their agendas. Analysing how

Box 5.1   Understanding professions

The understanding of professions has changed over time. Early approaches defined professions by specific traits (such as formal knowledge, long training and high social status) and by a positive role in society. However, these approaches have been criticized for taking the self-image of professions at face value and for remaining largely uncritical. Instead, later approaches focus on the social organization of power. Freidson (1994) for example defines professions as being primarily concerned with attaining and maintaining control. Control consists of autonomy (that is, control over the professions' own work) and dominance (that is, control over the work of others). Medical power is highlycomplex and has both an individual and a collective dimension, comprising the freedom of individual doctors to practise as they see fit as well as the activities of doctors' professional organizations. Here, Light (1995) further distinguishes among clinical and fiscal autonomy, practice and organizational autonomy, and organizational and institutional control. Elston (1991) adds cultural authority to her understanding of medical power. Cultural authority refers to the dominance of medical definitions of health and illness. At the same time, analysing professions across different countries has become an important concern for recent studies on the organization of expertise (Burau *et al.*, 2004). This builds on earlier historical analyses that emphasized the diversity of the phenomenon called 'professionalism' and exposed the Anglo-American centredness of many ideas about professions. For example, Johnson (1995) suggests that professions and the state have tended to be perceived as separate entities, which then relate to each other as autonomous professions and interventionist state. This makes it difficult to understand professions in Continental and Nordic countries, which have traditionally been 'state interventionist'.

health care reform affects doctors and their power is key. Equally, as much as doctors are entangled with health systems, changes in the regulation of medical work also give an indication of wider changes in health systems (Moran, 1999).

This chapter explores the issues of embeddedness, power and change. The first section provides an overview of the medical profession using OECD statistics. The second section locates the practice of doctors in the context of the health system, while the third directs attention to recent reforms and how they have affected doctors. The fourth section examines how doctors are paid and what this says about the relative power of doctors. This is followed by an analysis of the political organization of doctors and the role of doctors in the policy process. The concluding section summarizes relations between doctors, health policy and the state.

Who doctors are

Doctors are often thought of as a homogeneous group. The notion of profession suggests a cohesion that allows for dominance and autonomy. This corresponds to the idea that medical professionalism is a universal phenomenon (see Box 5.1). However, even a cursory look at statistics reveals considerable diversity among doctors across and within countries, for example in terms of the number of specialists or the percentage of female doctors. The analysis of statistics naturally remains on the surface, but as an overview it provides a useful starting point for comparison. Through highlighting similarities and differences, statistics raise 'why' questions which demand more detailed analysis. The number of doctors presented in Table 5.1 provides a first indication of the diversity that exists across countries.

In many countries, the trend in the number of doctors per 1,000 inhabitants since the early 1960s tells the familiar story of welfare state expansion, together with a shift towards curative, specialized medicine. In the majority of countries, the number of doctors has more or less doubled. Beyond the commonality of growth over time, the current number of doctors ranges from 1.5 doctors per 1,000 inhabitants in Singapore to 4.2 in Italy. However, Italy is a clear outlier. The remaining countries fall into roughly three groups: Britain, Japan and New Zealand with about 2 doctors per 1,000 inhabitants; Australia and the USA with

Table 5.1 *Number of practising doctors per 1,000 inhabitants*

	1979	1984	1989	1994	1999	2004[a]
Australia	n/a	1.8	2.1	2.4	2.4	2.6
France	1.8	2.5	3.0	3.2	3.3	3.4
Germany	n/a	n/a	n/a	3.0	3.2	3.4
Italy	n/a	n/a	n/a	3.7	4.2	4.2
Japan	1.2	1.4	n/a	1.8	n/a	2.0
Netherlands	1.8	2.2	2.4	n/a	3.1	3.6
New Zealand	1.5	1.7	1.9	2.0	2.2	2.2
Singapore	n/a	n/a	n/a	n/a	n/a	1.5
Sweden	2.0	2.5	2.8	2.8	3.0	3.3
UK	1.3	1.4	1.6	1.7	1.9	2.3
USA	n/a	n/a	n/a	2.1	2.2	2.4

[a] The figures for Australia, New Zealand and Sweden are from 2003.
n/a = not available

Sources: Data from OECD (2006) and Singapore Ministry of Health (2006).

about 2.5 doctors per 1,000 inhabitants; and France, Germany, the Netherlands and Sweden with about 3.5 doctors per 1,000 inhabitants. The variation is significant and, while there is no ready explanation for it, it may reflect differences in the levels of health care expenditure. It might also reflect government restrictions on the number doctors in the form of limits on the number of medical students or the number of doctors allowed to set up practice outside hospitals.

The disparity in the number of doctors also disguises regional variations in the distribution of doctors. This is particularly pertinent in large, unevenly populated countries. Australia is a case in point. There are no legal restrictions on the ability of doctors to establish a practice wherever they wish in Australia. This has resulted in a geographical maldistribution of doctor–patient ratios, which are much higher in the capital cities than in the remainder of each state, especially among specialists in the most rural areas (Palmer and Short, 2000: 196). Successive Commonwealth governments have attempted to address the shortage of doctors in the bush, but the imbalance in their distribution has proven persistent, in part reflecting lifestyle choices of doctors (Davies *et al.*, 2006; Hamilton, 2001). For example, there is one GP for every 1,000 residents of Australian capital cities, while small communities have a ratio of 1:1,700 (Birrell, 2002). Day *et al.* (2005) found the recent changes in bulk billing have done little to ameliorate geographical inequities. Hamilton (2001) argues that even though most doctors receive much of their income in the form of Medicare payments, the government has little control over where they practise. In 1996, the government did require graduating doctors without their full qualifications to take part in programmes designed to address this imbalance. As a result, the number of doctors practising in rural and remote areas increased from around 5,400 in 1996 to 6,200 in 2000, although rural areas remain underserved (Wooldridge, 2001).

The situation is similar in the USA. Rural areas tend to have physician shortages while urban areas have high concentrations of doctors, especially specialists. Despite incentive programmes through Medicare's massive subsidy for hospital-centred residency training of doctors, isolated areas find it difficult to retain doctors (Medicare and Graduate Medical Education, 1995). The fact that the USA is heavily skewed towards specialists compounds this problem because specialists are least likely to practise in rural areas (Medicare and Graduate Medical Education, 1995). In recent years, rural communities have come to depend heavily on foreign-trained doctors to fill the void (C. Busse, 1998).

Countries differ not only in terms of the number of doctors but also the diversity of the medical profession itself. One feature of this diversity is the fact that doctors are increasingly female and, as Table 5.2 shows, in

Table 5.2   *Female practising doctors, as a percentage of practising doctors, 2004*[a]

Australia	32.0
France	37.7
Germany	37.6
Italy	35.3
Japan	16.4
New Zealand	34.5
Sweden	41.2
UK	37.7
USA	28.1

[a] The figures for Australia, New Zealand and Sweden are from 2003.

Source: Data from OECD (2006).

the majority of countries about a third of doctors are women. This can be attributed to cultural and economic developments which have changed the position of women in society and also to more specific state-initiated measures which have strengthened the position of women doctors (Riska and Wegar, 1995). For example, the end to discriminatory practices has helped to increase the number of female medical students, as has the establishment of new medical schools with their emphasis on community and primary care medicine. Only in Japan with 16.4 per cent women doctors do they account for less than a quarter of all doctors. The traditional dominance of males in medicine in Japan has been resistant to change, although an increasing number of young women have entered medicine in recent years. The reason for the smaller proportion of female doctors in the USA (28.1 per cent) is less clear, but it might be linked to the fact that medical education in the USA tends to be considerably longer than in other countries (4 years of medical school after 4 years of university). Also, the strong emphasis on medical specialties instead of general practice might be less attractive to potential women candidates.

Another indication of the diversity of the medical profession is the division between generalist and specialist doctors. As Table 5.3 illustrates, in half the countries there are about twice as many specialists as generalists. One possible explanation is that in specialist practice and in relation to acute care the medical model of health and illness can excel. The ratio is even higher in Sweden, where the number of specialists per 1,000 inhabitants is three times that of generalists. This reflects the fact that hospitals have long been dominant in the provision of health care, with patients having direct access to specialists in outpatient hospital

Table 5.3   *Numbers of generalist and specialist doctors per 1,000 inhabitants*

	Generalist doctors	Specialist doctors[a]
Australia	1.4	1.2
France	1.7	1.7
Germany	1.0	2.4
Italy	0.9	n/a
Japan	n/a	n/a
Netherlands	0.5	0.9
New Zealand	0.7	0.7
Singapore	n/a	n/a
Sweden	0.6	1.8
UK	0.7	1.6
USA	1.0	1.4

[a] The figures for Australia, the Netherlands and Sweden are from 2003.

Source: Data from OECD (2006).

departments. In contrast, the provision of ambulatory care has been patchy. The other exception is France, where the numbers of generalists and specialists per 1,000 inhabitants are the same. Data for Japan are unavailable in part because, unlike Western countries, in Japan the generalist–specialist distinction is almost meaningless. Medical practitioners are all doctors of medical science, which includes some specialty. Significantly, there is no nationally recognized or formal system of specialty training or registration, and instead numerous academic societies have established their own training systems.

Types and settings of medical practice

In many ways medical practice goes to the heart of what doctors are about. It is here that doctors relate to patients and make decisions about the allocation of health care resources. This occurs at the micro-level of individual clinics, doctors' surgeries and ward rounds but it is also embedded in the respective health system. The sub-systems of funding, provision and governance frame the practice of doctors. The settings of medical practice describe the institutions in which medicine is organized and relate to what Moran and Wood (1993) call the 'regulation of market structures'. This section focuses on the settings where different

Table 5.4   *Types and settings of medical practice*

	Ambulatory settings (in either solo or group practice)	*Hospital settings*
Generalist/ specialist practitioners[a]	*Generalists only* Australia, Britain, Netherlands, New Zealand, Sweden, Singapore	*Mostly specialists* Australia, Britain, Germany, Netherlands, Sweden, Singapore, USA
Private/public practitioners	*Mostly public* Sweden	*Mostly public* Australia, Britain, New Zealand, Sweden, Singapore
	Mostly private Australia, Britain, Germany, Japan, Netherlands, New Zealand, Singapore, USA	*Mostly private* Japan, Netherlands,
		Public and private Germany, USA

[a] It is difficult to include Japan in this category as there is no clear distinction between generalist and specialist practitioners.

types of doctors work and the implications this has for the power of the medical profession.

As Table 5.4 illustrates, hospitals and ambulatory practices are the typical settings for doctors. Ambulatory settings can be further distinguished into solo and group practices. Different settings are closely associated with different types of medical practice (ambulatory settings with general practitioners and hospitals with specialists), although there are exceptions. As discussed in Chapter 3, in the majority of countries, patients have direct access to GPs, but need a medical referral to see specialists. In contrast, there is more diversity in terms of the public/private distinction, reflecting the public/private mix of the health systems in which medical practice is embedded.

Hospital doctors are either public or private practitioners, depending on the ownership of the hospital. As providers of specialist care, hospitals are complex organizations that rely on the division of labour across a wide range of health practitioners. This means that specialists depend to a great extent on the work of others when they practise in hospital settings. As complex organizations, hospitals also need management structures that coordinate the different parts of the labour process. In addition to being an organizing force, hospital managers personify the rationality of economics, which has come to the fore over concerns about cost pressures and containment. Not surprisingly, potential and real conflicts between managers and doctors have become a prominent issue, and highlight the contingency of medical power.

The introduction of market mechanisms and corresponding managerialist reforms are the key here. In Britain, an important juncture in the rise of hospital managers in the NHS was the introduction of 'general management' in 1987, replacing professionally based consensus management structures. The underlying idea was that health service management required first and foremost generic skills, particularly those to be found in the private sector, rather than professional judgements by doctors. This, together with the introduction of an internal market in the NHS in 1992, inevitably led to conflicts about the relative power of hospital managers and doctors (Harrison and Pollitt, 1994).

Similarly, in New Zealand before the health reforms of the 1980s and 1990s hospital boards were run by triumvirates composed of medical staff, nursing staff and administrators, with medical staff predominant on most boards. In large part, the reforms were an effort to wrest control from these boards, which critics felt were self-serving, inefficient and unconcerned with cost control. Beginning in 1983 with the government's setting of hospital budgets and culminating in the replacement of hospital boards with Area Health Boards in 1989, a series of steps was taken to create a structure for hospitals that would enable them to 'avoid capture by the medical community' (Blank, 1994). The continual erosion of the influence of the medical community over decision making and the shift in authority to managers and outside consultants has been a contentious issue that at times has resulted in near open warfare between the parties.

Conflicts between doctors and managers are less prominent in Japan where a majority of hospitals (though not usually the high-tech medical centres which are in the public sector) are owned and operated by individual doctors, most being expansions of private ambulatory practices. These hospitals rely on outpatient primary care for a large proportion of their revenues. Furthermore, in Japan the chief executive of all hospitals must be a physician (Nakahara, 1997).

The situation is different in smaller ambulatory settings where doctors tend to work as independent, private practitioners. Solo practice, the traditional way in which doctors have worked, provides the greatest independence, while group practices are more likely to circumscribe independence. In Germany and Japan the majority of doctors work in solo practices. The independence associated with solo practice is especially pronounced in Japan where doctors operate out of so-called 'clinics', about 40 per cent of which have some inpatient accommodation (Nakahara, 1997). Clinics can keep a patient for up to 48 hours and are legally defined as having fewer than 20 beds. Doctors working in ambulatory settings do not have access to hospital facilities, although most doctors have some degree of specialization.

In contrast, in the USA, Australia, Britain and Sweden, most primary care doctors work in group practices. The significance of group settings is particularly apparent in Sweden where they work in multi-disciplinary health centres where their role is not necessarily paramount. This reflects the fact that the provision of health care has long been dominated by hospitals (Harrison, 2004) and that the initiative to set up health centres came from political-administrative circles (including the Ministry for Health and Social Affairs) not the medical profession (Garpenby, 2001). Likewise, group practices are the norm in Australia with solo practitioners accounting for less than 15 per cent of total practices. Recently there has been a trend towards corporatization of practices with companies taking on the administration under contract to the practitioners.

However, operating in a group setting can also strengthen the position of doctors as demonstrated by the emergence of regional independent practice associations (IPAs) of ambulatory care doctors in New Zealand and Australia. The IPAs act as collective negotiators, contract and fund holders for doctors who are overwhelmingly generalists. In New Zealand, for example, IPAs were originally established to provide GPs with a critical mass for negotiating with the Regional Health Authorities (Finlayson, 2001). IPAs act as umbrella organizations for GPs in negotiations with purchasers and manage any resulting fund-holding relationships (Crampton, 2001). The increasing membership in IPAs has strengthened their negotiating power and protected their professional status (Malcolm and Powell, 1996). Currently over 75 per cent of New Zealand GPs are members of over 30 IPAs. Although developments in contracting and alternative methods of funding and managing services were initially either resisted or treated with caution by the majority of GPs, early successes in contracting, in budget holding for pharmaceutical and laboratory services and in establishing new services led to a progressive recruitment of IPA membership (Ashton, 2005).

Regardless of the relative size of the practice settings, the status of independent contractors is likely to give doctors in ambulatory settings considerable autonomy. Nevertheless, it is in specialist practice that the medical model with its emphasis on acute illness and specialist knowledge can excel, making hospitals the most prestigious setting within which doctors work. A notable exception is Japan, which places heavy emphasis on preventive medicine and primary care in ambulatory settings. As a result, the hospital admission rate is about one-third and the surgical procedure rate is only one-quarter of the USA (Ikegami and Campbell, 1999).

In the majority of countries, hospitals are the only places in which specialist doctors practise. Germany and the USA are unusual in this respect. In Germany, hospital work is seen as transitional and is used as a springboard to set up a specialist practice in ambulatory care. In the USA, many specialists practice in ambulatory settings. However, as a result of managed care, demand for GPs is growing because of their increased use as gatekeepers and to encourage the use of primary care doctors in lieu of more expensive specialists. These moves have generated vehement opposition by a US public which is used to being able to consult a specialist directly rather than having to be referred by a GP (Lamm and Blank, forthcoming).

The practice of doctors is embedded in the specific context of hospitals and ambulatory care and their relative position in the sub-systems of funding, provision and governance. This is a truism but nevertheless highly relevant to understanding medical practice. In the case of Germany, for example, hospitals have traditionally been less well integrated in health governance, reflecting not only the mix of public and private non-profit providers, typical of social insurance systems such as those found in Japan and the Netherlands, but also the absence of a system of self-administration. Instead, health governance has been fragmented into contracts between individual hospitals and insurance funds, and into coexisting competencies between the federal and state governments. The fragmentation of health governance (also typical of other federalist countries such as Australia and the USA) strengthened the position of the provider side and left hospitals and hospital doctors relatively untouched by health reforms in the 1980s (Schwartz and Busse, 1997). However, this has been changing and the practice of hospital doctors is now much more strongly integrated in and controlled by joint self-administration (see Burau, 2005). The funding of hospitals has moved away from prospective payments to payments based on DRGs, also flanked by extensive measures of quality assurance (see Luzio, 2004). The Joint Committee as the key body of the joint self-administration now has a separate sub-committee on hospital care. The sub-committee consists of the representatives from the hospital association, doctors and insurance funds, and is responsible for maintaining and extending the benefits catalogue for hospital care and for deciding on measures of quality assurance.

The situation is different in national health services such as those in Britain, New Zealand and Sweden, which have traditionally been characterized by a greater degree of public integration. Britain is a typical example of a system where the degree of integration of ambulatory care has actually increased since the early 1990s. As part of the introduction of the internal market, many GPs chose to become 'fund holders' and were given budgets to purchase diagnostic procedures and elective surgery for their patients. GPs thereby extended their managerial responsibilities beyond their own practice and moved closer to the mainstream of NHS management. The reforms under the New Labour government in 1998 took this development a step further. General practices became part of Primary Care Trusts, which are responsible not only for the provision of primary care but also for the commissioning of all other health services within a certain area (Peckham and Exworthy, 2003). GPs now work within an organization that is directly funded by and accountable to government. The Minister for Health appoints the chief executives of Primary Care Trusts and the Trust is subject to government guidance in the same way as hospital trusts. For example, the Primary Care Trusts have to follow the National Service Framework that includes guidelines about appropriate care for individual patients and preferred service models (Checkland, 2004). In short, government control over medical work in primary care has increased, pointing to the contingency of medical authority (Harrison and Lim, 2000).

Reforming medical practice

Positioning doctors in the context of health systems provides a sense of the type of settings where doctors work. More importantly, this also gives an insight into the relative permeability of medical practice when it comes to reform. Considering the centrality of doctors in the allocation of health care resources, any reform will, directly or indirectly, affect the practice of doctors. Measures to control expenditure at the macro-level are increasingly complemented by measures to control the allocation of health care resources at the micro-level, and it is these measures that can be expected to affect doctors most directly. Reforms directed at the micro-level have included changes to how doctors are paid (discussed in the next section), restrictions on available treatment and measures of quality management such as medical audit, clinical standards and, more recently, evidence-based medicine.

In any publicly funded health system, available treatment is naturally restricted in terms of both the range and the volume of services. By virtue of being contract based, social insurance systems such as those in Japan, Germany and the Netherlands have traditionally spelled out more explicitly what services are covered while the commitment to comprehensive coverage has remained more vague in national health services. In Germany, for example, the Social Code Book Five defines the scope of social insurance, which is complemented by the more specific provisions of self-administration. In contrast, the national health services in Britain, New Zealand and Sweden are based on the duty of government to provide services as opposed on the right of patients to receive them. As Harrison (2001: 279) observes in relation to the British NHS, '[t]his enables governments to "cash limit" (that is, cap) increasing proportions of the annual NHS budget'.

Concerns about cost pressures and containment, together with the move to a public contract model in national health services, however, have put the issue of restricting treatment high on the political agenda. This is well illustrated by New Zealand's attempts to define core services discussed in Chapter 4 (p. 117). Similarly, in the case of Britain, resources became tighter and health authorities were encouraged to manage their budgets by setting priorities. At the same time, rationing received considerable media and academic attention and as a result probably lost its innocence (Harrison *et al.*, 2002). A recent example is the National Institute for Clinical Excellence. The use of scientific and evidence-based criteria is supposed to give the Institute legitimacy, yet its work is often associated with explicit, national rationing (Syrett, 2003). In contrast, market-based systems like those in the USA and Singapore are unlikely to set limits on particular treatments or on routes to those treatments that a patient might need if they have the resources or insurance to cover the costs.

Even in national health services the explicit exclusion of treatment is notoriously controversial among patients and doctors because such measures directly constrain medical practice. In contrast, doctors (by exercising clinical freedom) have traditionally been secret accomplices in the rationing of health services (Harrison, 1998). By providing a medical rationale for the necessity of treatment in individual cases, doctors have given legitimacy to implicit rationing. Nevertheless, the alliance between doctors and the state has become fragile, reflecting more assertive and demanding patients, government challenges to medical autonomy as well more general cost concerns. In the case of Britain, for example, the national contract previously stated only that GPs had to provide their patients with 'all necessary and appropriate care'. In contrast, the latest contract from 2003 is more specific and lists the type of services GPs have to provide (Baggott, 2004).

The emergence and prominence of quality management in recent years has to be seen against the background of the controversies surrounding the explicit restrictions of available treatment and potentially challenges existing mechanisms for regulating medical work (see Box 5.2). Quality management promises to square the circle between restricting treatment, while at the same time ensuring the quality of health care and allowing for (and even using) medical judgement (Harrison, 1998). This solution is

Box 5.2   Professional self-regulation of medical work

Professional self-regulation has been the traditional approach to setting and ensuring standards of medical practice, and involves licensing and (by implication) education and training. Further, self regulation is a key indication of the 'professionalism' of doctors and is at the centre of the regulation of competitive practice in medicine (Moran and Wood, 1993). A typical example of professional self-regulation is the General Medical Council in Britain, which is responsible for keeping a register of doctors and for regulating their education, training and professional standards. The regulatory ideology underpinning the GMC has traditionally been rather narrow and isolationist and the Council has tended to focus on protecting doctors from market competition on the one hand and from interference from the state on the other (Moran, 1999: 103). Similar arrangements exist in Australia, Germany and the USA. However, as recent scandals in Britain have demonstrated, these arrangements are not necessarily successful at securing the quality of medical work and have led to policy reform. In Sweden and Japan, by contrast, professional self-regulation is less prominent. The bodies regulating medical work are government agencies that include doctors, but not exclusively so. In Sweden, for example, the Medical Responsibility Board, a government agency that assesses and decides on complaints and instances of malpractice, consists of members drawn from different stakeholders in the health service, including county councils, municipalities, the unions of health professionals and the public, all of whom are appointed by the government.

politically attractive because it diffuses blame for potentially unpopular decisions away from government while safeguarding the autonomy of doctors over clinical decision making. In Britain and New Zealand the prominence of quality management has coincided with a move away from purely market-based reforms. The reforms of the late 1980s and early 1990s were built on the belief in the superiority of the market and business style management. In contrast, quality management redirects the attention to medical practice, though one that is expected to adhere to explicitly defined standards. At the same time, the introduction of market mechanisms itself has stimulated the development of mechanisms of quality management. As Herk *et al.* argue in the case of the Netherlands '[t]he increasing importance of health insurers as negotiating partners of the providers put[s] increasing weight on measurable quality, on quality indicators, which could be objectified and specified in contracts' (2001: 1726). Initial legislation on quality goes back to the mid 1990s, but following limited implementation the government put renewed emphasis on quality and in 2004 introduced new, compulsory measures supervised by the Inspectorate of Health Care (Exter *et al.*, 2004).

The medical audit has been a long-standing measure of quality management. As an instrument to systematically evaluate clinical care and increase the accountability of doctors, it has been promoted heavily by governments. However, as Herk *et al.* demonstrate in their comparative study of the Netherlands and Britain, medical audit demonstrates 'the capability of the [medical] profession to maintain autonomy through re-negotiated mechanisms for self-control' (2001: 1721). As part of this process, professional controls have become more formalized and the freedom of individual doctors is circumscribed by collegial regulation through peer review.

The case of the Netherlands is indicative here. The professional organizations of doctors took the lead in developing medical audit in the late 1970s and this helped the medical profession maintain control. Doctors are well represented on the board of trustees of the Institute for Quality Assurance in Hospitals, and while medical audit has become compulsory, doctors have remained responsible for its organization. The system of site visits as the predominant form of medical audit emerged in the late 1980s (Lombarts and Klazinga, 2001). This was a time of increasing public concerns over health care expenditure and related questions about the (economic) autonomy and accountability of hospital doctors. Here, doctors 'traded' peer-controlled quality assurance in exchange for the government not interfering with the income of specialists. External peers, under the auspices of the specialist scientific societies, conduct the site visits. Being doctor-led and owned the results of individual reviews remain confidential and the implementation of recommendations is left to the group of specialists itself. As Dent (2003) suggests, the development of clinical guidelines tells a similar story. The Netherlands was one of the first countries to adapt and widely implement clinical guidelines, although importantly clinical guidelines mostly have taken the form of consensus guidelines combined with peer review.

Developments in New Zealand have been similar, although the medical audit takes a more individualized form. Doctors on general registration must work under the general oversight of a doctor who holds vocational registration in the same branch of medicine. An overseer is similar to a mentor and assists a doctor in his or her continuing education and audit. Doctors report to the Medical Council, the professional self-regulatory body, every year as part of their annual practising certificate application and each year some will be audited to ensure they are meeting requirements. This enhanced rigour of regulation, combined with the removal of the disciplinary function from the Council to a separate tribunal, were major innovations of the Medical Practitioners Act 1995.

However, in other countries, such as the USA and Australia, doctors have been less successful in exclusively controlling medical audit. The expanding role of Medicare and Medicaid in the USA has increased federal government activity through regulations and audits for hospitals that have Medicare/Medicaid patients (which means virtually all of them). The states, however, remain the key players in setting and enforcing quality assurance standards for doctors, hospitals and nursing homes. Although the rigour of such programmes varies by state, as noted above, concerns over cost containment have put great emphasis on quality and efficiency. The implementation of quality programmes is in the hands of State Medical Boards, which are government agencies dominated by doctors. This means that doctors have considerable influence over quality programmes, but enjoy less autonomy compared to doctors in the Netherlands and New Zealand.

In Australia, medical acts in each state also provide the principal control over the practice of medicine and conduct of medical audit, and are administered by state medical boards that are similar to the boards in the USA. Furthermore, in the early 1990s legislative action was taken to facilitate the monitoring of doctors in specified areas by the Health Insurance Commission under the Medicare programme. Doctors suspected of excessive ordering are referred to the Medical Services Committees of Inquiry, although the test of whether a particular treatment is acceptable practice falls on local medical community standards, which vary considerably across states (Palmer and Short, 2000: 195ff.). Nevertheless, this is an example of a quality programme that is clearly controlled by the payers of services rather than by doctors as the providers of services (see Box 5.3).

Box 5.3   Australian Primary Care Collaborative Program (APCCP)

The national APCCP is a large-scale coordinated programme of rapid change management to improve service delivery in general practices across the 4,300 general practices in Australia. The Divisions of General Practice are designated as the local organizers of the collaboratives. The Programme's initial objective is to involve 600 general practices, representing 20 percent of the practices in each geographical location. It is being funded under the Primary Care Providers Working Together component of the Focus on Prevention funding package and is managed or commissioned by the Primary Care Quality and Prevention Branch of the Australian Department of Health and Ageing. The National Primary Care Collaboratives aim to improve care in national priority disease areas, provide greater integration among providers in the primary care sector, and focus on prevention through better chronic disease management and accessible primary health care.

Source: Bertelsmann Foundation (2004e).

In some ways, clinical guidelines are the natural extension of medical audits because audits assume the existence of standards of good practice against which performance can be judged. Significantly, guidelines have become increasingly evidence-based, and '[t]he emphasis shifted from professional consensus to systematic evidence or from professional endorsement to authority derived from science' (Herk *et al.*, 2001: 1728). From the perspective of doctors, evidence-based medicine is ambivalent (Berg *et al.*, 2000). Evidence-based medicine promises to strengthen the scientific nature of medicine by reducing unwarranted variation in diagnostic and therapeutic practice. At the same time, guidelines encourage a standardized approach to practice and as such limit the leeway for professional judgement. Reflecting this ambivalence, Harrison (2002) suggests that clinical guidelines are part of a 'scientific-bureaucratic' model of medicine that gives primacy to knowledge derived from research and distilled into guidelines of best practice. Developments in Britain and Sweden illustrate the move to clinical guidelines, although initial rationales for introducing guidelines differed.

In Britain, setting, measuring and improving quality standards has been one of the priorities of the Labour Government. At the centre is a system of 'clinical governance' designed to set and monitor clinical standards (Salter, 2005). NHS managers are responsible for clinical quality, putting particular emphasis on cost-effectiveness. This builds on systems of medical technology assessment developed throughout the 1990s but, in contrast to its predecessors, the Labour Government established a set of institutions that supposedly ensures professional compliance (Harrison, 2002; Harrison *et al.*, 2002: 13). The National Institute for Clinical Excellence plays a central role in this and is responsible for evaluating new technologies and care guidelines with regard to their clinical and cost-effectiveness. As such, conflicts between medical and economic rationality are embedded in the Institute's work (Butler, 2002; Syrett, 2003). The Institute can rule against treatment that is proven clinically effective on the basis that the costs to the NHS are disproportionate to the long-term benefits. Technically, doctors can choose not to follow NICE guidance, although in practice this will be difficult. The establishment of NICE in 1999 must be seen in conjunction with the development of the National Service Framework which sets out patterns of care for specific diseases, disabilities and patient groups, and the establishment of the Commission for Health Improvement which is responsible for monitoring and improving standards at local level (Salter, 2005; also Dent, 2003).

In Sweden, by contrast, the development of quality standards was initially underpinned by the intention to counterbalance the increasing decentralization of the health system. The debate on quality assurance was initiated in the mid 1980s by a government agency, and the National

Board for Health and Welfare emerged as one of the key actors in quality management. The Board became responsible for collecting data on health outcomes and good practice and intensified its monitoring of health care personnel and health care providers. For the government, quality management became a 'new means of influencing and monitoring health care' (Garpenby, 1999: 409). Significantly, and in line with the emphasis on consensus building, national agencies only provide general guidelines, leaving considerable space for doctors to develop strategies independently at the local level (Garpenby, 1997: 197). At the same time, although doctors do not have any formal representation on the relevant government agencies and consultation committees, the Medical Quality Council, a body set up by doctors, serves as a pool for recruiting individual doctors into these agencies and committees.

Medical care is at the centre of health reform, reflecting the centrality of doctors in the definition, provision and allocation of health care resources. Macro-level reforms have increasingly been complemented by micro-level reforms which affect the practice of doctors more directly. However, the picture that emerges here is ambivalent. Doctors are certainly under greater pressure to account for their practice, but the turn to quality provides an opportunity for doctors to appropriate measures of control. In many ways, quality management marks the rebirth of medical practice, although under different, more closely defined terms.

Paying for medical care

How doctors are paid is not merely a technical issue; in fact, systems of remuneration are important pointers to power and are at the centre of the regulation of doctors (Moran and Wood, 1993). Power here refers to the privilege of doctors to be rewarded according to the medical treatment they provide. Systems of remuneration can either sustain or constrain this privilege (for an overview, see Jegers *et al.*, 2002). The fee-for-service system, under which doctors are paid for the individual services rendered to patients, supports this type of medical privilege most extensively. In contrast, with payment by salary there is little connection between the services rendered and the payment received by doctors. Between these two extremes is payment based on capitation, whereby doctors are paid according to the number of patients registered with their practice. Typically, hospital doctors receive a salary, whereas office-based doctors are paid on either a fee-for-service or a capitation basis. In addition to systems of payment, another indication of medical power is the role of doctors in the determination of fee schedules and payment structures.

Table 5.5   *Types of payment for different types of doctor*

	Predominantly salaried	Predominantly capitation payments	Predominantly fee-for-service payments
Ambulatory care doctors	Singapore (public) Sweden	Britain Netherlands New Zealand	Australia Germany Japan Singapore (private) USA[a]
Hospital doctors	Australia Britain Germany New Zealand Singapore (public) Sweden	Netherlands (lump sums)	Japan Singapore (private) USA

[a] The USA is undergoing a shift due to HMO movement but is still free-for-service based.

As Table 5.5 illustrates, the payment of doctors is characterized by variation and includes unexpected cases, such as salaried office-based doctors (in Sweden and in public health centres in Singapore) and hospital doctors paid on a fee-for-service basis (in Japan, the USA and in private hospitals in Singapore). Significantly, however, in most cases pay is not directly related to the volume of services, and even where this is the case, there are limitations on payments. If power refers to the privilege of doctors to be rewarded according to the medical treatment they provide, medical power is restricted.

Concerns for cost containment are likely to direct the attention to systems of remuneration, especially in countries (including Australia, Germany, Japan and the USA) where doctors are paid according to the volume of services provided. Germany and the USA are classical examples of the fee-for-service system and also illustrate its problems. In Germany, the Uniform Value Scale (*Einheitlicher Bewertungsmasstab*) lists the services that are reimbursed by health insurance funds, together with their relative weights for reimbursement, which are measured in points. The monetary value of each point varies and depends on the total reimbursement agreed by self-administration at state level on the one hand, and the total volume of services provided by doctors on the other. This constrains the total expenditure on ambulatory care, although not necessarily the incentive to maximize the volume of services at the level of the individual practice.

Nevertheless, the fee-for-service system in Germany remains problematic from the perspective of cost containment and has undergone several changes in recent years. Fee negotiations take place within legally set limits and there is a maximum ceiling for the number of points that can be reimbursed per doctor. In addition, doctors may be subject to utilization review, either randomly or if their levels of service provision are significantly higher than those of their colleagues. This has been accompanied by measures to change the system of payment itself including rewards for particular specialties (GPs in particular) and specific services (e.g. counselling rather than medical testing), together with blanket payments for certain sets of services.

Contraints also exist in the fee-for-service system in Australia. With the introduction of Medicare in 1984/85, Australia adopted a bulk billing system of payment under which a GP can choose to bill the government directly and receives 85 per cent of the scheduled fee thereby avoiding administrative costs and delay. This also ensures that services are effectively free to the patient at the point of service. However, if the GP chooses not to bulk bill or chooses to charge patients a co-payment, the patient pays the bill and is reimbursed by Medicare for 85 per cent of the scheduled fee. Although the proportion of bulk billing increased steadily until the mid 1990s, it declined significantly after 2000 (Swerissen, 2004). In response to concerns about the fall in the bulk billing rate, the Commonwealth Government proposed a Fairer Medicare later implemented as Medicare Plus. This package introduced a participating practice scheme under which GP practices that agreed to charge a no-gap fee to concessional patients were eligible for increased Medicare rebates for these patients.

In the USA, controlling doctors' pay is even more difficult. Ambulatory-care doctors are paid through a combination of methods, reflecting the fragmentation of health care funding. Fee-for-service payments include charges, discounted fees paid by private health plans, capitation rate contracts with private plans, public programmes and direct patient fees. However, the growth of Health Maintenance Organizations and other managed-care schemes has resulted in changes in the methods of payment away from fee-for-service reimbursement. HMO doctors may be salaried, paid a fee for service, or a paid a capitation fee for each person on their list. However, often there are financial incentives to the doctor to reduce services to their patients. A variation of the HMO is the Preferred Provider Organization (PPO) in which a limited number of providers – doctors, hospitals and others – agree to provide services to a specific group of people at a negotiated fee-for-service rate that is lower than the normal charge.

By contrast, in Britain, the Netherlands and increasingly also New Zealand ambulatory-care doctors are paid predominantly on a capitation basis, allowing for much more direct control of doctors' remuneration. Britain is typical here, and fixed sums per patient are complemented by allowances for providing enhanced services and for quality improvements.

In New Zealand, the capitation payments coexist with considerable co-payments, but this is changing. New Zealand's Primary Health Care Strategy (PHCS) was introduced in 2002 to reduce health disparities in access to general practice services and transformed publicly funded primary health care payments from targeted welfare benefits to universal, risk-rated insurance premium subsidies (Howell, 2005). Under PHCS, GPs are grouped under umbrella groups called Primary Health Organisations (PHOs) which are not-for-profit organizations funded on a capitation basis which contract with DHBs to provide a comprehensive set of preventive and treatment services for their enrolled populations. Government subsidies historically were paid on a fee-for-service basis targeted to low-income and high-risk people, but because the subsidy levels were not sufficiently tied to inflation and because GPs retained the right to set their own levels of co-payments, it resulted in a significant cost barrier to GP services for some people. In an effort to remove or reduce this cost barrier, the move to PHOs was also accompanied by the phased introduction of higher government subsidies for GP services and pharmaceuticals (Ashton, 2005).

Sweden is the only country where the majority of ambulatory-care doctors are public employees and paid a salary. This manifests the high degree of public integration of the health system, and doctors are firmly positioned in what is a very politically controlled health system (Garpenby, 2001: 263). In this respect Dent (2003: 53) suggests that the medical profession in Sweden appears more like civil servants than autonomous professionals. However, private providers of ambulatory care do exist, particularly in major cities, and their numbers increased after the introduction of patient choice for family doctor in the early 1990s (Harrison, 2004; Harrison and Calltorp, 2000). However, that scheme was abolished after a few years, reflecting the return of the Social Democratic Government and the fact that the emerging competition among doctors for funds threatened existing health centres. The providers are private in that their facilities are privately run, although the majority have contracts with the county councils. In 2003, a third of health centres and practitioners worked in privately run facilities (Glenngård *et al.*, 2005).

Unlike ambulatory-care doctors, hospital doctors tend to be salaried employees, although in many countries they have the right to treat private patients who represent an attractive source of additional income since services are often paid for on a fee-for-service basis and remuneration tends to be high. In Britain, for example, the right to practise privately was the condition on which hospital doctors agreed to become part of the NHS when it was set up in 1948. Hospital doctors were initially opposed to a tax-funded health service instead advocating the extension of the existing health insurance system, but they were won over by a number of concessions. Besides private practice and pay beds, they received large increases in salaries for those receiving distinction awards. This led the then Minister of Health to remark that he had 'stuffed their [the hospital doctors'] mouths with gold' (Abel-Smith, 1984: 480, quoted in Ham, 1999: 11). Senior hospital specialists are allowed to earn up to 10 per cent of their income from private practice, while there is no limit for specialists on part-time contracts.

Notable exceptions are the Netherlands and Japan, where hospital doctors are paid on a fee-for-service basis. In the Netherlands, medical specialists have traditionally been independent practitioners who have 'bought' the right to practise in a hospital and who practise in partnerships. As such, they contracted directly with patients and insurance funds and are reimbursed on a fee-for-service basis separately from the hospitals. However, this changed in 2000 and now doctors receive a lump sum directly from the hospital in which they practise. As a result, specialist medical services are now an integral part of the hospital contract and budget (Harrison, 2004), thus potentially providing a leverage for hospital managers to exercise greater control over the practice of medical specialists (Trappenburg and Groot, 2001). In Japan, hospital doctors are paid by a national fee schedule, not surprisingly since many doctors work as private entrepreneurs running their own hospitals.

A case on its own is Singapore, where the form of payment depends not on the practice setting, but rather on whether doctors work in public or private health care facilities. Doctors in government-owned facilities receive a civil service pay scale plus a clinical supplement. Those with very heavy clinical loads may opt for an incentive based on their total billings in place of the fixed supplement. Private doctors are generally paid on a fee-for-service basis. The Singapore Medical Association publishes guidelines on fees for billing in the private sector.

The involvement of doctors in the process of determining pay is another indication of medical power. As Table 5.6 illustrates, there is some variation here. However, in large part salaries and capitation/fee-for-service payments are negotiated between doctors and the payers of health services, although there may be some restrictions as in the Netherlands. Even where the government alone decides, the decision may be based on a broad range of evidence as in Britain or be limited in scope as in Singapore. Significantly, doctors enjoy considerable power relative to pay determination, although they can rarely act alone.

In the case of salaries, the process of pay bargaining involves the pay negotiations where medical power depends on the relative strength of unions and employer organizations, together with the overall economic

Table 5.6   *The involvement of doctors in systems of pay determinations*[a]

	Salaries	Capitation/fee-for-service payments
Set by government	Britain (with review body as intermediary); Singapore (for doctors in public health facilities)	Australia (de facto); Britain (with review body as intermediary); New Zealand (de facto)
Negotiated between doctors and payers of health services	Australia Germany New Zealand Sweden	Germany Japan Netherlands (government approval required)
Set by doctors		Singapore (for doctors in private health facilities)

[a] The USA has been omitted from this table as the system of pay bargaining is too fragmented.

climate. An interesting exception is Singapore, where doctors working in public health facilities are paid on the basis of the civil service pay scale, which is set by government with little input from the medical association.

The situation is more complicated in the case of capitation and fee payments, as they are the basis for many rounds of future remuneration. Negotiations of this type generally require extensive bargaining to reach an agreement. Countries operate different kinds of decision systems, ranging from payments set by government and negotiated with doctors to payments set by doctors themselves. Britain provides an interesting example of the first variant where the government determines capitation payments and allowances for GPs and salary scales for hospital specialists though the Minister for Health normally takes into account the recommendations of the Review Body on Doctors' and Dentists' Remuneration. The Review Body is an independent agency that is financed by government. The government also appoints the members of the Review Body, usually with the approval of the British Medical Association. The recommendations of the review body are based on demands submitted by the professional organizations and the government as well as other input, such as the budget plan and the evaluation of statistical material (see, e.g. Department of Health, 2006b).

By contrast, in Germany, Japan and the Netherlands doctors' organizations have more direct influence and negotiate directly with insurance funds as the payers of health services. However, in some cases the negotiation process has become curtailed in recent years. In Germany, for example, the autonomy of negotiations between doctors and insurance funds has been more constrained as control over funding has become more centralized (Rosenbrock and Gerlinger, 2004). This began with the introduction of legally fixed regional budgets for ambulatory medical care which replaced negotiated budgets after 1992. The regional budgets have now been substituted with a maximum ceiling for fees per doctor.

Turning to Japan, we have an example of a country where the influence of doctors on fee negotiations remains relatively unchallenged. The Japanese Medical Association (JMA) nominates all five doctors who sit on the fee-scheduling body and negotiates the fees with the Health Ministry's Health Insurance Bureau. The influence of doctors is further strengthened by the fact that '[i]n effect, those on the provider side must work through the JMA' since 'hospitals, pharmaceutical companies, and other important actors are not directly represented on the council' (Ikegami and Campbell, 1999: 63).

The organization of doctors' interests and access to the policy process

Issues around the practice and payment of doctors often concern medical practitioners as individuals. In contrast, the political organization of doctors' interests directs attention to doctors as a group and how doctors relate to policy process. The interests of doctors can be organized in different ways, through specialist scientific societies, professional associations and trade unions. An important indicator of power is the degree of cohesion (or fragmentation), that is, the extent to which a group of doctors speak with one voice, or at least with different voices complementing each other. This has become increasingly difficult as distributional struggles between diverse groups of doctors have intensified under pressures of cost containment. At the same time, countries offer dissimilar points of access to organized interests, reflecting the specific characteristics of the respective political and health systems. The power of doctors to a great extent depends on how states are organized and also on how powerful states are.

As Figure 5.1 suggests, in most countries the political organization of doctors is relatively cohesive with one organization acting as the main representative of doctors' interests. This normally goes hand-in-hand

Access to policy process

		As outsiders through lobbying	As insiders through corporatism
Organization of doctors' interests	Cohesive	Australia, Britain, Japan, New Zealand, Singapore, Sweden	
	Fragmented	USA	Germany, Netherlands

Figure 5.1   *The organization of doctors' interests and access to the policy process*

with a high membership among doctors. However, as Germany, the Netherlands and the USA show, divisions between different types of doctors have led to the fragmentation of the political organization of doctors. These divisions affect the distribution of financial resources and intensify under policies designed to contain costs. The relative collective strength of doctors coexists with varying degrees of access to the policy process, which as seen in Chapter 2 embody one indicator of how the power of the state is organized.

In most countries, doctors have to rely on lobbying the government from the outside. As Britain and Australia demonstrate, the extent of influence varies over time and the cohesion of interest organizations is only one factor. At the same time, lack of cohesion is not necessarily a bar to influence as the USA, Germany and the Netherlands demonstrate. The considerable influence of doctors in the USA reflects not only the economic power of the medical sectors, but also the weakness of the state in health governance. Germany and the Netherlands, to a lesser extent, are unusual in that doctors are an integral part of health governance and as such often have privileged access to the policy process. Being insiders gives doctors considerable influence, although this may come at the price of becoming agents of cost containment.

In the majority of countries the political organization of doctors shows a considerable degree of cohesion. This reflects a number of country-specific factors, including the type of political system and the size of the country. Cohesion can be expected to be most likely in small unitary countries such as New Zealand and Singapore. New Zealand, for example, has one primary medical association that has a high level of membership among doctors. The New Zealand Medical Association (NZMA) is a voluntary organization which claims membership of about 65 per cent of the country's doctors. As such, the Association has a broader-based membership than many national medical associations, maintains formal links with affiliates including the Royal Colleges and specialty organizations, and acts as the primary representative of the profession in dealings with the government. The New Zealand GP Association (NZGPA) is an offshoot of the NZMA and mainly represents the interests of GPs, although it has remained closely linked to its parent body (Crampton, 2001).

Even in larger unitary countries the organization of doctors' interests can be cohesive. Britain is a case in point. The British Medical Association (BMA) is at the centre of the political organization of doctors' interests and more than 80 per cent of doctors are members (European Observatory on Health Care Systems, 1999: 22). The BMA acts in a dual role as a professional organization and as a trade union. As a professional organization, it promotes medical education and professional development, whereas as a trade union it represents doctors' economic interests. This de facto monopoly puts the BMA in a strong position in principle, but also requires the BMA to cater for a diverse range of constituencies within the medical profession. Here, conflicts between GPs and hospital consultants have been particularly prominent (Giamo, 2002).

Likewise, as Sweden and Australia demonstrate, a more decentralized political system is no bar to a cohesive organization of doctors' interests. In Sweden, more than 90 per cent of doctors are members of the Swedish Medical Association (Garpenby, 2001: 261). The Association acts as a type of umbrella organization and the specific interests of its membership are channelled through seven professional organizations and 28 local bodies. The Swedish Medical Association coexists with a range of scientific societies and while the Swedish Society of Medicine is the largest with over 60 per cent of doctors being members, the smaller specialist societies are the more influential actors (Garpenby, 2001: 264). The Medical Association and the Society of Medicine have different responsibilities, although in relation to some issues the two organizations compete with each other (Garpenby, 1999). In Australia, the Divisions of General Practice are local area-based representative bodies for GPs and their national body, the Australian Divisions of General Practice (ADGP), which has a growing policy presense.

In comparison to the countries discussed so far, the political organization of doctors in Germany, the Netherlands and the USA is more fragmented. The USA represents a case of fragmentation between generalists and specialists, which is exacerbated by federalism and the sheer size of the profession. Although less than half of all practising doctors are members of the American Medical Association (AMA), it remains a very powerful political lobby group with significant influence in Washington, DC, and the state capitals. Many specialty medical groups have been established which concentrate on their own interests, often in conflict with the AMA.

There are literally hundreds, if not thousands, of medical associations at the local, state and national level in the USA, and although the AMA is the single most influential, the voice of the medical community is considerably more diverse than in other countries.

Germany provides another example where the organization of doctors' interests is divided, not only between different types of doctors, but also between different types of organization. The *Marburger Bund* is the main professional organization and trade union for hospital doctors, but the situation surrounding ambulatory care doctors is more complicated. The vast majority of these doctors cannot exclusively rely on private practice and instead have to provide services under the social health insurance. However, this requires joining one of the regional associations of insurance fund doctors (*Kassenärztliche Vereinigungen*) which assume an intermediate position between doctors and the state (Rosenbrock and Gerlinger, 2004). As public law bodies, the associations have the statutory responsibility of ensuring the provision of ambulatory care and organizing the remuneration of doctors, including control functions such as assessing the economic efficiency of the performance of individual doctors. At the same time, they represent the interests of doctors when the associations negotiate contracts and fees with insurance funds. The tensions inherent in this dual role have become more prominent; and intensifying distributional struggles have made it more difficult for the associations to integrate the conflicting interests of their membership (Burau, 2001). The distributional struggles result from a combination of the increasing number of doctors, falling income and more extensive government control. The heightened conflicts have also negatively affected the division of labour between the associations of insurance fund doctors and the two lobbying organizations for ambulatory-care doctors.

The relative cohesion of the political organization of doctors is only one measure of collective power of the medical profession. Another, complementary, measure of power is the role of doctors in the policy process, and different health and political systems provide different degrees and types of access. This demonstrates how the power of doctors is tied to the power of the state. In most countries, doctors' organizations have access to the policy process as outsiders, mostly through lobbying and some informal consultation.

Britain and Australia, countries with tax-funded health services embedded in a centralist and a federalist political system respectively, illustrate the ups and downs of the influence of doctors. In both countries, the relationship between the medical profession and the state has traditionally been close. However, access to the policy process has largely consisted of lobbying and informal consultation. In Britain, the fragility of this type of access became apparent in the late 1980s. Reform efforts in part were aimed at weakening the role of the profession in the governance of health care and this affected the influence of doctors in health policy, resulting in a widening rift between the parties. Significantly, the medical profession was practically excluded from the policy review that lead to a major reform in the early 1990s (Harrison, 2001). Similarly, Kay (2001) sees the conception, implementation and abolition of the GP fund holding scheme as an indication of the weaker influence of the medical profession. This stands in sharp contrast to the earlier corporatist settlement that was characterized by a strong insider role of doctors in government (Giamo, 2002). Similarly, in Australia, the Medical Association regressed from a comfortable corporate-style partnership to an awkward pressure group when the political struggles over national health insurance legislation erupted in 1972 (De Voe and Short, 2003). Government leaders faced strong opposition from key players in the health arena and created fractures in the medical establishment. This resulted in a realignment of the power structures in health policy.

In the USA, by contrast, the medical profession seems to have been more successful at maintaining its traditionally compelling influence over health policy. The medical sector is consistently ranked among the best organized and financed sectors in influencing politicians at the national and state levels by the Congressional Quarterly Service. This reflects the strength of the 'health care industry', which coincides with a policy process that is typically driven by lobbying and one where winning is largely manifested in blocking change.

In Germany, and to a lesser extent in the Netherlands, corporatism means that doctors are an integral part of health governance and this often gives them access to the policy process as insiders (see Giamo, 2002; Kuhlmann, 2006). However, as the example of Germany shows, even as insiders the influence of doctors is variable. Together with the insurance funds, doctors form a self-administration, which is responsible, not only for negotiating contracts, but also for implementing health care legislation. Here, the Joint Committee is key and responsibilities include defining the benefits catalogue, clinical guidelines and measures of quality assurance (see Busse and Riesberg, 2004). The role of doctors in the health system is highly institutionalized and codified in the relevant Social Code Book Five. In addition, the federal structure of health governance offers doctors multiple points of access. Significantly, however, doctors are involved in a public role granted to them by the state, and are not first and foremost involved as representatives of private interests. This can lead to the kinds of conflict of interest discussed above and can also constrain the collective power of doctors.

Over the last decade the federal government has expanded the scope of self-administration while at the same time circumscribing its activities. For example, the joint committee is now also responsible for evaluating the medical efficacy and economic efficiency of existing treatments.

Issuing such guidance may be subject to a timetable with the possibility of a unilateral decision by the ministry. The pendulum has swung from autonomous negotiations towards hierarchical decisions by the state (Burau, 2005; Luzio, 2004; Wendt *et al.*, 2005). The government has defined more precisely the substantive issues to be decided and has set deadlines by which agreement has to be reached. Doctors have become key agents of cost containment through self-administration precisely because the system of self-administration is adaptable and depoliticizes the implementation of potentially problematic policies (Giamo and Manow, 1999: 978). Yet, recent years have been characterized by a greater scepticism about the capacity of the Associations of Insurance Fund Doctors. Since it is now possible to complete contracts with specific groups of doctors rather than the Associations, there has been open discussion about abolishing the Associations (see Greß *et al.*, 2004).

Doctors, the state and health policy

Doctors are deeply embedded in health systems, and since the state looms large in health systems and policy, doctors inevitably have a close relationship with the state. This means two things: medical power will always be contingent on the state, but states cannot do without doctors. Light's (1995) notion of 'countervailing powers' offers one way of understanding the close, but above all changeable, relationship between doctors and the state. Here, medical power is seen to oscillate between highs and lows. Highs of medical power (dominance) produce imbalances and provoke countervailing powers originating from the state, third-party payers and patients. This in turn and over time weakens medical dominance and strengthens the power of the state.

In his discussion of the Foucauldian notion of 'governmentality' Johnson (1995) goes one step further and suggests that doctors and the state are inextricably linked through the process of governing. Johnson (1995: 9) observes that '[e]xpertise, as it became increasingly institutionalized in its professional form, became part of the process of governing'. It is impossible to distinguish clearly between doctors and the state: the state depends on the independence of doctors to secure its capacity to govern, a process through which doctors become agents of governing. However, acknowledging independence does not mean denying shifts in relations between the doctors and the state. Over the last two decades, states have become more interventionist, reflecting the need of states to assert their agency in times of concerns about costs. This has noticeably changed the institutional context in which doctors work, but, importantly, has not necessarily reduced their power (Moran, 1999).

Chapter 6

Beyond the Hospital: Health Care in the Home

Care outside hospitals has traditionally been the poor relation of health systems. Health systems are concerned first and foremost with the provision of medical care and focus on acute illness. Doctors are the key professionals shaping the delivery of health care and hospitals are the primary location. The emphasis is on *curing* as opposed long-term *caring*. Less acute, more long-term health care is typically characterized by considerable diversity in terms of the range of services, the user groups, the localities of service provision and the professionals involved.

Care outside hospitals includes basic care to help with daily living, mobility and self-care; medical and nursing care to help with physical and mental health problems; therapy, counselling and emotional support to promote well-being; and other social, educational and leisure activities (Tester, 1996). User groups are equally diverse and reflect the support required at different stages of the life span, ranging from severally ill infants to people at the end of life. Other beneficiaries include people with mental illness and handicap, physical disability, drug-related disorders and progressive illness (Means *et al.*, 2003). Care outside hospitals is also located in different settings, such as residential care and nursing homes, day hospitals and sheltered housing, as well as people's own homes. The professionals involved are equally diverse and include nurses, mental health nurses, care assistants, home helps, counsellors and physiotherapists.

The diversity of care outside hospitals reflects the varied yet interlocking needs of people who require long-term care. Diversity makes care outside hospitals interesting, but also difficult to define, analyse and compare. At the same time, care services are often locally specific and even tailored to particular individuals and it is difficult to identify the typical, let alone to generalize. For example, in their comparative analysis of community care policies in Finland and Britain, Burau and Kröger (2004) highlight the distinct local nature of policies together with the importance of local politics. Antonnen *et al.* (2003b) go even further and suggest that because of the interchangeability with informal care, the use of formal care services is highly individualized and does not follow any methodical patterns. Furthermore, although care services outside hospitals are central to the health of individuals, they can be remote from the health system. In the context of our comparative analysis of health policy we therefore need to focus on a specific aspect of care outside hospitals, and notably an aspect of care that is closely related to health systems.

This chapter focuses on home care for older people. Older people represent the largest user group of care outside hospitals and in the face of ageing societies have attracted considerable attention in health policy terms. Home care for older people is also closely related to health systems, as demonstrated by the involvement of nurses. Tester (1996: 76) describes home care as 'any type of care and support offered to older people in their homes, whether ordinary or specialized settings, by formal and informal carers'. Home care involves a wide range of activities, from basic, physical and mental care to counselling, support for informal carers and giving information. With home care the underlying disease is of secondary importance and instead help with basic activities of daily living is the focus. It encompasses a wide range of tasks and cuts across boundaries between health and social care, and between formal and informal care. It also involves nurses rather than doctors and, most importantly, principally women as informal care givers. Indeed, unpaid care givers deliver the majority of home care; it is estimated that formal care represents only one-fifth of the total help older people receive (OECD, 2005). This further contributes to the marginal position of home care in health systems. This chapter focuses on home health care: the health care aspects of home care and the services provided by home nurses. However, given the nature of home care it is important to explore the interfaces with other aspects of home care, particularly informal care, but also social care.

Although health systems continue to focus on curing acute illness, interest in home care is growing and it is becoming a higher priority on the health policy agenda in many countries (Kröger, 2001). It is indicative that the recently completed Health Project by the OECD included a study of 'long-term care for older people' (OECD, 2005). This change reflects demographic as well as cost pressures. As the number of older (and very old) people increases, both in absolute terms and as a proportion of the total population, so does the need for long-term care (for data see Chapter 1). Combined with falling birth rates, this also means a greater need for formal care, since the pool of potential informal carers becomes smaller.

Unfortunately, this increase in the need for long-term care comes at a time of intense concerns about costs and efforts to contain the public spending on health care as discussed in Chapter 4. However, for many observers home care promises to square the circle between demographic and cost pressures (Duff, 2001). This is based on the assumption that care in the home is much less costly than that in high-tech hospitals and labour-intensive nursing homes. Substituting care in the home for institutionally based care is also said to provide better quality care because it allows for more autonomy and flexibility. Moreover, home care settings make it easier to combine formal and informal care arrangements. The shift in priorities also reflects the critical views towards the institutionalization of older people that emerged in the 1970s (Jenson and Jacobzone, 2000).

There is no shortage of political debate about the value of care in the home and the appropriate balance between individual and collective responsibilities. However, it is less certain what is happening beyond the level of political rhetoric and at the level of policy. This question is interesting particularly from a comparative perspective because home care policies are pushed by demography and costs, but are shaped by country-specific factors. Key factors include how the funding and provision of health care is organized, where health systems draw the boundary between health and social care, and cultural assumptions about the appropriate relations between the generations and between women and men, what Pfau-Effinger (2004) calls 'gender cultures'.

Analysing the policies of home care is not only topical, but also offers new perspectives on health policy and systems. Home care highlights the complex interrelationships among different sectors of health care provision and between health care and other welfare services, as well as between formal and informal health care. This forcefully demonstrates the multifaceted embeddedness of health care raised in Chapter 1. Home care, as well as public health (Chapter 7), also demonstrate that many services now central to health are at the margins of health systems. Finally, home care makes for an interesting study of the politics of health care because the medical profession is less directly involved: other actors are pushing the reform agendas here.

This chapter provides an analysis of home care and home care policies for older people. A first section examines the size and importance of home care through an analysis of available data. The next section looks more closely at the provision of home care and how the organization and the level of provision are shaped by the type of health system within which it is embedded. Provision is closely tied to the funding of home care, which is discussed next. The relative security and generosity of funding are favourable conditions for the growth and development of home care as a distinct sector of health care provision. Another important factor is the relative strength of policies that explicitly support the substitution of formal home care for both institutionally based care and informal care (Boom, 2001).

The fourth section looks more closely at the interface between formal and informal care and the underpinning cultural expectations about the role of women in care giving. This linkage is important because the majority of home care continues to be provided by unpaid care givers. Under the banner of a greater welfare mix, the objectives of reforms are to integrate care givers more explicitly into formal care arrangements and to support care givers through payments and related benefits.

The final section of this chapter compares and contrasts key trends in recent policy initiatives on home care and evaluates the extent of change. Has home care merely been redefined by acknowledging the importance of informal care and externalizing costs into the community (Duff, 2001)? Or have there been serious attempts at substituting formal home care for informal and institutional care?

Home care statistics

Compared to other sectors of the health systems, international statistics on home care are scarce and often non-existent. This paucity of data illustrates the marginal position of home care in health systems. Diverse, sporadic and often non-public sources of funding make it difficult to capture in one single figure how much is spent on home care. Also, the organization of home care is often highly decentralized, making it more difficult to gather standardized figures across different localities, let alone different countries. As a result, the statistics discussed here are incomplete and often not directly about home care. Thus, the analysis looks at trends in institutionally based care, for which more statistics are available, in order to get a sense of the degrees of de-institutionalization. However, the question as to whether de-institutionalization has been followed by the development of formal home care services remains open.

The total spending on long-term care in Table 6.1, which includes home and institutionally based care, gives a first indication of the relative size of this sector of health care provision. The majority of countries spend very little on long-term care, around 0.5 per cent of GDP. The notable exceptions are the Netherlands and Sweden, which spend 0.6 and 0.82 per cent of their GDP on long-term care. Moreover, it is likely that most goes to institutionally based care, which is more expensive than home care.

The percentage of 65-year-olds and over receiving formal home care in Table 6.2 offers a more direct indication of the relative size of home care services. In Australia, the Netherlands and the UK, more than 12 per cent of older people receive formal help at home. In other countries between 2.8 per cent (USA) and 9.1 per cent (Sweden) receive formal home care services. Although only a minority of older people receives formal help in all countries, the variation is striking. With the exception of the USA, the percentage of older people receiving formal home care is greater than the

Table 6.1   *Estimated spending on long-term home care (2000)*
as a percentage of GDP

	Total spending	Public spending
Australia	0.38	0.30
France	n/a	n/a
Germany	0.47	0.43
Italy	n/a	n/a
Japan	0.25	0.25
Netherlands	0.60	0.56
Sweden	0.82	0.78
UK	0.41	0.32
USA	0.39	0.17

n/a = not available

Source: Data from OECD (2005).

Table 6.2   *Population aged 65 and over in different care settings as a*
percentage of the total population*

	In institutions	Receiving home care benefits
Australia	5.5	14.7
France	n/a	n/a
Germany	3.9	7.1
Italy	n/a	n/a
Japan	3.2	5.5
Netherlands	2.4	12.3
Sweden	7.9	9.1
UK	5.1	20.3
USA	4.3	2.8

n/a = not available
* Various years 1999–2003

Source: Data from OECD (2005).

percentage living in institutions, thus highlighting the importance of home care for older people.

The growth of institutionalization rates in Table 6.3 offers a more detailed picture of how the relative importance of institutionally based care has been changing over time. With the exception of Sweden, growth

Table 6.3   *The growth of institutionalization rates of people aged 65 and over (%)*

Australia[a]	−0.4
Austria[b]	−0.2
Norway[c]	−0.2
Sweden[c]	1.5
USA[d]	−0.2

[a] Figure refers to growth between 1995 and 2003.
[b] Figure refers to growth between 1996/1997 and 2000.
[c] Figure refers to growth between 1991 and 2000.
[d] Figure refers to growth between 1973/1974 and 1999.

Source: Data from OECD (2005).

Table 6.4   *Number of long-term care beds per 1,000 people*

	1978	1983	1988	1993	1998	2003
Australia	4.1	4.7	4.4	4.2	4.5,	5.0
France	n/a	n/a	n/a	n/a	n/a	9.9
Germany	n/a	n/a	n/a	3.7	n/a	8.6
Italy	n/a	n/a	n/a	n/a	n/a	2.7
Netherlands	3.1	3.3	3.4	3.5	3.7	3.8
Sweden	n/a	n/a	n/a	n/a	n/a	n/a
UK	n/a	n/a	1.4	3.3	3.8	3.1

n/a = not available

Source: Data from OECD (2006).

rates are negative and are about 0.2 per cent. In most countries, then, fewer people tend to live in institutions. In part, this reflects policies explicitly aimed at de-institutionalization. However, as Table 6.4 indicates, this does not mean that the number of long-term care beds has fallen. In the majority of countries, the number of beds per 1,000 people has increased over the last two decades. In Australia and the Netherlands the increases have been moderate, whereas in Germany and Britain the number of long-term beds has about doubled. In short, in most countries institutionally based care continues to be important.

Irrespective of the inconclusive trends in the provision of institutionally based care, the spending on other types of services for the elderly and disabled has increased significantly. Table 6.5 lists per capita public

Table 6.5   *Per capita public expenditure on services for the elderly and disabled (US$)*

	1983	1988	1993	1998	2003
Australia	n/a	n/a	n/a	4	n/a
France	n/a	n/a	6	9	12
Germany	2	6	38	129	157
Italy	n/a	n/a	n/a	n/a	n/a
Japan	n/a	n/a	n/a	4	10
Netherlands	27	37	118	68	n/a
New Zealand	n/a	n/a	n/a	n/a	n/a
Sweden	n/a	n/a	n/a	n/a	n/a
UK	13	26	n/a	n/a	n/a
USA	18	34	84	120	131

n/a = not available

Source: Data from OECD (2006).

expenditure on day care, rehabilitation, home help services and other services in kind. Despite the inconclusive trends in the provision of institutionally based care, the spending on other types of services for the elderly and disabled seems to h ave increased.

The analysis of the very limited available statistics has given a first impression of home care in our countries. In terms of both funding and provision, home nursing is marginal in all countries, in some more so than in others. At the same time, there is little evidence of a systematic move away from institutionally based care. In some countries institutionalization rates have fallen, but in most the number of long-term care beds has increased. Nevertheless, more public money is being spent on alternative services for older people, such as day centres and home helps.

Providing home health care

Home care is embedded in health systems and, as such, its provision is closely related to that of health systems. However, as the poor relation, home care is often not fully integrated in the institutional fabric of health systems, thus creating distinct features in the provision of services. More broadly, this relates to the respective boundaries between health and social care services and the relative integration between the two services. The degree to which this is the case is an interesting question from a comparative perspective.

The provision of home care reflects the level and security of funding but is also influenced by other factors. This includes policies explicitly aimed at substituting formal home care for institutionally based care and informal care, together with cultural expectations about the role of the family in care giving, discussed in more detail later in this chapter. Substitution policies refer to a set of policies that are intended to replace institutionally based care with care in the home and related settings. Motivations are both financial and humanitarian. These policies have focused on de-institutionalization (see OECD, 2005), although any effects are partly offset by the increasing number of older and very old people (Jacobzone *et al.*, 1999). Policies have focused less explicitly on developing non-institutional care settings, often resulting in additional demands on women as informal carers (Jenson and Jacobzone, 2000). When assessing the provision of home care, it is important to look at how services are organized and who provides these services. Again, both aspects give an indication of the degree to which home care is integrated in health systems and influence the level of service provision.

Considering the diversity of health systems, it is not surprising that the provision of home care services shows wide variation (see Figure 6.1). Only in Britain and Sweden are home nursing services provided publicly and firmly integrated into the health system. This situation is typical of national health services, which are characterized by a high degree of public integration (see Chapter 3). However, this does not necessarily guarantee a high level of service provision. In Sweden, home health care is embedded in a gender culture that combines ideas of universal access to services and individual independence from families as sources of financial and care support. In contrast, in Britain targeting and shifting responsibilities to less well integrated social care services has undermined the traditional entitlement for home nursing. The push towards a more mixed provision of services has paradoxical consequences, because the fragmentation of services not only requires more coordination, but also makes it more difficult. Trudie Knijn (2000) in her analysis of the

Predominant Type of Provision

		Public	Non-profit
Level of Provision	High	Sweden	Netherlands
	Low	Britain	Australia, Germany, Japan, New Zealand, Singapore, USA

Figure 6.1   *The provision of home health care*

Netherlands identifies this as one of the central tensions underlying contemporary market reforms.

The Netherlands is an unusual case, where private, non-profit providers are part of a universal system of service provision, resulting in a high level of this provision. This reflects a long-standing commitment to home care, together with service provision, which combines health and social care as well as secure funding (this last element is discussed in the following section). In all other countries, the provision of home care is highly mixed and less well integrated into the health system, thus reflecting either a strong legacy of informal care (as in Germany, Japan and Singapore), health systems with a strong liberal element (as in Australia and the USA) and/or weaker demographic pressures (as in New Zealand). However, with ever-present demographic and cost pressures, some countries have adopted more explicit policies. In response, Japan and Germany have extended their social insurance to cover home care, whereas Australia has introduced a tax-funded home care programme.

Sweden is the paradigmatic case of a country where the level of service provision is high and where the public provision of services dominates. Home care is embedded in a national health service, which makes for strong public integration. This also reflects a strong commitment to the primacy of formal care services over informal care that resonates with a gender culture where universal access to formal care is seen as a central means to secure the independence of individuals, both as potential employees and care recipients. Yet, this coexists with a high degree of decentralization, and some suggest that the wide differences at local level make it more appropriate to talk about a multitude of 'welfare municipalities' rather than a single welfare state (Trydegård and Thorslund, 2001). Not surprisingly, the organization of services is characterized by diversity. In half of the localities, county councils have delegated the responsibility for home nursing to municipalities (National Board of Health and Welfare, 2000). This results in a highly integrated service provision since municipalities also provide other long-term nursing services in institutional settings together with social-care-oriented home help services. In the other half, county councils continue to organize home care as part of primary care services.

As the international statistics discussed earlier indicate, Sweden has a high percentage of older people receiving formal home help. Services for older people with long-term care needs have long been well developed and the social preferences for home care, together with the need for de-institutionalization, were recognized very early (see Gough, 1994; Trydegard, 2000). However, financial constraints combined with an emerging ideology of welfare mix have put a strain on the system. The number of non-public providers delivering home care for municipalities increased by 146 per cent between 1995 and 1998 (National Board of

Health and Welfare, 2000) although the overall number remains small. The targeting of services also disguises an overall reduction of service levels. Home-based care services have been concentrated in very old people and in older people living alone; that is, in older people who need help most. As a consequence, the number of older people receiving extensive help has increased significantly (Trydegard, 2003). These changes illustrate a gradual move away from universal welfare policies and contrast with earlier reforms, while the overall commitment to tax funding, female employment and universalism remains unchanged (Theobald, 2003).

In contrast, the case of England demonstrates that high public integration can facilitate but does not necessarily safeguard high levels of service provision. Home nursing services are provided publicly with GP-led Primary Care Trusts responsible for organizing the provision of services. The Primary Care Trusts are intended to commission home help services and this should help to integrate better the provision of home-based care services across the health and social care divide. However, the level of service provision is low not least reflecting lower overall spending on health care (see Chapter 3), as well as the hollowing out of entitlements to tax-funded home nursing. Instead, home-based health care over the last decade has focused on acute care needs, while other care needs have been redefined as social care for which older people have to pay (Lewis, 2001). As a consequence, substitution policies that could have helped expand the provision of home nursing services have been weak, if not non-existent. The same applies to social care-oriented services where speedier discharge of older people from hospitals and the reduction of long-term care facilities has not been matched by comparable public funding to stimulate the development of home-based services (Gibson and Means, 2000; Glendinning, 1998a). More broadly, this reflects a gender culture where, in contrast to Sweden, family care is only partly to be shared with the state. As a result, the availability of social care service is uneven (Brodhurst and Glendinning, 2001).

The cases of Sweden and Britain suggest that public provision makes for publicly integrated home care. However, as the case of the Netherlands demonstrates, a similar degree of integration in the health system can also be achieved with a more mixed provision of services, which is dominated by non-profit providers. In the Netherlands, the provision of home care is in the hands of non-profit organizations, the regional Cross Associations. Only one organization operates in any one area and provides skilled nursing services, personal care and prevention (Tester, 1996). In the past, separate organizations existed for home nursing and home help services, but in the early 1990s the two started to merge with the aim of increasing the efficiency of service delivery (Kerkstra, 1996). Integrated provision of services coincides with a high overall level of service provision, which is comparable to Sweden and which reflects a long-standing commitment to formal care services dating back to the late 1960s (Knijn 1998). Interestingly, the Netherlands also had a higher proportion of people living in institutions than any other European country and it was only in the 1980s that policies focused more explicitly on substitution (Loo *et al.*, 1999).

The Netherlands contrasts with the remaining countries, where a predominantly mixed provision of home care services coincides with low levels of integration of services in the health system as well as low levels of service provision. Germany (together with Japan and Singapore) is a classical example of a country where the development of home care services has been impeded by a deeply embedded gender culture that gives preference to informal care. The principle of subsidiarity defines home care first and foremost as the responsibility of the family. The introduction of long-term care insurance in Germany has only partly changed this. Security of funding coexists with basic coverage, which is cash limited and not needs-based, and there is an explicit emphasis on informal care in the form of cash benefits for informal care givers. Fee-for-service payments also encourage the provision of services which are closely tailored to the conditions under which services are reimbursed by the insurance. As a result, services often remain highly segmented, prescribed and inflexible (Theobald, 2004). Having said that, the end of the monopoly of the five main non-profit providers has led to the escalation of alternative (46 per cent privately owned) providers, which increased from 4,300 in 1992 to 11,800 in 1999 (Cuellar and Wiener, 2000: 19). This has resulted in greater diversity in the provision of home care, though not necessarily significant increases in the level of service provision. At the same time, the sharp separation between health and social care, acute care and rehabilitation, and ambulatory and hospital care continues to exist (Theobald, 2004). As Boom *et al.* (2000) suggest, policies have been concerned more with closing gaps in the provision of long-term care, not specifically with home care as such. Instead, the support for informal care has been strongest and most explicit.

In contrast, Australia and the USA are examples of countries where the development of home care services has been impeded by strong liberal elements in the health and welfare system. In Australia, the historical emphasis on private funding and the heavy role of charitable agencies in providing care for older people, combined with the provision of health care by the states and not the Commonwealth, resulted in a highly fragmented provision of home care. However, this situation changed with a series of steps in the early 1980s culminating in the introduction of the Home and Community Care Program (HACC) in 1985, which provides secure funding for home care and encourages the states to fund more home care services.

HACC is a central element of the Australian Government's aged care policy, providing community care services to the frail aged and younger people with disabilities. The aims of the Program are to provide a 'comprehensive, coordinated and integrated range of basic maintenance and support services' for frail elderly people and their care givers to enable them to be more independent, thus enhancing their quality of life and preventing their inappropriate admission to long term residential care (Australian Department of Health and Ageing, 2006a). The type of services funded include nursing care, allied health care, meals, personal care, respite care and counselling. Some services charge a small fee depending on ability to pay and the number of services used but this varies from state to state. Despite HACC, one national conference concluded that 'rampant bureaucracy' meant Australia's home care programmes for the elderly were in dire need of an overhaul. Experts and advocates agreed that caring for the elderly in their homes needed to be simplified and better funded. They criticized the buck-passing between the Commonwealth and the states and argued the system would be better run by one or the other (Wroe, 2003). In response to such criticism, in 2004 the Ministry released *A New Strategy for Community Care – The Way Forward* that outlined the Australian Government's vision for streamlining Commonwealth-funded programmes and providing a more consistent and coordinated community care sector (Australian Department of Health and Ageing, 2006b).

There is a similar move towards greater public involvement in New Zealand. Under the national 'Ageing in Place' programme in New Zealand, home care services are increasingly publicly subsidized. As a result, government home support expenditure more than doubled between 1995/6 and 2002/3 (New Zealand Ministry of Health, 2003: 40). The government partially or fully subsidizes a wide range of home care services, particularly those that depend upon professional expertise such as nursing. Eligibility and level of service are determined by needs assessment. These recent developments are typical of a care regime that combines very limited universality with means-testing and where privately paid and charitable services complement family care. In relation to the last aspect, it is also indicative that there are additional community support services that are not publicly funded such as transportation which are also often provided free of charge to persons in need. The main source of funds for these services is the Lottery Grants Board which provides funds to not-for-profit organizations.

Funding home health care

The ways in which home care is funded are significant in two respects. Security of funding, together with the relative level of public funding, are important factors shaping the provision of home care services. Funding arrangements also give an indication of the extent to which home care is an integral part of a health system.

The funding of home care ranges from taxes and social insurance contributions to out-of-pocket payments and private insurance. The first two provide secure funding, whereas out-of-pocket payments are a much less reliable source of funding. The funding of home care is typically highly mixed as funding from public sources is often insufficient, and a substantial amount of home care is funded from private, out-of-pocket payments. The importance of non-public sources of funding is even greater if the indirect costs incurred by unpaid care givers are taken into consideration. At the same time, different approaches to funding create different types of access. In countries with tax funding, patients tend to have direct access to services. In contrast, in countries with social insurance funding patients often need a medical referral to access services.

As Table 6.6 shows, there is considerable variation in relation to the funding of home care that reflects the respective health systems. In contrast to medical care, public funding of home care often only provides basic coverage which has to be supplemented by substantial amounts of out-of-pocket payments and/or unpaid informal care. The degree to which this is the case is influenced by the broader gender culture and the relative state support for formal care services more generally. In Britain, New Zealand and Sweden, tax funding of home nursing (and home help services in Sweden) is embedded in a health system which is universal in its orientation. This leads to generous entitlements in principle. In Australia, home care is also tax funded, but this is part of a health system with strong private elements and entitlements are means-tested.

The social insurance funding in Germany, Japan and the Netherlands

Table 6.6 *Funding home health care*[a]

Predominantly tax-based funding	*Predominantly social insurance contributions*	*Predominantly private funding*
Australia	Germany	Singapore
Britain	Netherlands	USA
New Zealand		
Sweden		

[a] Japan is difficult to categorize as home health care is funded by taxes and social insurance contributions to equal extents.

makes home care an individually earned right, although individual benefits are often needs-based. Integrated funding of health and social care (as
is the case in Australia, the Netherlands and Sweden) can add further
security to funding arrangements. In contrast, the USA and to a lesser
extent Singapore rely heavily on private funding (Teo *et al.*, 2003). This
undermines the security of funding for individuals. At the same time,
entitlements to tax-funded home care have also been reduced as services
have been targeted to the very needy (as in Sweden) or defined as means-
tested social care (as in Britain). This reflects financial pressures together
with an ideological turn towards welfare mix. Nevertheless, other countries have seen the introduction of tax-funded programmes covering
home care (as in Australia and the USA) and even the introduction of new
additions to social insurance (as in Germany and Japan).

Britain and Sweden are typical examples of national health services in
which public provision of home nursing coincides with tax funding. New
Zealand is another national health service where home nursing care is
tax funded, although the provision is mixed and in the hands of non-
profit providers. Taxes may be combined with complementary sources of
funding such as out-of-pocket payments in Sweden that constitute 10 per
cent of expenditure (National Board of Health and Welfare, 2000: 6).
Tax funding represents a high degree of public integration and security of
funding, although the levels of funding vary among countries and over
time. In Britain, for example, home nursing services are part of the NHS
and, as such, are funded out of general taxation and are free at the point
of use. Although this implies generous entitlements in principle, in practice the use of home nursing services is restricted, reflecting the tight cash
limits under which the NHS operates. Over the last decade, more and
more services have been defined as social rather than health care, and as
such they incur charges. Combined with targeting of services by local
authorities, this means that older people increasingly have to rely either
on their own funds or on the help of families and friends in order to pay
for services and stay in their own homes (Baldock, 2003). Brodhurst and
Glendinning (2001) suggest that this strategy effects a considerable
reduction of citizenship rights in what was a universal system until the
early 1980s.

In 2002 Scotland established a social right to home care. In addition to
home nursing, patients now also have access to free personal (social)
care, which covers personal assistance and hygiene, together with simple
treatments. The only condition is that patients be over 65 and that their
care needs have been assessed (see Marnoch, 2003). The introduction of
free home care is an example of the emerging health care federalism in the
UK and distinct health policies in Scotland since, under the 1997 devolution legislation, the Scottish Parliament can pass its own laws on social
issues and also raise additional taxes (Woods, 2004).

Australia illustrates a country where tax funding is embedded in a health system with strong elements of private funding. Significantly, the HACC, which covers home nursing and home help services, was only set up in 1985. Its services are means tested. The HACC, an integral part of a set of changes known as the Aged Care Reform Strategy, was the product of a 1982 Commonwealth inquiry which recommended that the entire system of aged care support be overhauled and more home care services provided to enable people to stay in their own homes (Jenson and Jacobzone, 2000: 59). Nevertheless, funding for home care remains a combination of public, private, charitable and individual funding, as the testing of assets are used for home care support. Also, public funding is a complex combination of different sources.

HACC is a joint Commonwealth, State and Territory cost-shared programme with the Commonwealth contributing 60 per cent and the States and Territories providing 40 per cent. While the Commonwealth and State/Territory governments jointly allocate funds to HACC regions based on agreed targets for service outputs, the sub-national governments are solely responsible for its administration and for allocating funds to services within regions and for the day-to-day operation of the programme. As at September 2005 there were approximately 3,100 HACC-funded organizations that provided services to approximately 750,000 people. The HACC also funds a wide range of non-profit organizations (Australian Department of Health and Ageing, 2006a). The impact of HACC has been a radical shift in balance from nursing home to hospice and home-based care. Between 1985 and 1990, for instance, while Commonwealth expenditure on nursing home care increased by 9 per cent, the corresponding increases in expenditure for home care and hospices were 95 per cent and 127 per cent, respectively (Australian Department of Health and Ageing, 2003).

The public funding of home care has traditionally been less well established in social insurance systems, reflecting an implicit focus on the working population, together with an often strong communitarian orientation that puts self-help by individuals and communities first (see Chapter 2). Here, the principle of subsidiarity underpinning German social policy is indicative. The principle of subsidiarity says that social, political and economic activity is undertaken at the lowest appropriate level of social organization (Freeman and Clasen, 1994). This principle is the cornerstone of Catholic social teaching, which has been very influential. Subsidiarity assigns primary responsibility for welfare to the individual and to the family and resonates with a gender culture that builds on part-time caring by women and full-time paid employment by men. Furthermore, welfare is funded through social insurance and is provided as an earned right rather than on the basis of need. In terms of the provision of formal services, priority is given to non-government, non-profit organizations. Not surprisingly, the introduction of social insurance for home care has been a relatively recent phenomenon in Germany as well as Japan.

In 1989, faced with a fast-growing elderly population and the problem of social hospitalization, the government in Japan instituted the Gold Plan to expand services for older people. One goal of this Plan was to facilitate access to care services by challenging the assumption that home care is to be provided by family alone and by shifting resources from hospitals to social support services, such as home nursing and social care. Two criticisms of the policy were that it was not matched by government attention to the quality of care and that it failed to adequately reimburse home health care (Kobayashi and Reich, 1993).

As a result of these shortcomings, the Gold Plan was expanded in 1997, when Japan enacted the Public Long-term Care Act, which marked a clear shift towards funding a comprehensive programme of long-term care, both health and social care.

Under Japan's New Ten-Year Strategy to Promote Health Care and Welfare for the Elderly (The New Gold Plan) that came into effect on 1 April 2000, municipalities are the insurer and the national government, prefectures and medical care insurers provide multi-layers of support (Japan Ministry of Health, Labour and Welfare, 1999). Half of the cost of long-term care insurance administered by the Financial Stability Fund is borne by the premium payments of the insured and the other half is funded by public funds. Of the public funds, the ratio among the national government, prefectures and local municipalities is fixed at 2:1:1. In addition, the national government pays towards making adjustments to the financial gaps among municipalities, which occur because of the differences in the ratio of subscribers in their advanced elderly age and their abilities to bear the burden (Japan Ministry of Health, Labour and Welfare, 2004), paying half of the cost for the new administrative work. To ensure impartiality between service users and non-users, in principle the users are required to pay a 10 per cent co-payment for long-term care. However, in the case of the low-income elderly, a maximum amount of burden is set (Japan Ministry of Health, Labour and Welfare, 1999).

In contrast, in Germany the so-called long-term care insurance is funded entirely by insurance contributions. Another distinct feature is that the insurance includes cash benefits, which older people can use to pay informal care givers. This was designed to encourage informal care by the family and wider network (Meyer, 1996) and, despite the freedom of choice, a clear majority of beneficiaries receiving care at home choose cash benefits. Furthermore, the security of the new funding arrangement contrasts with the limited levels of funding available and many older people must continue to rely on out-of-pocket payments and/or unpaid care givers (Cuellar and Wiener, 2000: 17).

In comparison to Japan and Germany, the Netherlands is something of a pioneer. Home care is covered by a separate health insurance which was introduced in the late 1960s and covers a range of exceptional medical risks (Knijn, 1998). The insurance is compulsory for all employees irrespective of income and is supplemented by central government funds and out-of-pocket payments. This represents a strong element of universalism in a health system in which almost one-fifth of the population is covered by private health insurance. The Netherlands is unusual in that the insurance covers both home nursing and home help services. Integrated funding means that the scope of the insurance is relatively extensive, which in turn has led to a high level of service provision and use of formal services (Coolen and Weekers, 1998: 50). However, concerns about expenditure coupled with a renewed emphasis on subsidiarity and the primacy of self-help in relation to informal care have begun to weaken the universalist orientation of home care in the Netherlands (Visser-Jansen and Knipscheer, 2004).

In comparison to the countries discussed so far, Singapore largely relies on private funding of home care with users expected to pay for home care services out of their Medisave accounts or through the private or public insurance they can purchase with those accounts (Cheah, 2001; Teo *et al.*, 2003). Health care services for the elderly in Singapore are mostly run by the voluntary welfare organizations, although government financial assistance is provided to them. To address the concerns over heightened health needs by the rapidly ageing population, the Inter-Ministerial Committee on Health Care for the Elderly (IMC) was created in 1997 to provide strategies for the provision of health care for the elderly. The IMC has consistently emphasized that the elderly are to be cared for in their own homes for as long as possible with institutionalization being a measure of last resort. The Government recognizes that these care services can be expensive and provides financial assistance in the form of subsidies to the elderly who lack adequate resources. To ensure that the subsidy goes to those who need it, means testing was introduced in 2000. The subsidy goes directly to the service providers to offset the bill for the care fees and charges.

In June 2002, a public long-term disability insurance scheme, ElderShield, was introduced to provide basic financial protection against expenses required in the event of severe disabilities. The ElderShield payouts are set at $300 per month, up to a maximum of 60 months which is considered sufficient to cover a substantial portion of a patient's share of subsidized nursing home charges and defray the expenses of those who choose home care. Once an ElderShield policy holder starts paying premiums, she is covered for the rest of her life after she finishes paying all the premiums at age 65 under the Regular Premium Plan or a lump sum premium under the Single Premium Plan. For those who are not eligible for ElderShield or who exhaust their benefits, the government assistance scheme Interim Disability Assistance Programme for the Elderly offers means tested support of $100 or $150 a month, up to 60 months, per life time for those with monthly household incomes under $1000 (Singapore Ministry of Health, 2006). Moreover, in October 2000, the Ministry of Health launched the Primary Care Partnership Scheme to bring affordable health care to needy elderly who do not live near to the polyclinics that normally provide affordable health care to them.

In the USA, home care is also predominantly funded from private sources, either out-of-pocket and/or private insurance. As can be expected in a market-based health care system, public sources of funding are marginal, often means-tested, and highly fragmented. Until recently, reimbursement for home care services has been minimal except for the indigent. Depending on the case, Medicare and Medicaid may pay some home care costs that are related to medical care, but do not pay for informal care givers. In recent years, however, to reduce costs Medicare has initiated programmes targeted to home care to encourage people to stay at home (Sloane, 2005; Wilensky, 2005). All Medicaid beneficiaries are eligible for home nursing care if they meet certain conditions, though these conditions vary widely from one state to another (see Centers for Medicare and Medicaid Services, 2006). Services supported by Medicare are more narrowly construed as medical and it does not pay for 24-hour care at home, drugs, meals or home help services.

Recently, however, there have been a number of new programmes to provide public funding for home care, the most important of which is the Program of All Inclusive Care for the Elderly (PACE). After more than a decade operating as a federally supported demonstration project, PACE is now recognized as a permanent provider under Medicare and a state option under Medicaid for people over 55 years of age who are frail enough to meet their state's standards for nursing home care (Centers for Medicare and Medicaid Services, 2006). For most patients, the comprehensive service package permits them to continue living at home rather than be institutionalized. A team of doctors, nurses and other health professionals assess participant needs, develops care plans and deliver a mix of services integrated into a complete health care plan. The PACE organization must offer a service package that includes all Medicare and Medicaid services provided by that state as well as an additional 16 services including primary care, social services, restorative therapies, personal care and supportive services, nutritional counselling, recreational therapy and meals. The PACE organization receives a fixed monthly payment per patient from Medicare and Medicaid, regardless of the services an enrollee uses. Persons enrolled in PACE also may have to pay a monthly premium, depending on their eligibility for Medicare and Medicaid.

The interface between formal and informal care

As the analysis above suggests, home care is a complex policy field. Public funding is often insecure and insufficient and has to be supplemented by out-of-pocket payments. Moreover, publicly funded services increasingly are targeted at highly dependent older people and, in many instances, the entitlement to publicly funded services is being hollowed out. Furthermore, often the level of service provision is basic and involves a diverse range of providers. As a result, the emphasis on welfare mix competes with the policy goal to integrate services across varied providers and with the boundary between health and social care.

The analysis thus far has focused only on formal home care – the care provided by paid staff with formal training/qualifications. The policy field becomes even more complex when it is realized that the bulk of home care traditionally has been (and still is) provided by family and friends: that is to say, informal, unpaid care givers. Tester (1996) in her comparison of community care in a number of European countries and the USA, estimates that informal care givers provide 75 to 80 per cent of care. With cost containment in health care and inadequate resources to develop home care services, the burden on informal care givers has actually increased in recent years. Substitution policies also mean that home care services are directed at highly dependent older people who would otherwise require institutional care. Significantly, informal care work is viewed as women's work and an overwhelming amount of care work is still being done by women in family settings (Jenson and Jacobzone, 2000; OECD, 2005).

Informal care is important in all countries, but there are interesting variations in regard to the underlying cultural assumptions about the relations between generations and between women and men (Pfau-Effinger, 2004). In those countries where family bonds and collectivist values are traditionally strong, the care-giving responsibilities of families are extensive. The inverse applies to countries where values of individual independence dominate. Here, it is more accepted that care giving be in the hands of paid professionals, or at least that they complement informal care. These clusters of values and cultural traditions coincide with different types of care regimes (Burau *et al.*, forthcoming), as shown in Figure 6.2.

Sweden is the classic example of a public service care regime where equality and individual independence are the key and which is characterized by high female employment (see Rauch, 2005; Trydegard, 2000). Many responsibilities traditionally associated with families, such as care of older people and children, have been taken on by the public sector and formal care has been chosen over informal care. The overall commitment to this principle remains strong, although recent years have seen a much

Value Orientations

Care Regime		Individual Independence	Family Responsibility
	Public Service	Sweden	The Netherlands
	Means-tested		Australia, Britain, New Zealand, USA
	Subsidiarity		Germany, Japan, Singapore

Note: Japan and Singapore do not easily fit into (European) types of welfare regime. However, with Germany they share an explicit emphasis on family responsibility.

Figure 6.2   *Value orientations in informal care and welfare regimes*

more explicit concern with the role of the family in care giving. In the Netherlands, the attitude towards the role of women in care giving is more ambivalent and ideas of family care coexist with a strong emphasis on formal care. The new insurance for exceptional medical risks compensated for weakening traditional divisions in Dutch Society (Alber, 1995) and marked the introduction of universalist elements into what otherwise was a conservative welfare state (Knijn, 2001).

In contrast, Britain is an example of a care regime with increasingly strong liberal elements and where means-testing tends to prevail (Baldock, 2003; Means *et al.*, 2003). The NHS is an exception to the rule that the public funding and provision of welfare is often minimal, designed as a safety net for those who cannot provide for themselves. While services are defined universally, in practice they are often means tested or income related. The responsibility of the individual (and the family) is central, whereas that of the state is residual. In relation to older people, it is assumed that families take on caring responsibilities. Australia has been most active in the expansion of public support for families, while New Zealand with its younger population has largely depended on private resources and long-standing charitable organizations to serve this function. Like the UK, though, New Zealand serves a residual role and provides a safety net through means-tested subsidies to the poor. Although the US government is beginning to accept some responsibility for long-term care of the elderly, by and large it continues to be the responsibility of the family to arrange and fund this care through private insurance or personal resources.

Germany is the archetypal example of a subsidiarity care regime that places great importance on the family as an organizing principle of society (Alber and Schöllkopf, 1999). This reflects Catholic teachings on the family. However, Germany is unusual in the explicitness with which demands are made on the family. In this respect the idea of subsidiarity is key where self-help is understood as the responsibility of individuals. If self-help is no longer possible, then it is the responsibility of the family to take over from the individual, followed by voluntary organizations, and, only if all else fails, will the state then step in.

In Japan, direct relatives, including children, grandchildren and siblings, may be legally required to provide financial support to maintain their elderly relatives. Traditionally, it has been the case that elderly parents live with their eldest son's family with an arrangement for sharing resources. Moreover, this strong filial duty to care for elderly family members often falls on the daughter-in-law. Thus, in some cases, a woman might be caring for two sets of parents simultaneously. One of the major factors driving reform in home care in Japan is the ongoing decline in the supply of in-family care givers due to the ageing process and the increasing labour market participation of younger women (Jenson and Jacobzone, 2000). The situation is similar in Singapore, where there is also a strong filial tradition that daughters be care givers for elderly parents. As in Japan, the Asian cultural context has produced tensions between institutionalized and home care as the Singapore population ages.

With home care on the political agenda of many health systems, there has been a corresponding interest in informal care. Expectations of a gap in informal family care as well as research findings on the significance of informal care have opened up the political debate (Hochschild, 1995). Home care inevitably involves informal care. Home is where older people live with their spouses and partners, and home is also one of the places where older people meet with friends and family. The spatial interface of personal relationships and home care facilitates the provision of informal care. Policies on home care have acknowledged the importance of informal care (see Burau *et al.*, forthcoming; Lundsgaard, 2004); and from a comparative perspective the interesting question is what form this formalization takes and how policies define the interface between formal and informal care.

Here, a number of considerations come into play. In times of resource constraints, it seems inevitable that health systems continue to rely on informal care. Compared to formal care, this is the cheaper option, but only if the costs associated with informal care such as lost income and pension entitlements are ignored (Jacobzone, 1999; Jamieson, 1996). Another consideration is that the expansion of formal care might reduce the provision of informal care and even create new, expanded demands for formal care (Jamieson, 1996). This can be either a desirable or an undesirable policy outcome, although studies indicate that substitution is not straightforward. For moderately disabled older people, home-based care is likely to be the best (and most efficient) option, whereas for severely disabled older people, institutional care is more appropriate (Jacobzone, 1999). If anything, this suggests that substitution needs to be tailored to the particular circumstances of individuals (see Low *et al.*, 2000). Moreover, even in countries with relatively high levels of publicly funded formal care, families continue to play a significant role as informal care givers. For example, even in Sweden an estimated two-thirds of the total volume of home care is provided informally (Johansson, 2000).

Policies on the informal aspects of home care pick and mix considerations about the interface between the formal and the informal in distinct ways, which are shaped by cultural assumptions about relations between the generations and between women and men. At the same time, it is interesting that in recent years many countries have experienced in one way or another a more explicit integration of informal care into the (formal) health system. Twigg (1989) has developed a typology for understanding the range of relationships that exist between welfare agencies and informal care givers. She distinguishes among care givers as resources, when they are taken for granted; care givers as co-workers, when they are treated instrumentally to ensure the continuation of their caring activities; care givers as co-clients, when agencies are concerned with the needs of care givers in their own right; and superseded care givers, when agencies aim to replace them with paid formal care staff.

Looking at the interface between formal and informal care, similarities within differences are most striking. Countries vary significantly in terms of their expectations about the role of women in care giving. Sweden and the Netherlands have traditionally favoured formal care, whereas Japan, Singapore and Germany explicitly expect women to take on caring responsibilities. This attitude also exists, but more implicitly, in Australia, Britain, New Zealand and the USA with their liberal welfare regimes. However, despite these differences, most countries – with the exception of Singapore, New Zealand and the USA – have begun integrating informal care into the formal system of funding home care. In this regard, payments for informal care givers have been vital. Although payments are largely symbolic (rather than reimbursements for a service), they are important indicators of a turn towards welfare societies.

With their traditionally strong preference for formal care, recent developments in Sweden and the Netherlands underline the pertinence of the emphasis on informal care and the move towards a welfare society. As Daatland (1996: 257) observes in relation to Sweden, '[t]he policy rhetoric encourages family care, voluntarism, and welfare pluralism'. For example, in the late 1990s the municipalities received additional funding to increase support for caring relatives that can take a number of forms

(Szebehely, 2005). Municipalities can employ informal care givers as care assistants. Alternatively, older people can receive grants to pay informal care givers for the help they receive at home. Nevertheless, the importance of such forms of support remain limited and in 1999 only 2 per cent of people receiving formal care services were cared for by informal care givers employed by the municipality (National Board of Health and Welfare, 2000: 86).

In the Netherlands, financial support for informal care givers came as part the introduction of a personal budget (a cash benefit) in 1995. The budget provides care receivers with the opportunity to establish their own care provision including the right to employ a family member. The introduction of the budget has been a part of care service reforms in the 1990s aimed at introducing more market elements, especially choice, into health care. The notions of autonomy and independence resonated with the criticisms of the self-help movement against paternalistic service provision; and carers organizations voted for care budgets as an opportunity to compensate for informal care giving (Kremer, 2005; Tjadens and Duijnstee, 2000). However, the implementation of the cash benefits has been piecemeal and in 2003 only 0.8 per cent of the elderly used care budgets for their care provision (Lundsgaard, 2004). Also, the preference for formal care services remains strong and only 37 per cent of older people decided to use their personal budget to pay informal care givers (Coolen and Weekers, 1998: 61).

Considering the conservative orientation of its welfare regime and the explicit emphasis on family responsibility, it is not surprising that in Germany the introduction of the long-term care insurance also extended the commitment to unpaid informal care. The demands made on the families of older people are now complemented by a range of support mechanisms that are meant to help maintain informal care (Theobald, 2004). Besides benefits in kind, insurance offers financial benefits which older people can use to pay their informal care givers and also pays contributions to the pension and accident insurance of informal care givers who qualify. In addition, insurance offers respite care as an annual benefit for older people cared for by the family. Although the monetary value of the financial benefits is only half that of the benefits in kind, the majority of beneficiaries receiving care at home choose cash benefits (Burau *et al.*, forthcoming). This reflects the continued strength of cultural norms about the role of the family in care giving (Wenger, 2001).

By comparison, the emphasis on informal care has typically been implicit in liberal welfare regimes while the explicit support of informal care givers has been weak. Significantly, in neither the USA, Singapore nor New Zealand do public payments to informal care givers exist. In the first two countries, this reflects strong private elements in the provision and funding of home care. In the USA, this is exacerbated by the high degree of fragmentation in public funding. As noted earlier, in Singapore a strong emphasis on obligations of female care givers plays an important role, as does the fact that individuals in effect control their own health care accounts and can use them for long-term care insurance should they so decide. In New Zealand, the relative youthfulness of the population is a possible explanation for the absence of formal support for care givers although public debate on this issue has begun.

Australia is an outlier among countries with a liberal welfare regime and has a tradition of paying family members for home care work. The Department of Families, Community Services and Indigenous Affairs administers two allowances for care givers, the Carer Allowance and the Carer Payment (Australia Department of Health and Ageing, 2006a). The Carer Allowance is an income supplement available to people who provide daily care and attention at home to a person who has a disability or severe medical condition. It is a non-means or asset-tested, non-taxable payment of small (25 per cent of average weekly full-time earnings) cash benefits to family members who support a person who requires continuous nursing care at home and who would otherwise be eligible for admission to a nursing home. To be eligible for Carer Allowance, a person must be providing care and daily attention to a person likely to suffer from the disability permanently or for a period of at least 12 months. The Carer Payment is an income support payment for people who are unable to participate in the workforce full time as a result of their caring responsibilities. Carer Payment is subject to income and asset tests and is paid at the same rate as other social security pensions. The level of benefit is the same as a retirement pension, similar in level to unemployment benefit, which is quite low, but ensures that carers have an adequate level of income and maximizes the opportunities available to participate in their community.

Policy trends and developments

Home care is full of contradictions. Home care is varied and diverse, yet it is a basic health need across countries. Home care is hardly visible in international statistics, yet it is central to the health of an increasing number of people. Home care funding and provision is often fragmented, yet home care is high on the health policy agenda of many countries. These are some of the salient contradictions in home care. The interesting question is what, if anything, recent policy trends and developments have changed regarding home care.

The provision of home care services is diverse, reflecting a political emphasis on a mixed economy of welfare and competition. Diversity means a greater number and wider range of providers. This requires greater coordination, but at the same time makes coordination (and ultimately the integration into the health system) more difficult. Problems of coordination can be exacerbated by a sharp divide between different types of care (e.g. health and social care in Britain), the absence of national legislation (as in the USA) or highly decentralized governance structures (as in Sweden). Also, diversity of provision does not necessarily translate into adequate levels of provision. This gives credence to the general tenet that in times of cost containment, diversity of provision often coincides with a targeting of services to those in greatest need (as in Britain and Sweden) or to those without any other means (as in Australia, and for social care in Britain and New Zealand).

At the same time, the funding of home care remains insecure and continues to rely largely on private funding and unpaid informal care. Only in Singapore and the USA does the insecurity of funding arise from the absence of public funding schemes. All other countries have schemes funded either from taxes or social insurance contributions, but which are restricted because of needs and/or means testing or because the scheme provides only basic coverage (as in the case of the long-term care insurance in Germany). Notwithstanding the continued insecurity of funding and the limits on funding, three countries have witnessed the wholesale introduction of new schemes over the last two decades. In Germany and Japan this took the form of the extension of social insurance and in Australia it took the form of a tax-funded programme. Even in the USA, states participating in the publicly funded PACE programme include a home care component.

Regardless of the policy trends in the provision and funding of services, however, home care remains overwhelmingly informal, women's work. Most countries acknowledge the centrality of informal care, although this takes different forms, reflecting differences among care regimes and gender cultures. Policy responses range from the gender-blindness of liberal welfare traditions (USA) and gender-specific expectations in male-dominated, collectivist societies (Japan and Singapore), to the ideology of the welfare society (Britain and Sweden), the revival of subsidiarity (Germany), and symbolic payments to care givers (Australia, Germany, and the Netherlands).

Chapter 7

Public Health

Until now the focus of this book has been on health care policy. We have been concerned with hospitals, doctors and other health care professionals and the funding, delivery and governance of health care services. Largely, it has centred on the care of individual patients. Chapter 5 demonstrated the wide range of settings and activities needed for the delivery of modern medical care. Chapter 6 extended this need to integrate health care with non-health arenas by demonstrating that with home care it is not possible to disconnect health care from social care. The health of the client is as dependent on personal care as it is on medical care, perhaps in many cases more so. Even this more inclusive picture of health care, however, can be criticized for minimizing what according to some observers are its most important dimensions: health promotion and disease prevention, which together are often termed public health. Due to the breadth and rather amorphous nature of public health, this chapter is more an overview of the policy concerns facing our countries than a comparative analysis as in previous chapters. Examples from our countries, however, are used throughout the discussion to demonstrate the wide scope of public health issues facing all countries.

The biggest advances in human health and longevity in the 20th century were the result of improved hygiene and clean water supplies, vaccines to prevent viral infections, and antibiotics to combat bacterial infections. Historically, they have constituted the backbone of public health, although as we will see in this chapter public health is much more expansive today. Simply put, public health is concerned with the health of the community as a whole. Although public health can be defined in many ways, common denotations of the term include health promotion, disease prevention, primary care, community health and population health. Public health encompasses a wide range of activities including the management of diseases that threaten the health of the population, the assessment of the health needs of specific populations and health education and promotion.

Although great strides have been made in conquering the health scourges of the past, many new threats to public health require continued vigilance. These include events like terrorism and natural disasters as well as longer-term health threats like viral and bacterial infections and high-risk behaviour. For instance, in the first half of 2006 among the

Box 7.1   The growing threat of tuberculosis in Europe

New drug-resistant strains of tuberculosis pose the disease's greatest threat to Europe since World War II. '[O]ur message to EU leaders is: Wake up. Do not delay. Do not let this problem get further out of hand', states Markuu Niskala, secretary-general of the International Federation of Red Cross and Red Crescent Societies. Tuberculosis, a respiratory illness spread by coughing and sneezing, is the world's deadliest curable infectious disease which WHO estimates killed 1.7 million people in 2004. The high levels of multi-drug resistant tuberculosis in Baltic countries, Eastern Europe and Central Asia, and the emergence of a new extremely drug-resistant strain known as XDR-TB have led international public health officials to create the 'Stop TB Partnership in Europe'. In Europe, 50 people get sick and eight people die of the disease every hour. The rate of incidence of TB in the Western European countries that comprised the EU before it enlarged in 2004 is 13 cases per 100,000 people every year. That number doubles in the ten newest EU members. It doubles again to 53 in Romania and Bulgaria and yet again to 98 in the former-Soviet republics farther East. But migration and EU expansion change things. For instance, TB cases in London have been increasing every year for almost 10 years and in some London areas with many immigrants, rates are as high as 100 per 100,000 (Bulman, 2006).

World Health Organization (WHO) Epidemic and Pandemic Alert and Responses (EPR) were anthrax, avian influenza, ebola haemorrhagic fever, E. Coli outbreaks, hepatitis, influenza, meningococcal disease, plague, severe acute respiratory syndrome (SARS), smallpox, tularaemia and yellow fever. Although many of these diseases are endemic to Third World countries, developed nations are at risk due to immigration, air travel and the global economy. As illustrated by Box 7.1 even diseases that we had thought we had conquered remain a concern of public health experts.

Until World War II health care was largely centred on public health measures. Hospitals were largely charity institutions for those who could not afford a personal physician, and few medical technologies or life-saving procedures were available. Since the leading causes of premature death were infectious diseases such as tuberculosis, typhoid and cholera, attention was focused on ameliorating the conditions under which they spread across populations. To contain the spread of a contagious illness, public health authorities rely on many strategies including isolation and quarantine (Centers for Disease Control, 2003). Isolation of people who have a specific illness separates them from healthy people and restricts their movement to stop the spread of that illness. It allows for the focused delivery of specialized health care to people who are ill and protects healthy people from getting sick. People in isolation may be cared for in their homes, in hospitals, or at designated health care facilities. In most cases, isolation is voluntary; however, governments have broad authority to compel isolation of sick people to protect the public.

Quarantine, in contrast, applies to people who have been exposed and may or may not be infected but are not yet ill. Separating exposed people and restricting their movements is intended to stop the spread of that illness and quarantine has proved most effective in protecting the public from disease. Although governments generally have wide authority to declare and enforce quarantine within their borders, often it is problematic politically because of its severe human rights ramifications when targeting specific groups and its potential economic impact. The political nature and dangers of quarantine are well illustrated by reactive calls to segregate AIDS victims in the mid 1980s before the mechanism of HIV transmission was understood.

Protecting the public health also entails a wide range of monitoring and inspection mechanisms designed to prevent the spread of disease through food and water supplies, environmental assaults and risky workplaces. As highlighted in Box 7.2, because of the transportation of food across long distances, often across national boundaries, the threat of contaminated food products can occur far from the origin of the

Box 7.2   E. coli threats to public health

Less than a week after the US Food and Drug Administration lifted its warning on spinach grown in California, a brand of lettuce grown there was recalled over concerns about E. coli contamination. Pathogenic Escherichia coli bacteria or E. coli can proliferate in uncooked produce, raw milk, un-pasteurized juice, contaminated water and meat. The lettuce scare comes amid other government warnings that shipments of beef could cause grave health risks including paralysis, respiratory failure and death. Epidemiologists also warned consumers to stay away from some bottled carrot juice after a woman was paralyzed and two people in Toronto died apparently due to botulism poisoning. Although most healthy adults recover within a week without long-term side effects, young children, senior citizens and people with compromised immune systems are vulnerable in extreme cases to kidney damage or death. The outbreaks have sparked demands to create a new federal agency in charge of food safety. 'This recent outbreak must be a wake-up call to get our food safety house in order, because right now it's in pure disarray', according the US Senator Schumer. 'We need to have one agency take charge to ensure the next outbreak isn't far worse.'

Source: Konrad (2006).

product or processing facility and affect wide populations. The case of Mad Cow Disease in the 1990s and the more recent possibility of the spread of bird flu through humans highlight the need for continued watchfulness. Moreover, threats of biological terrorism and the emergence of even more aggressive strains of viruses clearly require proactive attention with regard to public health and funding. Specific public health strategies, then, run the gamut from quarantining individuals suspected of having communicable diseases deemed to be threats to the public health, to regulating the workplace for health and safety, to reducing unemployment and economic disparities, to reducing greenhouse emissions and the depletion of the ozone layer.

Although public health is often viewed as a distant and esoteric field in which people are regarded as mere statistics, the spread of SARS in 2003 highlights the importance of public health and the fact that, because infectious diseases do not respect borders, international cooperation is essential. SARS is transmitted via droplets from infected individuals which, as a result of coughing, carry the virus to close contacts. Although the 2003 epidemic of SARS dissipated after several months, during that time it caused a great deal of concern and economic costs. SARS began in China but was quickly spread around the world by travellers. Researchers found evidence of the virus in the civet cat which is eaten as a delicacy by some Chinese (Ross, 2003), but most SARS victims contracted it after being in close contact with an infected person. Although the number of persons killed by SARS was small by disease standards, it demonstrated how vulnerable to the rapid spread of communicable diseases we are in an age of air travel and concentrated health care facilities where, ironically, many of the victims were infected.

China's early handling of the disease, in particular, was seen by many observers as reprehensible. When the first SARS cases appeared in southern China in March, Beijing denied it and tried to suppress the news, thus allowing the disease to be spread beyond its borders by unsuspecting victims. In May, 2003, Henen Province in central China punished 800 health workers for failing to perform their duties to protect the public health (Yahoo News, 2003). One of the key lessons resulting from China's delay in reporting the outbreak and the disease's rapid spread, according to Alfred Lam Ping Yan, deputy director of health in Hong Kong, is that 'We need stronger public health systems and more coordinated ways to handle emerging infections. It's not a problem of an individual city or country. This is a global problem' (cited in Manning, 2003).

As might have been predicted given its strong community-centred culture, Singapore instituted an aggressive home-quarantine system in response to SARS. Whereas health officials in Toronto, Canada, simply asked citizens suspected of SARS exposure to self-quarantine, Singapore took more extreme steps to enforce quarantine, including the use of video cameras and electronic bracelets to monitor the movements of those suspected of incubating the disease. It also passed a bill requiring quarantine-breakers to be fined up to $5,000 without being charged in court. The Health Minister also warned that the government might name and shame quarantine-breakers. Although criticized by some Westerners, Singapore's tough approach was supported by WHO (Greenlee, 2003). In the end, SARS was controlled (at least for the time being) but only after more rigorous public health policies were adopted. WHO credited old-fashioned quarantines with breaking the back of the outbreak (Wong, 2003).

Soon after the passing of the SARS story, in early 2004 the media began to report the spread of avian influenza across South East Asia. Although the 'bird flu' differs from SARS in that its transmission is from infected birds to humans, public health experts fear that it might mutate to enable it to spread from human to human. It is too early to predict whether it might be the next infectious pandemic, but it has raised serious concern among health experts. Another continuing public health threat is anthrax. Humans can become infected with anthrax by handling animal products or eating undercooked meat from infected animals, although its manufacture and use as a weapon for bioterrorism has generated the most anxiety. Anthrax raises the possibility of investigation of terrorist suspects alongside investigation of the outbreak of the infectious disease as well as a likelihood of public panic and the flooding of public health officials with reports of suspicious white powder (Howse, 2004).

The individual and public health

Generally, disease prevention activities focus on the health of communities or populations rather than individuals; but De Ferranti (1985: 67) makes a valuable distinction between patient-related and non-patient-related preventive care. Patient-related approaches are generally defined as primary care, take place in a clinical setting and include immunization, health education between patients and GPs, and cancer, cholesterol and prostate screening programmes. Non-patient-related preventive approaches include such disparate activities as improved sanitation and water systems, promotion of health and hygiene, provision of adequate housing, control of pests, food safety and the monitoring of disease patterns (epidemiology).

Although an integral part of health care, public health – including primary care services for well patients, health education, disease prevention, immunization programmes and health promotion activities – consistently receives only minor shares of health care budgets. For instance, in Australia the total public health expenditure comprises less than 2 per cent of the total recurrent health budget (Hilless and Healy, 2001). In the USA, it fares even worse with less than 1 per cent of the health care budget devoted to public health. Despite the AIDS epidemic and heightened costs of substance abuse, violence and teenage pregnancy, public health spending as a proportion of the health care budget fell by 25 per cent between 1981 and 1993. For example, while $3,007 was spent per person on medical care in the USA in 1992, only $34 was spent on prevention (US Public Health Service, 1995). Furthermore, in recent years US state governments struggling with large deficits have preferred to sacrifice the personnel and services of their public health agencies rather than cut medical care to individual patients (Sultz and Young, 1999: 353). In other countries, moves towards efficiency and cost containment have exacerbated the withdrawal of support from public health activities.

Despite a recent shift in many countries back towards a more public-health-oriented approach, there is evidence that even the most attentive countries would be well served to put a significantly larger proportion of their health care budgets into public health efforts (Blank, 1997: 87ff). Mounting evidence demonstrates that the most significant improvements in health come from public health measures, not curative medicine, even though the latter efforts are the most dramatic and therefore the most easily funded (Fries *et al.*, 1993). For instance, it is estimated that while 99 per cent of health spending in the USA goes to medical treatment, this spending prevents only 10 per cent of early deaths. In contrast, population wide, public health approaches have the potential to help prevent some 70 per cent of early deaths through measures targeted at the social, environmental and behavioural factors that contribute to those deaths (Sultz and Young, 1999: 352). The intention here is not to undermine medical care, but rather to restore a proper balance between patient-centred and population-centred health care.

Framing a public health policy

Despite general accord that it is more humane and cost-effective to avoid a condition of ill health in the first place than to have to treat it later, modern health systems continue to emphasize curative approaches – treating the ill rather than keeping people healthy. In part this is because the medical community has an intrinsic interest in curative medicine and, as illustrated in Chapter 5, it is a dominant force in all systems. In addition, prevention deals with statistical, future lives while curative medicine deals with identifiable patients who need help now. When a patient is facing imminent death, the individual, his or her family, and society as a whole are willing to pay heavily for any innovation that offers even a small promise of postponing death. In contrast, we are less likely to demand preventive innovations that will save many more lives in the distant future, because while health promotion/preventive programmes also ultimately help individuals, it is difficult to identify who they might be. Curative medicine, on the other hand, relates to specific patients in a 'direct, immediate and documentable way' (Baird, 1993: 347).

In spite of convincing evidence that the most significant advances in the health of populations have come from outside medicine, particularly through improved sanitation, housing, nutrition and education, many forces including the medical professions and the health care industry have strong economic interests in maintaining or increasing funding for treatment. In combination with patients (remember, virtually every one is a potential patient) and a public strongly influenced by optimistic media coverage, these groups have aggrandized curative medicine at the expense of public health. Human-interest stories and favourable media coverage naturally follow technological breakthroughs in treatment, not public health efforts. Television dramas exalt those who save individual lives such as trauma teams and surgeons, not public health nurses or epidemiologists. Together, these forces provide formidable obstacles against a reallocation of scarce resources from curative medicine to public health strategies. If the goal of the health care system is to improve the health of the population, however, public health programmes, particularly those that effect changes to healthier lifestyles, are critical.

Many observers contend that a reallocation towards disease prevention and health promotion would not only enhance health but also save money. For instance, for Cundiff and McCarthy it is 'essential that preventive medicine be emphasized if costs are to be contained while overall quality of care is improved' (1994: 11). Likewise, for Mueller, the 'three goals of health policy – cost containment, quality and access – can all be well served by policies related to promoting health' (1993: 152). Richmond and Fein (1995: 71) agree that efforts towards prevention and promotion have 'borne much fruit' and that we are on the threshold of being able to do even better. Even a modest increase, they argue, would yield significant benefits.

Other observers, however, are more sceptical of the savings from preventive strategies. In fact, many studies on programmes for hypertension screening, reducing high blood cholesterol by diet or drugs, and cancer screening tests demonstrate that the net costs per year of lives saved are exceedingly high. A review by the US Office of Technology Assessment reported that of all the preventive services it evaluated, only three were potentially cost saving (childhood immunizations, prenatal care for poor women and selected neonatal tests for congenital disorders). Similarly, screening for high blood pressure generally costs more than treating heart attack and stroke victims (Leutwyler, 1995: 124). The low per-unit cost of some population screening procedures obscures their true cost, which is the cost of achieving the desired outcome for the few who will benefit. Even though the cost of a single procedure might be low, if the condition is rare, a huge number of such procedures might be necessary to identify and prevent one case.

The fact that prevention does not always save money should not detract from the need to rebalance health care budgets towards disease prevention and health promotion. The investment in better health in itself is a worthwhile goal even when the immediate costs are high. The rationale behind spending more on public health, then, is the intrinsic value we place on the health it confers on the population, not its monetary savings. Commitment to public health is a measure of concern for the future. Any investment in preventive/promotion programmes shifts benefits from present patients to statistical persons who will enjoy healthier lives in the future because of these investments. Prevention can also compress morbidity by extending a person's healthy years and thereby reducing the individual and social burden of illness. By postponing the time at which we become victims of a chronic disease, prevention allows people to live healthier and more active lives, even though it might not necessarily extend their life span.

There is one other caution regarding preventive/promotion strategies that deal with behaviour-linked illnesses which today represent major contributors to ill health. Even though some of the linkages between lifestyle and health remain speculative, to be successful prevention programmes must change people's behaviour. Furthermore, even where evidence of danger is convincing, such as smoking, alcohol abuse or obesity, there is considerable debate over how effective preventive measures alone can be in changing such behaviour. Also, the dual motivation underlying health promotion – healthier individuals *and* saving future resources – often conflict with the goals and ethics of the medical establishment. To effect necessary behavioural changes requires investment of considerable resources for preventive programmes as well as for research to better understand the linkages between social and personal factors. Despite these limitations, health promotion is a decisive element of health care reform and extensive efforts must be made to educate, encourage and motivate essential behavioural changes.

Although modern medicine is by no means fruitless, Western cultures have overestimated its effectiveness and underestimated its limitations (Palmer and Short, 2000: 52). 'Reform of the medical delivery system and improvements in access to medical care alone will make possible only limited gains in health, the remaining gains require community-level interventions that public health provides' (US Public Health Service, 1995: 6). Later in the chapter, we raise the question of whether it might not be a more effectual health care strategy to actually reduce health care budgets and put the money saved into social and educational areas. The political trade-off is that while this is more likely to improve the health of the population, it does so at the expense of individual patients.

There are now strong motivations for Western countries to shift priority back towards primary care/prevention/health promotion activities. Ageing populations and the resulting changes in disease structures certainly favour movement towards chronic care facilities and less expensive nursing home care as opposed to more costly hospital care. These moves are politically challenging because they are often justified on the grounds of cost-effectiveness and because they are viewed as threats to the medical establishment. Furthermore, they give the appearance of sacrificing the lives of a vulnerable group of identifiable patients for a more nebulous aggregate population. Also, because of the unpredictable nature of disease, few members of the public are able to distance themselves from the plight of individual patients and their need for immediate and often costly support.

Public health responsibility and funding

While public health continues to be under-funded compared to curative medicine, all countries covered have extensive public health programmes, although as with other areas of health care, each country brings with it a particular orientation for organizing public health services. For instance, while Singapore has a highly centralized and vigorous public health policy, in most countries at least the non-medical aspects of public health are locally administered programmes. The major responsibility for public health falls on states, municipalities or other sub-national units, although in recent years some governments, such as Australia's, have tried to provide central coordination and increased funding to the localities in order to strengthen public health programmes.

Next to Singapore, New Zealand has the most centralized framework for public health, with responsibility vested in the Ministry of Health, but even here many public health activities are carried out through local programmes or the District Health Boards. The National Health Committee is an autonomous committee appointed by and reporting directly to the Minister of Health. Moreover, Section 14 of the Public Health and Disability Act of 2000 commissioned the Public Health Advisory Committee as a sub-committee of the National Health Committee (New Zealand Ministry of Health, 2003). Its role is to provide independent advice on public health issues, including factors influencing the health of people and communities, the promotion of public health and the monitoring of public health. The Committee's mandate includes giving advice on measures that would deliver the greatest benefit to the health of the population. It has also conducted extensive research on the social, cultural and economic determinants of health.

In Britain, central government, health authorities and GPs share responsibility for public health (Baggott, 2004). Within central government, public health falls under the remit of the Department of Health, although only since 1997 has there been a separate minister devoted to public health. The Primary Care Trusts are responsible for delivering public health and reducing health inequalities, both within the framework set by the Department of Health. It is indicative that the assessment of the performance of trusts includes indicators of health improvement. Primary Care Trusts have taken over responsibilities from the health authorities which marks the culmination of earlier policy developments. Although GPs have traditionally focused on the demands of individual patients, they have increasingly been integrated in public health initiatives. The 1990 contract included financial incentives for GPs to achieve immunization and disease screening targets. This was complemented by performance-related payments for health promotion and chronic disease programmes.

In contrast to Britain, responsibility for public health in Germany has always been more decentralized, reflecting its federal structure. As in Australia and the USA, public health has traditionally been the remit of the states and included activities ranging from monitoring of communicable diseases and environmental health to health education/promotion and physical examinations of school children (Busse and Riesberg, 2004). The range of services covered varies from state to state, as does the structure of the local public health offices responsible for the delivery of services. However, since the 1970s an increasing number of public health activities, particularly health promotion and disease prevention measures, have become part of social health insurance and responsibility has shifted from the public health offices to ambulatory care doctors. The provision of public health services has become more standardized as a result because doctors are legally obliged to deliver public services as part of the benefits catalogue of the health insurance. However, the focus of ambulatory care doctors on individual patients, together with the fact that many practise single-handedly, potentially undermines the public orientation of measures of health promotion and disease prevention. Significantly, immunization rates are relatively low by international standards (Busse and Riesberg, 2004: 93). The role of local public health offices is now mainly supervisory, focusing on controlling food safety and drinking water and compiling health statistics (Greiner and Schulenburg, 1997).

Sweden resembles Germany in that the responsibility for public health is decentralized and rests with county councils and municipalities as

service providers (Glenngard *et al.*, 2005), though preventive and population-based measures are more integrated into the delivery of primary
care services. Health centres employ school nurses to provide health
education to children, and doctors provide one-to-one health education
on diet and alcohol consumption, run well-women clinics and immunize
children. Complementing this at the national level is the National
Institute for Public Health, which is responsible for national programmes
of health promotion and disease prevention. As in other areas of health
care provision, the National Board of Health and Welfare is responsible
for supervising and monitoring what is happening at the level of county
councils and municipalities.

Compared to Sweden, the responsibility for public health is more
decentralized in the Netherlands. Following the 1989 Public Prevention
Act, some core responsibilities for public health services, including health
monitoring and dealing with contagious diseases, have been delegated to
local authorities. The activities of local public health agencies are only
loosely prescribed, but typically focus on the young, elderly and minority
groups and include health promotion and education, vaccination and
public health research projects (Maarse, 1997). The considerable autonomy at local level has resulted in substantial diversity in the delivery of
public health services (Okma, 2001). In response to concerns about
inequalities in access to public health services, a commission was established and in 1998 recommended that local authorities present an annual
review of their public health activities. It also recommended that the
Ministry of Health define a basic set of services which all local authorities must provide. Furthermore, the activities of the local authorities are
overseen by the Inspectorate of Health, which is responsible for monitoring the quality of health services and health protection measures
(Exter *et al.*, 2004).

As in the Netherlands and Sweden, a large share of the responsibility
for public health services in Japan falls on the local governments and to
a lesser extent the prefectures. Each of the municipalities has a division
responsible for health and the employment of public health nurses
(Nakahara, 1997: 123). In 2005, approximately 3,200 municipalities
were reduced to 2,300 in a policy aimed at strengthening the financial
basis of local governments and reducing administrative costs
(Bertelsmann Foundation, 2005c). In addition to basic environmental
services such as water supply and waste disposal, under the Community
Health Law of 1994 these primary local governments administer
community health programmes including maternal and child care,
immunization, nutrition guidance, health education, health screening
and health examinations for those over 40.

As decentralized as the organization of public health is in these countries, it is even more so in the federal systems of the USA and Australia.

As noted earlier, the USA is a federal system with responsibility for many functions falling on the sub-national units. Moreover, the US Constitution explicitly gives to the states the authority to protect the health of their residents. Each of the 50 states has its own public health agency or department. In addition, there are 3,066 counties that have public health responsibilities as well as tens of thousands of cities, towns and other municipalities, all of which have some public health activities, many quite extensive. At the federal level, the Centers for Disease Control and Prevention has primary responsibility for monitoring and policy making in disease prevention, but it relies on compliance from the state and local agencies to implement its guidelines. Despite many recent federal initiatives, an authoritative report (*The Future of Public Health in the 21st Century*) concluded that much yet needs to be done to provide 'a strong governmental public health infrastructure' that is needed in order to 'protect and promote health and well-being' of Americans (Institute of Medicine, 2002).

Public health in Australia too is a small, highly fragmented component of the health system that has been funded 'poorly and unsystematically' (Lin and Robinson, 2005). This is not surprising since like the USA and Germany, Australia is a federal system in which the states have primary responsibility for public health and the delivery of population health services (Box 7.3). In recent years, however, there have been many disparate efforts to increase coordination nationally. The Commonwealth Population Health Division has responsibility to keep Australians healthy

Box 7.3 Decentralized public health in Australia

Without a specific head of power, the Commonwealth has limited ability to legislate with respect to public health. As a result, there are no Commonwealth emergency health powers except quarantine powers that are currently restricted to isolation at the border of the country of people, plants, and animals to prevent the spread of disease. States and Territories have an array of emergency powers in their existing public health legislation including powers to support disease surveillance, contact tracing and orders to restrict movement of individuals. They also have other intrusive powers to recall food, search premises, seize property, and close buildings. Currently, in a public health emergency caused by the spread of an emerging infectious disease, Australia would need to rely on a patchwork of legislative measures. If an outbreak occurred on a border, or in some area where jurisdiction may be in doubt there could be confusion over jurisdiction since State and Territory public health acts do not adequately provide for inter-jurisdictional communication and cooperation.

Source: Howse (2004).

by helping them avoid illness and injury (Australia Department of Health and Ageing, 2002). Furthermore, the National Public Health Partnership was created between the Commonwealth and states in 1996 to strengthen collaboration and improve the health of Australians through a national approach to population health. The Commonwealth invests in population health activity through a combination of Public Health Outcome Funding Agreements and direct grants to states/territories and community organizations, as well as through supporting population health activity undertaken by GPs and their divisions. Moreover, the Communicable Diseases Network of Australia and New Zealand coordinates the surveillance of communicable disease and responds to significant outbreaks. Despite these varied activities, however, Commonwealth support for public health programmes accounts for only about one-third of public health expenditure with the bulk coming from state and local governments.

Health promotion

The health promotion efforts have taken different intensity, form and focus and to some extent their approaches and commitment reflects the general health goals predominant in each country. In countries such as Germany, New Zealand and Sweden, where the prevailing culture is more communitarian and egalitarian, health promotion strategies have focused on social factors. In contrast, more individualistic countries such as Singapore and the USA tend to focus on individual factors. Another variation is the extent to which health promotion is directed towards the population at large or at specific groups such as smokers, pregnant women or children. Furthermore, some countries have tended to target promotion policies at specific diseases or issues while others have taken more comprehensive approaches. In all cases, the health promotion strategies reflect the organizational variation in public health activities in general, with some countries displaying rigorous national programmes and others largely delegating it to various sub-units.

Although health promotion is but one aspect of public health, it has received more attention recently as the links between individual behaviour and health have been elucidated. Even those countries that lack well-established health promotion policies realize that promoting healthy lifestyles is not only an effective way of improving the health of their populations, but also a crucial strategy for reining in escalating health care costs, in other words, a key factor in cost containment. Not surprisingly, then, countries across the full range of health systems have instituted various initiatives for health promotion and disease prevention. A sample of highlights and orientations of these disparate programmes is presented here.

In Germany, the fragmented structure of public health and its increasing medicalization over past decades have tended to mitigate against a national strategy for health promotion. Public health has traditionally been the remit of the states, although an increasing range of public health responsibilities have been integrated into the services offered by ambulatory-care doctors (Busse and Riesberg, 2004). At federal level, responsibility for health promotion falls under the Ministry of Health, although the Federal Centre for Health Education is responsible for initiating and coordinating national health promotion campaigns. Significantly, however, the work of the Federal Centre has focused on a number of selected campaigns. Long-term campaigns include AIDS, drugs and sex education, whereas recent campaigns have been concerned with encouraging organ and blood donation.

As in other European countries, Dutch patients have access to a wide range of health services and the availability of publicly mandated insurance schemes makes this access practically universal. This is complemented by programmes for vaccinations, screening for cancers and pre- and post-natal screening, many of which have expanded over recent years. Recent policy initiatives have focused more specifically on promoting healthy lifestyles, reducing alcohol and tobacco consumption and targeting new diseases such as HIV/AIDS, as well as health problems related to socio-economic status (Okma, 2001). A recent National Contract for Public Health (2001) also stresses the need for cooperation among local and national levels as well as different sectors of health care provision.

By international comparison, people in Sweden enjoy good health and life expectancy is one of the highest. However, there have been concerns about health inequalities among certain social groups and, in 1991, a national strategy for public health was published (Whitehead, 1998). The strategy emphasized the importance of cooperation among different levels and coincided with the creation of the National Institute of Public Health, which is responsible for national programmes. In 2000, this was complemented by the publication of national goals in public health, which reiterated the need to reduce health gaps among different social groups (Ministry of Health and Social Affairs, 2001). These developments culminated in a government bill on public health objectives in 2003 that commits to ensuring social conditions that ensure good health for the entire population (Glenngård *et al.*, 2005).

Britain, too, has seen many initiatives in health promotion, but the White Paper, *The Health of the Nation*, in 1992 provided the first national strategy for England (Baggott, 2004). The White Paper identified priorities for health promotion and also set specific targets in relation to heart disease, strokes, cancers, mental illness, sexual health and accidents. The underlying view was that individual behaviour is the key factor responsible for poor health. This strong individualist orientation is not surprising considering the New Right orientation of the government at the time. The emphasis has changed somewhat since the Labour government came into power in 1997. The new strategy, encapsulated in the 1999 White Paper, *Saving Lives: Our Healthier Nation*, combines health promotion focused on the individual with an acknowledgement that social factors such as poverty also cause poor health. There is now a greater focus on improving the health of disadvantaged people and narrowing health gaps using health improvement programmes and designated health action zones. A central feature of these initiatives is that they rely on collaboration with a wide range of actors, from central government and health authorities to local government and voluntary organizations, and even private businesses.

As a prime example of an egalitarian country, it is not surprising that New Zealand has taken a broad health promotion approach that emphasizes social factors. In 2002, the New Zealand Ministry of Health launched *Achieving Health for All People*. The purpose of this document is to provide a framework for a broad health promotion action under the New Zealand Health Strategy which emphasizes the importance of taking a population health approach to the improvement of health and the reduction of inequalities. A key theme of this initiative is that 'public health action is not the responsibility of public health services alone, or even of health services as a whole. It is about the organised efforts of society' (New Zealand Ministry of Health, 2003). The Health Promotion Forum is a national umbrella organization representing over 200 groups nationwide that provides national leadership and support for good health promotion practice. The Forum provides advocacy, training and skills development to both member organizations and the health promotion workforce at large and facilitates networking, informed debate and contributions to policy development at regional, national and international levels.

Likewise, Japan launched its broadly based First National Movement for Health Promotion in 1978 and the second wave in 1988. A major measure taken in the first movement was the creation of Municipal Health Centres (MHCs) in every municipality to coordinate health promotional activities. The second wave was dubbed 'Active 80 Health Plan' because its purpose was to promote a prolonged life span of 80 years. After more than 20 years since its inception, these health promotional activities are beginning to bear fruit as reflected in the third wave of the national health promotion movement, 'Healthy Japan 21'. The period covered is between the years 2000 and 2010 with a defined set of goals in health promotion. In this wave, emphasis is placed in the prolongation of the 'healthy life span' which means a life span without disability. This emphasis reflects the problem of many elderly with disability in the face of the world's longest life span. In a research project conducted by the Tokyo Citizens' Council for Health Promotion, the implementation of Healthy Town initiatives stressed the importance to citizens of a health-conducive physical living environment; social networks and mutual help; and societal discipline/rules and good access to services (Takano and Nakamura, 2004).

Although the delivery of most health promotion activities in the USA is at the sub-national levels, the US Office of Public Health and Science serves as the Secretary's primary advisor on matters involving the nation's public health and oversees the Public Health Service (PHS). In turn, the Office of Disease Prevention and Health Promotion is mandated to provide national leadership for disease prevention and health promotion through the 'formulation of national health goals and objectives; the coordination of the Department of Health and Human Services activities in disease prevention, health promotion, preventive health services, and health information and education with respect to the appropriate use of health care; and the stimulation of public and private programs and strategies to enhance the health of the Nation'.

Like the UK, the USA has a very individualist orientation in its health promotion initiatives. As a result, much health promotion is oriented primarily through screening and prescription of drugs to reduce cholesterol and high blood pressure. In 2002, the PHS released *Healthy People 2010: A Systematic Approach to Health Improvement,* a set of health objectives for the nation to achieve over the first decade of the 21st century. It is to be used by states, communities and professional organizations to help them develop programmes to improve health. The report emphasizes the central role of the individual and posits that both the individual and the community need to do their parts to increase life expectancy and improve quality of life. 'Healthy People 2010 seeks to increase life expectancy and quality of life over the next 10 years by helping individuals gain the knowledge, motivation, and opportunities they need to make informed decisions about their health. At the same time, Healthy People 2010 encourages local and State leaders to develop community wide and state wide efforts that promote healthy behaviors, create healthy environments, and increase access to high-quality health care'. (p. 5)

Similarly, this heavy emphasis on individual responsibility in health care is reflected in the ambitious health promotion activities of Singapore. In 1992, Prime Minister Goh Chok Tong launched the National Healthy Lifestyle Programme designed to educate Singaporeans about the importance of leading a healthy lifestyle and to encourage them to participate in regular exercise, eat healthily, avoid smoking and manage stress. The Programme takes an integrated approach that includes creating a supportive social and physical environment to encourage individuals to practise healthy behaviour. Between its inception in 1992 and 2001, the percentage of Singaporeans aged 18 to 69 years who exercised regularly increased from 17 to 20 per cent and those smoking dropped from 18 to 14 per cent (Singapore Ministry of Health, 2002c). However, because the diet of Singaporeans has not improved and is still linked to high blood cholesterol and high blood pressure, the 2002 National Healthy Lifestyle Campaign focused on the promotion of healthier food choices (Singapore Ministry of Health, 2002b).

Health promotion, then, is an arena of increasing attention by many governments. This trend would represent going full circle back to the roots of health care if not for the fact that the resources being put into health promotion remain but a small fraction of what is put into curative, acute care. Also, because health is so tied to lifestyle choice, the success or failure of these health promotion initiatives is heavily dependent on the capacity to alter individual behaviour. Increasingly, public health will come up against the notion of the right to live one's preferred life free from government constraint. This tension is starkly illustrated in policies aimed to stem obesity, smoking and alcohol abuse.

Obesity and health

According to the World Health Organization, obesity is increasing at an alarming rate throughout the world (2004). Similarly, the 2006 International Congress on Obesity warned that an 'obesity pandemic threatens to overwhelm health systems around the globe . . . It is as big a threat as global warming and bird flu'. It is estimated that worldwide there are over 1 billion adults who are overweight and 300 million who are obese. Obesity is defined as a condition of excess body fat and is associated with a large number of debilitating and life-threatening disorders (generally the term overweight applies to those persons with a Body Mass Index (BMI) between 25.0 and 29.9 and obese to those with a BMI 30 or above). The prevalence of obesity is increasing in most of the world, affecting men, women and children.

In 2006, the European Commission warned that obesity is now 'an urgent public health issue' that requires coordinated action by the EU and member states. It reported that up to 27 per cent of European men and 38 per cent of women are now considered obese and that obesity-related illnesses account for as much as 7 per cent of total health care costs in the EU (Haddon, 2006). In the USA the situation is even grimmer. Lang and Rayner (2005) suggest that the US is widely accepted as the benchmark for the extent of obesity. A 2000 National Health and Nutrition Examination Survey estimated that 65 per cent of adults are either overweight or obese, up from 47 per cent in 1980 and 56 per cent in 1994. Moreover, based on current trends, it is predicted that by the

---

Box 7.4   Britain is the fattest country in Europe

Britain's status as the fat man of Europe has been confirmed by a government report showing that many citizens are losing the battle of the bulge and slipping into obesity. The Health Profile of England report quoted figures from the OECD showing that adult obesity rates in Britain were the highest in Europe at 24 percent. The Department of Health warned that 13 million people in England would be obese by 2010 if nothing was done to tackle the problem. Prime Minister Tony Blair told BBC television Tuesday that people had to take some personal responsibility for their health. 'We can't really afford a decent healthcare system going forward unless healthcare is not just about treating you when you are sick but also about looking after your fitness, your healthcare, and that requires people to take some personal responsibility for what they do', he said.

Source: Haddon (2006).

---

year 2025 levels of obesity could be as high as 45 to 50 per cent in the USA and between 30 to 40 per cent in Australia, the UK and other EU countries (Haddon, 2006).

Of major concern is the skyrocketing rate of obesity among young children and adolescents. Of the 14 million overweight children in Europe, three million are considered obese. This reflects significant rises in obsesity over the last decades (Lang and Rayner, 2005: 304). In the USA the percentage of overweight children aged 5 to 14 years has doubled in the last 30 years, from 15 to 32 per cent. It was estimated in 2000 that six million American children were obese enough to endanger their health and this number is still rising. According to Nancy Krebs 'An obese adolescent has a greater than 75% chance of becoming an obese adult' (as quoted in McConahy, 2002). Overweight children five to ten years of age are 9.7 times more likely to have two risk factors for type 2 diabetes and 43.5 times more likely to have three risk factors. As with adults, all diseases are exacerbated in children who are obese.

The tracking of obesity from childhood to adulthood is well substantiated and findings suggest that childhood obesity is likely to make them much more prone to chronic diseases and thus have a detrimental impact on their health in adulthood. It has been suggested that the children of this generation may be the first to die before their parents because of health problems related to weight that will shave years off their lives. According to health expert Jay Olshansky, 'within the next 50 years, life expectancy at birth will decline, and it will be the direct result of the obesity epidemic that will creep through all ages like a human tsunami. ... There has been a dramatic increase in obesity among the younger generation and it is a storm that is approaching' (Reuters, 2005).

Similarly, Brian McCrindle, a childhood obesity expert, warns the resulting 'wave of heart disease and stroke could totally swamp the public health care system'. Lawmakers had to take a broader view of this 'looming problem' and consider actions such as banning trans fats and direct advertising of junk food towards children (quoted in 'Reuters, 2005).

Recent studies demonstrate that the social environment and individual behaviour are key factors in the obesity epidemic (for a discussion of different factors, see Lang and Rayner, 2005). For the past 30 years changes in Western societies, and more recently Japan and Singapore, have encouraged high-calorie, fast food diets. Reinforcing this shift are trends towards more sedentary jobs; the replacement of physical activity with television, the Internet and video games as primary recreation activities for many families; and schools cutting back on physical education programmes. As a result, activity levels of both children and adults have decreased markedly.

Obesity has many negative health and social ramifications. Mortality and morbidity rates are higher among overweight and obese individuals than average-weight people. A person who is 40 per cent overweight is twice as likely to die prematurely as a person of average weight. Obesity is a known risk factor for heart disease, stroke, hypertension, sleep apnea, osteoarthritis and some forms of cancer (Thorpe *et al.*, 2004a). An estimated 70 per cent of diabetes risk is attributed to excess weight, and obesity has been identified as a major independent risk factor for coronary heart disease (American Obesity Association, 1997). In addition to the physical health consequences, obesity creates a social burden and been described as the 'last remaining socially acceptable form of prejudice' (Stunkard and Sobal, 1995: 417). This prejudice exists not only among the general public but also among many health care professionals, attitudes that can seriously impede the treatment of overweight and obese patients.

Obesity also has negative economic consequences for societies and individuals. Regardless of how one calculates these costs, obesity and the conditions related to it comprise an increasing share of health care expenditures (Reidpath *et al.*, 2002). In addition to its direct costs there are indirect costs for individuals including ill health and reduced quality of life and for society though loss of productivity due to sick leave and premature pensions.

Policies and strategies to combat obesity

Given the variations found in terms of the priority they place on health promotion, we expect similar disparities across countries in their response to obesity. As noted above, although obesity is a global problem that transcends national boundaries its prevalence varies considerably country by country. This section examines a sampling of policy strategies and programmes. Because of the magnitude of its problem, the USA has taken the lead, although Australia and New Zealand offer good examples of the range of strategies available (including food policy and collective/individualized public health strategies). Singapore offers a rather radical example of compulsion that is unlikely to work in other countries while Japan has taken a more measured approach to the emerging problem. Again, the importance of the cultural context of health policy is readily apparent in these different responses.

Although the Australian government took notice in 1995 by convening the National Health and Medical Research Council on the Prevention of Obesity, by 2000, 17 per cent of men and 20 per cent of women were classified as obese, with a further 49 per cent of men and 27 per cent of women overweight, ranking it second in the world behind the USA (Nathan *et al.*, 2005). In response, the National Obesity Taskforce was established to develop a national approach to address the problem and identify initiatives required to prevent obesity (Lin and Robinson, 2005). By 2005, Australia improved its ranking for obesity to sixth but when those figures are combined with the number of people considered to be overweight, Australia still ranks fourth behind the USA, Mexico and the UK. The government aims to halve the number of overweight children by 2015 and announced an extension to the $15 million Healthy Schools Program, which provides grants for initiatives such as improving school menus. The federal government also launched a $6 million national physical activity campaign in 2006 aimed at children and adolescents.

Singapore has been one of the most proactive, and some might say draconian, countries with a strong commitment to reduce the prevalence of overweightness and obesity (see Box 7.5). Since it introduced the 'Fit and Trim' programme in schools, levels of obesity among students have dropped and fitness improved. The government also has initiatives to mobilize its adult population, of which about 6 per cent are obese, to adopt healthier lifestyles. Singapore holds a month-long fitness campaign each September aimed at getting the entire population to eat better and stay active. The theme for the 2004 campaign was 'Fighting Obesity' and it was launched with a mass aerobic workout class of 12,000 people. Despite these efforts, a continuing trend towards overweight citizens is attributed to a shift in diet towards Western fast foods. In response to studies that show that many Asians have more fat as a proportion of total body weight than Caucasians of the same age, sex and BMI, and in response to the recommendations of the WHO, the Health Promotion Board lowered the BMI score for obesity to compensate for these differences.

Although the Japanese are far from being as overweight as Americans (24 per cent as compared to 65 per cent), there is concern over changes in eating patterns. Men in all age groups have grown heavier in the past two

Box 7.5   Fighting obesity in Singapore

The fight against obesity starts young in Singapore. Overweight children are separated from their classmates and ordered to exercise more until they lose weight. For example, as a member of a Singapore primary school's 'Health Club' where membership is compulsory for overweight kids, Siow does special exercises on top of the regular physical education curriculum. Teachers monitor her height and weight every month. While the school does not put restrictions on what she can eat, teachers meet her parents regularly to recommend healthier ways to prepare their daughter's meals at home. More than a decade ago, Singapore decided that the best way to fight the war on expanding waistlines, and ballooning health care costs, was to begin with the young. The government created a school-based intervention program that includes rigorous exercise for overweight children and recommendations on food sold in canteens. The health clubs have reduced the proportion of overweight students from 14 percent in 1992 to 10 percent in 2003, but many, like Siow, have not lost weight. If she fails to do so, she is doomed to stay in the program until she completes her pre-university schooling.

Source: Associated Press (2006).

decades, with the highest rate of obesity (34 per cent in 2003) among men in their 40s. The government has set aside about $600,000 in the 2006–2007 Budget to combat childhood obesity (Inagaki, 2006). Health Japan 21 is a ten-year national plan for health promotion and disease prevention established by the Ministry of Health, Labour and Welfare. The plan covers nine focus areas, including nutrition and physical activity, which set goals for decreasing obesity in adults and school children. Early detection of overweight students and education on healthy body weight take place in most primary and secondary schools in Japan (Matsushita *et al.*, 2004).

More than half of New Zealand adults are now obese (17 per cent) or overweight (35 per cent). Obesity in New Zealand increased by 55 per cent between 1989 and 1997 and is predicted to increase to 29 per cent of all adults by 2011 if no changes are instituted. In response, the New Zealand Health Strategy targeted the reduction of the rate of obesity as one of the 13 priority areas for population health. District Health Boards (DHBs) are required to report annually on progress towards each of these priority areas. In 2001 a toolkit was promulgated to provide guidance to DHBs on the importance of obesity as a public health issue and the most effective ways to reduce it in their populations. It notes that any effort to reduce the incidence of obesity or prevent any further increases must include key partners outside the health sector including non-government organizations such as Agencies for Nutrition Action, Heart Foundation, New Zealand Nutrition Foundation, and Diabetes New Zealand; government agencies such as Child, Youth and Family Services, the Recreation and Sport Agency, and the ministries of Youth Affairs and Education; the media; local councils; Pacific health initiatives and church groups; and the food and weight-loss industries.

As part of a four-year bid to reduce its escalating obesity levels, in 2006 New Zealand banned fatty, sugary foods and drinks from school shops (*Associated Press*, 2006). Prime Minister Helen Clark said at the launch of the NZ$67 million anti-obesity campaign that over 30 per cent of children are either overweight or obese and that improving nutrition and encouraging a more active lifestyle is the first step in fighting this epidemic. Imminent steps include introducing healthy food, drink and exercise policies into all government agencies. A labelling system for food and drinks will be implemented ahead of the 2007 school year, and although the government will not regulate to bring about change, school boards are required to develop policies that promote and achieve healthy nutrition and reduce consumption of unhealthy foods and drinks.

Obesity has become an acrimonious political issue in the USA as well (see US Department of Health and Human Services, 2001, 2005). In 2001, the US Surgeon General's Call to Action emphasized the need to create supportive environments which provide accessible and affordable healthy food choices and convenient opportunities for regular physical activity (US Department of Health and Human Services, 2001). In May 2002, a $4.1 million USDA Team Nutrition programme began to teach children healthy eating habits (Kersh and Morone, 2002) and in June of that year the White House implemented the Health and Fitness Initiative to highlight physical activity (US Department of Health and Human Services, 2004). Unlike other countries, however, policies in the individualistic USA have been aimed more at ensuring that obese patients are not discriminated against by medical professionals and less at encouraging behavioural changes. In fact, there has been considerable emphasis on making allowances for obese patients so as not to make them feel inferior (see Box 7.6). Medicare redefined obesity as a medical problem and approved payment for a wide array of surgical weight-loss procedures for obese elderly patients (MSNBC, 2006). As a result, the number of *bariatric* surgeries performed quadrupled since 2000 and are predicted to burgeon, according to the American Society for Bariatric Surgery (2006). Obesity-related hip and knee replacements are predicted to grow by 600 per cent in the coming decade. Furthermore, the US Social Security Administration now allows obesity to qualify for disability income (American Obesity Association, 2006), and, as of 2002, the Internal Revenue Service acknowledged the medical importance of treating

Box 7.6   Preparing for large patients

As Americans keep getting bigger, hospitals are revamping themselves to accommodate an influx of obese patients. When these patients check into a hospital, they are increasingly likely to find themselves in a room with a wider doorway than the 42-inch standard, a bed that holds up to 1,000 pounds and a ceiling lift system to move them to the bathroom. Toilets in such a room are extra-sturdy and mounted to the floor instead of a wall. The obese are also more likely to suffer from chronic medical ailments like diabetes and severe joint problems, bringing them into the hospital. As a result, more hospitals are making capital investments to set up separate wings and whole floors for obese patients to keep up with demand.

Source: Reuters (2006).

obesity, making physician-prescribed weight-loss programmes deductible medical expenses (Shortt, 2004).

Although the national level remains the primary focus of public health policies on obesity, there are increasingly initiatives at the international level. In the context of Europe, the Regional Office of the World Health Organization has been particularly active since the late 1990s. Initial consultations among member states culminated in a commitment in 2000 to create Nutrition Action Plans (Lang and Rayner, 2005). This has been followed up by other initiatives, most recently the European Charter on Counteracting Obesity (WHO, Regional Office for Europe, 2006). In contrast, the EU has remained more passive, not least reflecting the marginal position of health policy in relation to other policy issues. Any policy initiative on obesity also has to compete with other, more high public health issues such as food safety.

Box 7.7   Obese people denied some surgical procedures in a bid to cut costs in the NHS

Three Suffolk primary care trusts have ruled patients with a body mass index (BMI) of over 30 will not get operations like hip and knee replacements. A person of average weight would have a BMI of between 18.5 and 24.9. Dr Brian Keeble, a director of Ipswich PCT, said: 'We cannot pretend that this work wasn't stimulated by pressing financial problems.' Under new guidelines surgery will not be performed unless 'the patient has a body mass index below 30 and conservative means have failed to alleviate the patient's pain and disability'.

Source: BBC News (2005).

Tobacco and alcohol policy

Cumulatively, tobacco, alcohol and illicit drugs 'prematurely kill about 7 million people world wide each year and the number is rising' (Reuters, 2003). Therefore, most countries have instituted public health measures designed to reduce the incidence of smoking. These include raising the price of tobacco products through taxes, restricting where people are allowed to smoke, banning certain types of advertising, requiring health warnings on tobacco products, and enforcing the minimum purchasing age (for specific country regulations, see www5.who.int/tobacco/). Some countries, like Singapore, have very restrictive and severe policies (see Box 7.8).

Although systematic comparative estimates on the costs of smoking and alcohol abuse are unavailable, smoking causes a significant number of deaths, and smokers generally consume more health care resources than non-smokers. In the USA, for example, it is estimated that 19 per cent of all premature deaths (about 400,000 annually) are caused by tobacco use (McGinnis and Foege, 1993). Given that the USA has mid-range levels of smoking (see Table 7.1), death rates from smoking in other countries are assumed to be similar, if not higher.

Box 7.8   Graphic health warning on cigarette packets

Singapore's latest anti-smoking strategy consists of showing the gruesome effects of smoking on cigarette packs. As part of the Smoking Regulations 2003 cigarette packets sold in Singapore must carry graphic images of the harmful effects of smoking such as bleeding brains, toothless gums, and blackened lungs aimed at making smokers face up to the serious health effects of smoking. One picture shows a hospitalized man on life support with the slogan 'smoking can cause a slow painful death', while another depicts a mother playing with two children while the father puffs away behind them, meant to warn of the dangers of second-hand smoke. Singapore also has comprehensive tobacco control policies and programmes. Smoking is prohibited in most areas such as public transportation, elevators, government offices, cinemas, air-conditioned restaurants, and other areas where No Smoking signs are displayed. Moreover, a national smoking control campaign with extensive mass media support is held annually to raise awareness on the harmful effects of smoking and encourage smokers to quit smoking. Innovative publicity events and programmes are organised to elicit maximum media coverage. Since the launch of the National Smoking Control Programme in 1986, the smoking prevalence in Singapore has declined from 20 to 14 percent, one of the lowest in the world.

Source: Bertelsmann Foundation (2004d).

Table 7.1   *Smoking rates, men and women (%), ranked by women, 2004*

	% women who smoke	% men who smoke
Netherlands	26.0	34.0
UK	23.0	26.0
Germany	19.1	29.8
France	19.0	28.0
Italy	17.6	31.4
Sweden	17.5	15.0
Australia	16.5	18.9
USA	15.1	19.0
Japan	13.2	46.9
Singapore	3.1	26.9

Sources: Data from OECD (2006) and Singapore Ministry of Health (2006).

Table 7.1 illustrates that smoking rates vary significantly across countries, especially among women. In Singapore, high prices and strict regulations have cut overall smoking rates, but obviously the extremely low rate for women is cultural since male smoking is near the average. Similarly, Japan's low rates for women are cultural because, comparatively speaking, Japan has relatively relaxed regulations and by far the highest rate of male smoking. Evidence suggests, however, that laws can make a difference and that public health and education programmes reduce smoking rates. Data from ten European countries where rigorous tobacco control policies have been implemented, including France, Italy, Sweden and the UK, show a decrease in the number of tobacco-related deaths in recent years (WHO, 2003a). The most effective control measures include high prices on tobacco products, total bans on advertising, support for cessation treatment, and policies requiring the creation of smoke-free environments.

According to WHO (2003), most countries could strengthen anti-tobacco controls even more. For example, less than 25 per cent of countries in the European Region earmark any tobacco tax revenues for control measures and health promotion, and only five countries allocate more than 1 per cent. However, there are new European Union directives and a Framework Convention on Tobacco Control that aims to counter the industry's ability to undermine national controls (WHO, 2003a).

The European report on tobacco control policy shows that, while smoking rates stabilized at 30 per cent for the region as a whole (38 per cent for men and 23 per cent for women) over the last five years, increases in population meant that the number of smokers rose (WHO, 2003a). Most countries show a gap in smoking rates between the lowest and highest socio-economic groups. In some countries, the poorest smoke three times as much as the richest. This report further found that smoking rates among young people across Europe are converging, eliminating former differences according to gender and geography, and that although several countries reported reductions in adult smoking, none showed significant reductions in smoking by young people. In addition, the gender gap has become less significant among teenagers: in 12 countries girls smoked as much as, or more than, boys (WHO, 2003a).

Like smoking, alcohol causes severe health problems, and there is 'sufficient evidence to indicate that alcohol is a significant threat to world health' (WHO, 2001). In fact, alcohol contributes far more years of life lost to death or disability than tobacco and illegal drugs combined (WHO, 2001). To date, most countries have not been as rigorous in their attempts to reduce alcohol consumption as they have tobacco, but instead have focused on reducing drinking and driving and other alcohol-related behaviour. Table 7.2 illustrates the range of consumption. Not surprisingly, wine-producing countries in Europe have traditionally had the highest rates, but since 1995 the trend indicates that the UK (see Box 7.9) is closing the gap (Institute of Alcohol Studies, 2002). Sweden, due to high prices, and Singapore, due to high prices, strict regulations and its emphasis on personal responsibility for health, display the lowest consumption rates.

Table 7.2 *Alcohol consumption, per capita in litres (16 and over)*

Country	1995	2000	2003
France	15.3	14.2	14.0
Germany	11.1	10.5	10.2
Italy	10.4	9.0	8.0
Netherlands	9.6	9.8	9.8
Australia	9.6	9.8	9.8
UK	9.4	10.7	11.2
New Zealand	9.4	8.9	8.9
USA	8.1	8.3	8.4
Japan	7.9	7.6	7.6
Sweden	6.2	6.2	7.0
Singapore	1.6	1.5	n/a

n/a = not available

Source: Data from OECD (2006).

Box 7.9   Alcohol Deaths Soar in Britain

The number of middle-aged men drinking themselves to death in Britain has more than doubled since 1991. Deaths among women in the same age group also nearly doubled, fuelling concerns over binge-drinking and rising alcohol consumption in Britain. Campaigners said the link between people drinking more and the rise in alcohol-related deaths was established more than 50 years ago. The number of alcohol-related deaths in 2005 stood at 8,386, compared to 4,144 in 1991. Death rates among middle-aged men more than doubled to 30 per 100,000 of the population, with the highest rate of deaths among men and women in the 55 to 74 age bracket. The Liberal Democrat party said the government had 'failed miserably' to deal with alcohol abuse. Last year's changes in the law to allow pubs to open longer were criticized as an invitation for people to drink more. The government rejected the claims, saying the changes would encourage sensible drinking.

Source: Griffiths (2006).

The most common form of alcohol regulation is the setting of a minimum age for purchase or consumption. Studies have found that such restrictions are effective in reducing motor vehicle crash fatalities even with relatively low levels of enforcement (Wagenaar and Wolfson, 1995). At present, Australia, the Netherlands and the UK have set the legal drinking age at 18; Japan, New Zealand and Sweden at 20; the US states generally at 21; and France, Italy and Germany at 16 for beer and wine and 18 for distilled spirits (WHO, 2002). Key to the effectiveness of such preventive efforts is enforcement, which varies considerably both across and within countries.

Other alcohol control policies include prohibition, monopolies over production and/or sale, licensing, warning labels, restrictions on advertising and promotion, education and taxation. Central to any comprehensive health strategy for alcohol is the provision of adequate treatment facilities for alcohol dependence, but according to WHO, very few countries have 'systematically evaluated various forms of treatment and the resources allocated for treatment are often very scarce, if existent. Globally, access to affordable and effective treatment is still largely inadequate' (2001: 13). No attempt is made here to summarize the specific control policies, but it is important to reiterate that across our countries, with the possible exception of Singapore, public health measures towards alcohol remain ambiguous and inadequately funded, thus undermining their effectiveness to combat the types of health problems it raises.

So far this chapter has examined the structures and funding sources of public health and health promotion strategies and activities, particularly those surrounding obesity and tobacco and alcohol use. It is evident that many of these efforts lead us far from health care as medicine into the realm of health education and social welfare policy. The next two sections extend these linkages even further afield into housing and environmental policy areas, among others. Still other dimensions of public health that we are unable to discuss here due to space limitations are occupational health, food safety, crime/violence, drug abuse and mental illness. In combination, they raise major health concerns overlooked by the prevailing medical model.

Homelessness and inadequate housing

One health factor virtually ignored by the medical model, but which takes on meaning in the more inclusive social model, is housing. Lack of housing obviously puts people, particularly children, at serious health risk. While homeless people suffer from the same acute and chronic illnesses as those in the general population, they do so at much higher rates. 'Because the homeless have little or no access to adequate bathing and hygienic facilities, survive on the streets or in unsafe and generally unsanitary shelters, smoke and drink to excess, and suffer from inadequate diets, their physical health is compromised' (Institute of Medicine, 1993: 210). As a result upper respiratory tract infections, trauma and skin ailments are commonplace. High levels of alcohol abuse, drug abuse and mental illness complicate the picture.

Although the health impact of a lack of housing is most severe, even inadequate housing can lead to poor health. Poor housing is linked to a wide array of physical and mental health problems as described in Box 7.10. Substandard housing is related to house fires and increased accidents. Furthermore, damp and cold living conditions are associated with respiratory ailments, while improperly ventilated housing is linked to heat-related health problems. In combination with overall poverty, unemployment, poor education, and violence and crime, inadequate housing remains a health hazard for many citizens. These factors share in common their isolation from the medical model. Although medical care is beneficial for many individuals affected by these health-threatening factors, 'medical care cannot compensate for economic deprivation, social disorganization, personal alienation, and low levels of education and social integration' (Mechanic, 1994: 3). In the end, solutions to these problems lie fully outside the medical community. Unfortunately, as argued by Kassler (1994: 166), health care reformers have focused so much on medical care that they have ignored those factors that ultimately make the biggest difference in people's health.

Box 7.10   Homelessness, poor housing and health in Britain

The poor health of homeless people is made worse by inadequate access to health services, as two reports on the health of 'rough sleepers' in the UK suggest. A report by the housing charity Crisis highlights the fact that homeless people are often denied the right to register with a GP (Carvel, 2002b). Instead, homeless people have to rely on overstretched casualty departments in hospitals when their health problem has become an emergency. Medical treatment can also be rendered useless when homeless people are discharged back on to the streets without any adequate support. This is echoed by a government report, which states that the health needs of homeless people are not met in a systematic and effective way (Ward, 2002). For example, only one-third of health improvement plans of Primary Care Trusts mention homeless people.

One need not be homeless to suffer adverse health effects, however. A report by the London School of Hygiene and Tropical Medicine (1999) lists the many health aspects on which housing has an impact, including excess winter morbidity because of inadequate home heating, respiratory problems because of damp and mould, and noise disturbance because of poor sound insulation. However, it is difficult to quantify the amount of ill health caused by poor housing because many health effects are qualitative in nature and concern poor quality of life and social isolation. Housing-related health problems are particularly acute in London, where the housing stock is comparatively old and often of poor quality. London also has some of the most deprived populations in the UK and a high proportion of residents from ethnic minorities.

Environmental health

Global environmental change is ultimately a matter of health. However, while the health effects of environmental change have received considerable press coverage, serious policy attention has been more subdued, in part because they are viewed as transnational problems. Although local and national environmental health hazards have always been endemic (see Quah and Boon, 2003), concern has recently been raised over new global threats. For instance, global climate change resulting from the accumulation of greenhouse gases is likely to have a significant impact on the health of the population (Keatinge and Donaldson, 2004; Smith *et al.*, 2003). If global warming predictions are accurate, the increase in the number of days with temperatures over 100°F (38°C) will produce a sharp rise in heat-related mortality from heat strokes, heart attacks and cerebral strokes, especially among the very young, the elderly, and those with chronic respiratory diseases (as evidenced by events in France in the summer of 2003 where an estimated 15,000 died from the heat). Moreover, global warming and changing patterns of rainfall could result in the spread of infectious diseases as insects carrying the agents move into areas that until now have been too cold for their survival. Although the full health impact of global warming and as yet unanticipated outcomes is unlikely in the near future, evidence suggests that commitment is needed now to avert these threats and prevent major health problems (Aron and Patz, 2001).

Similarly, depletion of the ozone layer poses severe health risks that are emerging already. Higher levels of ultraviolet B radiation (UVB) reaching the surface of the earth can damage DNA and proteins and kill cells in all living organisms. There is evidence that heightened exposure of humans to UVB leads to an increase in all forms of skin cancer (Garvin and Eyles, 2001). Most at risk are Australia and New Zealand, although the incidence of malignant melanomas, with mortality rates of 25 per cent, have increased faster than any other cancer – even in Scotland where the incidence of melanoma for men tripled between 1980 and 2000 (British United Provident Association, 2002). Worldwide, WHO estimates there are 132,000 new cases of malignant melanoma (the most dangerous form of skin cancer) and 66,000 deaths from this and other skin cancers annually (Box 7.11). One in three cancers worldwide is skin-related and in the USA that figure is one in two. The American Cancer Society estimates that 7,600 people die each year in the USA from fully preventable malignant melanomas, many of them young (Doneny, 2003).

Box 7.11   It's not only the Sun

In 2005 WHO warned that sunbed use poses a risk of skin cancer, and that no person under 18 years of age should use one (WHO, 2005). There is evidence that young people who get burnt from exposure to UV will have a greater risk of developing melanoma later in life and recent studies demonstrate the direct link between the use of sunbeds and cancer. WHO called on countries to legislate against this practice but at present, only a few of our countries have regulations: France and Sweden limit the maximum proportion of UVB to 1.5 percent of the UV output and France requires that all UV appliances be registered, prohibits use by minors, mandates that trained personnel supervise all commercial tanning establishments, and forbids them to claim any health benefit. The state of California also prohibits use of tanning salons by minors. However, many governmental agencies with responsibility for environmental health and safety inspections are overwhelmed with other duties, leaving an unsupervised tanning industry to give the false impression that sunless tanning is safe.

Source: Ferguson (2005).

Australia has the highest rate of skin cancer in the world with exposure to ultraviolet radiation emitted by the sun being the primary cause. Not surprisingly, this is a significant public health issue and the country has been a world leader in efforts to protect the ozone layer, the main line of defence against the ultraviolet radiation emitted by the Sun. State cancer councils have developed Sun safety and awareness campaigns, such as 'Slip! Slop! Slap!' and 'SunSmart', to educate the population about sun exposure and encourage early detection of skin cancers.

In addition to promoting cancer, burns, loss of elasticity, wrinkling and freckling of the skin, excess UV exposure can also harm the eyes and may compromise immune function. In terms of numbers, cataracts represent an even wider health threat. Some 20 million people worldwide are blinded by cataracts, 20 per cent of which have resulted from UV exposure (WHO, 2005). Because UVB exposure can be reduced by 90 per cent though a combination of the use of plastic lens glasses and a hat, this is one area where relatively straightforward strategies could easily be integrated in health promotion programmes such as that of Singapore to avert considerable health problems and costs.

Alongside the health threats of long-term environmental changes, more immediate and localized conditions can have considerable adverse health consequences for exposed populations. Despite efforts to reduce their impact, air and water pollution levels remain high in many locales and continue to put large numbers of persons at risk. Respiratory problems in urban areas caused or aggravated by air pollution are also likely to be exacerbated by global warming and population concentration (Epstein, 2000). Drinking water systems are not only threatened by industrial and waste disposal contamination, but also by the methods used for disinfecting them due to the toxic effects of the disinfectants and their by-products. The imminent breakdown of old and deteriorating water and sewage systems in some of the larger urban centres of many countries represents a growing health concern that requires urgent attention. Unfortunately, infrastructure funding in many countries has decreased as medical care consumes larger shares of state and local budgets.

All this is not to say that there have been no efforts to deal with environmental health problems. At the international level, a number of initiatives have arisen from the 1984 WHO's 'Health for All' strategy. Its definition of health as physical, mental and social well-being directed attention to the importance of the environment for promoting health. In 1989, the Member States of the WHO's European region agreed on a 'European Charter on Environment and Health', which recognizes the right to an environment conducive to health and the right to relevant information. In 1994, this was followed by an 'Environmental Action Plan for Europe' prepared by the WHO. The Plan calls for management instruments in the area of environmental protection where this is relevant to health. The participating Member States committed themselves to implementing the Plan through 'National Action Plans on Environment and Health' (WHO, Regional Office for Europe, 2003c). WHO set up the European Environment and Health Committee to support the implementation of the Action Plan (WHO, Regional Office for Europe, 2003a). The member states of the WHO European Region have reconfirmed their commitment to earlier policies as part of the Fourth Ministerial Conference on Environment and Health in 2004 (WHO, Regional Office for Europe, 2004). The work of the Committee is complemented by the WHO Programme on Global Change and Health, which is concerned with assessing and monitoring the health impact of global environmental changes (WHO, Regional Office for Europe, 2003b).

Sweden considers environmental health an important issue and has had a pioneering role in environmental policies (Glenngård *et al.*, 2005). In Sweden, the municipalities are responsible for a wide range of areas of environmental health, including disease prevention, food quality, water management and chemical control. Municipalities are also experimenting with new forms of auditing and accounting as well as with new tariffs to improve environmental protection and food security. They have also been at the forefront of implementing the UN's Local Agenda 21, a participatory process aimed at sustainable development, which includes health issues (Eckerberg *et al.*, 1998).

Public health: putting the medical model in perspective

While there is no doubt that medical care can be decisive in individual cases, there is substantial evidence that it is a relatively minor factor in the health of populations. If the goal of health care is to improve the health of populations, then our blind acceptance of the medical model must be reassessed. Three decades ago, Ivan Illich (1976) vehemently criticized modern medicine as a nemesis and a cause, not a cure, of illness. Although Illich's criticisms of medicine were unduly harsh, he raised many legitimate questions and forced placement of medicine in a social context. There is strong support, for instance, for his conclusion that major improvements in health derive from changes in the way in which people are able to live, thus suggesting the need to replace the medical model with one based in subjective reality. Too much medicine is not good for health! Not only does it divert resources from more useful endeavours, but it also produces ill health and disrupts traditional social and cultural institutions and values that are central to good health in the broader sense. Medical misadventure alone contributes to many deaths each year, over 100,000 in the USA alone (Kohn *et al.*, 1999; Starfield, 2000).

Furthermore, health must be put into perspective along with a wide array of requisites of a good life including art, entertainment, music and work, as well as family and social interaction. To place health above everything else risks underestimating the contribution of these many other factors to the fulfilment of our goals and the enhancement of the human condition. According to Richard Lamm (2003), we cannot live by health alone, but must invest in education, infrastructure and other essential components. Although health is important, it is not all-important. It makes little sense to invest disproportionate amounts of societal resources into health at the expense of those things that make life worth living. It appears that while Western nations accept the notion that health is but one aspect of well-being at the personal level, as societies we expect the health care systems to resolve many problems that at their core are social, not medical, ones.

This nearly exclusive focus on medical care is flawed not only because it tends to emphasize only one dimension of health but also because it elevates health as the primary goal instead of as a means to broader life goals. Implicit in the conventional health care model is the assumption that improved health status is achieved primarily by higher expenditures on medical care. Although the health status of individuals is influenced by medical care and it has the potential to improve quality of life or save the lives of some persons, there is little correlation between how much money is spent on doctors and hospitals and how healthy a society is. As illustrated in Table 7.3, countries that expend the highest amounts on health do not score higher on health outcomes and, in fact, often do less well. Any relationship between medical care and health, even in its narrow physical sense, is minimal compared to other determinants of health status such as heredity, personal behaviour, and the physical and social environment. The impact of medical care is further limited because many health conditions are self-limiting, some are incurable, and for many others there is little or no effective treatment. The cases where health care is effective and significantly affects health outcomes 'comprise only a small proportion of total medical care – too small to make a discernible impact on the statistics in populations' (Fuchs, 1994: 109).

Moreover, in those cases where health gains have been presumed to be the result of medical intervention, data indicate that medical technology has, in fact, not played the principal role. For instance, it has been estimated that at least two-thirds of the reduction in mortality rates during the 1970s and 98 per cent of the modest mortality rate improvement in the 1980s was tied to the reduction in death from cardiovascular disease (Drake, 1994: 133). Under the medical model, the reduction in deaths

Table 7.3   *Total health care expenditure, life expectancy at birth and infant mortality, 2004 (ranked by % GDP)*

	Total health care expenditure (as percentage of GDP)	Life expectancy at birth (in years)	Infant mortality (in deaths per 1,000 live births)
USA	15.3	77.5	6.9
Germany	10.9	78.6	4.1
France	10.5	80.3	3.9
Netherlands	9.2	79.2	4.1
Australia	9.2	80.6	4.7
Sweden	9.1	80.6	3.1
Italy	8.4	79.7	4.1
New Zealand	8.4	79.2	6.2
UK	8.3	78.5	5.1
Japan	8.0	82.1	2.8
Singapore	3.8	78.9	2.5

Sources: Data from OECD (2006) and Singapore Ministry of Health (2006).

from cardiovascular disease is assumed to be the result of impressive innovations in treatment, especially coronary by-pass surgery and angioplasty. However, evidence suggests that most, if not all, of this drop is attributable to lifestyle changes reflected in the decline in smoking, increase in exercise, and decrease in saturated fat consumption. 'Only a small part, if any, can be attributed to medical technology' (Cundiff and McCarthy, 1994: 18). Similarly, Bunker *et al.* conclude that 'current data provide no evidence that medical care has reduced mortality when all cancers are added together' (1994: 233).

These findings regarding the inability to explain health status by health care alone have significant implications for any efforts to restructure the health care system. If a system really wants to achieve the goal of maximizing the health of its population, resources would better be directed towards alleviating poverty, reducing crime, changing lifestyles and so forth. A healthy person does not need medical care! As noted by Hurowitz, 'Good health often does not require access to medical care and is largely dependent on the condition of society' (1993: 130).

On these grounds, recent efforts to reform health care systems may be misguided because no amount of restructuring health care along the lines proposed by the reformers will have a major impact on the health of their populations. Reforms for universal access, improved quality of care and cost containment might improve the medical care system, but they cannot be expected to improve substantially the public health. As a result, 'there is little evidence . . . to suggest that providing universal coverage or changing the delivery system will have significant favorable effects on health, either in the aggregate or for particular socio-economic groups' (Fuchs, 1994: 109).

Chapter 8

Understanding Health Policy Comparatively

In analysing health policy in a comparative context, the preceding chapters have covered a wide range of topics including the historical and cultural trajectories of health policy; systems of funding, providing and governing health care; policies of allocating health resources; health care in the home; and the diverse policies that constitute public health. As in any cross-country comparison, a tension emerges between similarities and differences, between common policy trends, such as the ubiquity of rationing, and policy divergence, such as welfare mix in the provision of hospital services.

This brings us back to cross-country comparison and the question of what analysing a range of countries can contribute to our understanding of health policy. Comparison can help by juxtaposing health systems and health policies in different countries. This allows us to get a better idea about the range of variation that exists and also helps to avoid both false particularism ('everywhere is special') and false universalism ('everywhere is the same'). Importantly, exploration often leads to deeper questions about why it is we find certain differences and similarities. As such, comparison can provide an important lever for explanation. Finally, comparison can also offer a basis for evaluation as a way of assessing the relative success and failure of specific health policies. The first rationale is central to the analysis presented in the preceding chapters and the next section critically discusses to what extent the concept of the health system indeed helps to explain health policies (see also Burau and Blank, 2006). The following section extends the discussion and assesses the potential for policy learning based on evaluating health policies across different countries.

Health systems and explaining health policies

The use of the notion of different health systems (ordered in a typology of health systems) has been central to the comparative turn in health policy analysis and they have been used to conceptualize the (institutional) context in which health policies are embedded and the institutions of health care (among others) which shape health policies (and politics) (see, e.g., Freeman, 2000; Ham, 1997b; Raffel, 1997; Scott, 2001; Wall, 1996). Cross-country comparison generates an abundance of information, and ordering this information by using a typology of health systems is central to using comparison to build, review and revise explanations about health policy emergence and health policy making. Against this background, the following analysis critically discusses two things: the importance of institutional embeddedness beyond the health system, and the use of the concept of the health system in relation to non-medical health policies. The key issue here is whether the concept of the health system helps us to discover how countries vary (or are similar) in the health policies they adopt and whether we can gain insights into why these differences (or similarities) exist.

Health systems and institutional embeddedness

Table 8.1 maps out our countries using the typology of health systems introduced in Chapter 1 as a basis, but it also defines in more detail different aspects of government involvement in the funding and provision of health care following on from the discussion in preceding chapters. The institutions of governing the funding of health care are concerned with the mechanisms by which individual patients have access to services (such as social citizenship and earned insurance entitlements) and the mechanisms that decide on the total volume of resources allocated to the financing of health care (such as governing through public management and setting regulatory frameworks). In contrast, the institutions of governing the provision of health care include the mechanisms for regulating hospitals (such as the amount of public regulation and the mix of differently owned hospitals) and the regulation of doctors (especially different forms of private interest government). This reflects the centrality of hospitals and doctors for the provision of health care.

Looking at the health systems in these countries across the different types and respective dimensions of governing health care, several findings stand out. Only four out of the nine countries included in the study fully fit one of the three types of health system (Britain, Sweden, Germany and the US). In contrast, the remaining countries are more or less only close approximations of the individual ideal types. This highlights the fact that the institutional contexts of the governing of health care are more complex than suggested by the definition of the health system. Instead, institutional contexts are often highly specific in terms of how individual aspects combine themselves in individual countries. Such specificities also point to additional aspects of institutional context. Consequently, within a country the two sets of institutions associated with the governance of funding may actually fit different types of health

Table 8.1   *Health systems and their policies*

	Governance of funding • Extent of public access to health care • Extent of public control of total health care costs	Governance of provision • Extent of public control of hospitals[1] • Extent of constraints on private interest government of doctors[2]
National health service • Extensive public access, high public control of costs • High public control of hospitals, highly constrained private interest government of doctors	BRITAIN SWEDEN Australia (access/control) Japan (cost control) New Zealand (access) Netherlands (cost control) Singapore (cost control)	BRITAIN SWEDEN New Zealand
Social insurance systems • De facto public access, moderate public control of costs • Moderate public control of hospitals, some constraints on private interest government of doctors	GERMANY Japan (access) Netherlands (access) New Zealand (cost control)	GERMANY Australia Japan Netherlands Singapore
Private insurance system • Limited public access, low public control of costs • Little public control of hospitals, few constraints on private interest government of doctors	US Singapore (access)	US

[1] Share of hospitals in public ownership with degree of public regulation used as a proxy for extent of public control of hospitals.
[2] Share of publicly employed (hospital) doctors together with degree of professional self-regulation used as a proxy for exent of constraints on self-government of doctors.

systems thus making categorization problematic. The same problem might also apply to the comparison of the governance of funding and provision.

According to the typology, public control of the total resources allocated to health care can be expected to be highest in national health services with access to health care based on social citizenship and lowest in private insurance systems where access to health care is based on private insurance, with public control in social insurance health systems lying in between. This is true for four of our countries, but the picture is more complex in the remaining five countries, pointing to the importance of country-specific institutional contexts. In Australia, for example, federalism combined with the legacy of the private insurance systems weakens government authority over funding (Palmer and Short, 2000). In contrast, the unitary political system in Japan helps to concentrate authority in the hands of central government (Campbell and Ikegami, 1998). Despite significant decentralization of health services and insurance plans, for example, all billing and payment in Japan is centralized through the payment fund of the National Health Insurance.

The Netherlands and Singapore are particularly interesting examples of how country-specific institutional contexts shape the public control of health care costs, thus making differences between countries particularly pertinent. In the Netherlands, the high public control of funding reflects the unusual combination of a social insurance with strong universalist elements (for an overview, see Exter *et al.*, 2004; Maarse, 1997). Health funding combines a considerable diversity of sources, including private insurance for acute medical risks for those with earnings above a certain level, and compulsory social insurance contributions to cover exceptional medical risks. This reflects the historical legacy of a society segmented into different groupings and the gradual weakening of this legacy in the Netherlands. The semi-federal political system also helps to concentrate authority in the hands of the central government, and, in contrast to Germany, corporatism is confined to the national level.

In Singapore, country-specific institutional contexts are such that public control is strong not only in relation to health care costs but also to other key aspects of health care (for an overview, see Barr, 2001; Ham, 2001). Strong government control of funding coexists with health care funding that is predominantly based on individual responsibility and limited familial risk pooling. Health care is funded by individual savings accounts, which are compulsory. The government also caps contribution rates, while out-of-pocket payments are high. As such, Singapore defies the dictum that private funding is unlikely to make for public control. The strength of government control reflects not only the spatial concentration of political power typical of city-states, but also a strongly centralized approach to health policy. Government education programmes are aimed at lowering the demand for health care and also emphasize the importance of primary health care and prevention over hospital care. Not surprisingly, public health policies are strong, and the government heavily subsidizes health promotion and disease prevention programmes that emphasize the responsibility of the individual to look after his or her own health.

The importance of country specific institutional contexts also applies, though to a lesser extent, when comparing the governance of funding and provision. Singapore, for example, and as mentioned above, has a highly controlled health system but one based on individual savings accounts that give the impression of minimal government control over funding. Thus, it crosses the line between a social insurance and a private insurance health system. Furthermore, Singapore gives those persons with sufficient Medisave account balances considerable freedom of choice as to public and private doctors and hospitals as well as allowing them to purchase private insurance with their account should they so desire. While provision best fits a private insurance health system, a large proportion of health care is provided in publicly owned hospitals by government-set salaried doctors. Despite this, there are few controls on medical intervention in Singapore because in the end individuals have the choice of what services to use with their compulsory but private accounts.

The analysis suggests two things. First, the concept of the health system holds as an approximation of 'real' health systems. It is therefore a classical ideal type that is useful as a heuristic device that simplifies the complex real world of governing health care (following Weber, 1949). Thereby, the concept of the health system helps to move the analysis beyond the specificity of individual cases and towards more generalized observations, overcoming a salient tension inherent in comparative enquiry (Goodin and Smitsman, 2000). The health system as an ideal type, therefore, does not need to fit the real types completely in order to be useful.

Second, it is important to remember that it is primarily through the comparison and contrast with real types that explanations can be advanced (see Arts and Glissen, 2002). The central question, then, is how to explain the extent to which 'real' health systems do or do not fit the ideal types. The different degrees of 'misfits' among these nine countries and the types of health systems presented in the analysis raises many such 'why' questions. In turn, this underlines the fact that the concept of the health system indeed only provides a starting point for a comparative analysis and must be complemented by additional, more specific, institutional explanations. The importance of a detailed study of institutional contexts is well recognized in the comparative study of health policy (see, e.g., Döhler, 1991; Immergut, 1992; Wilsford, 1994).

Significantly, then, there is institutional embeddedness beyond the health system. As the analysis of our countries suggests, governing health care is embedded in institutional contexts that are broader than those institutions making up the health system, and institutional contexts that are often also highly specific to individual countries. Our analysis, for example, points to the importance of the specific characteristics of political systems (such as federalism in Australia), social structures (such as the legacy of societal pillars in the Netherlands) and social values (such as the high degree of individual self-reliance in Singapore). The governing of health care reflects specific configurations of these different aspects of institutional context, all of which are changeable over time. Therefore, more often than not, health policies follow trajectories that are highly complex and specific.

Health systems and non-medical health policies

The analysis above suggests that the institutional context of governing health care itself is highly complex. This echoes Freeman's (2000: 7) observation that the organization of health care is actually not very systematic. The complex historical emergence of policies of health care often defies the order implied by the notion of a *system*. As a result, the health system perspective may be looking for order where there is little. Instead, the institutional context of governing health care is highly differentiated, to the extent that such contexts are often somewhat specific to individual countries. Importantly, there is also specificity in relation to sub-sectors of health care and policy. This is particularly apparent in relation to those sub-sectors that have traditionally been at the margins of the 'health system', but that are increasingly relevent to health policy. Focusing on home and community based health care as an example, this section assesses the use of the concept of the health system for capturing the institutions central to non-medical health care and for explaining such 'new' health policies across countries.

Debates about ageing populations and their implications for health care costs and services have put home and community-based health care on the health policy agenda. At international level it is indicative, for example, that long-term care for elderly people was one of the components of the recent OECD Health Project (OECD, 2005a). The OECD Health Project echoes developments across the countries included in our study in which there are many examples of major policy initiatives relating to home and community based health care (see, e.g., Jacobzone, 1999; Jenson and Jacobzone, 2000). Such policies often aim at the expansion of existing services to support informal care givers by integrating home and community based health care into the regular organization of health care. The expansion of social insurance in Germany and

Japan are indicative examples. Starting in the late 1980s, the government in Japan introduced a publicly funded scheme, the so-called Gold Plan, to expand care services for older people. The scheme was extended in the late 1990s and in effect became a separate branch of social insurance, funded by a mixture of social insurance premiums and taxes. Considering the traditional strength of family responsibility for care of the elderly, this is a significant policy development (Furuse, 1996).

This emergence of non-medical based health care raises the question of how policies related to home and community based health care fit into the concept of the health system. The concept focuses on institutions and policies related to medical care. In contrast, home and community based health care is located on two sets of interfaces: between formal and informal care, and between health and social care. In relation to the first aspect, it is indicative that few older people receive home nursing care and even when they do it only accounts for a small share of their care. Instead, home care predominantly means unpaid (informal) care by women and often also includes social care, such as help with domestic tasks. This reflects not only the inadequacy of existing home nursing services, but also the fact many of the health care needs of older people are often not principally medically related.

This puts a number of limitations on using the concept of the health system for capturing the institutions governing home and community based health care and for explaining corresponding health policies. The institutions related to the governance of funding are relevant to the extent that home and community based health care is part of the organization of medical health care. Traditionally, parts of home and community based health care have by default been funded by the same scheme as medical health care. At the same time, parallel funding schemes relating to social care have existed. In Germany, for example, before the introduction of the long-term care insurance, funding for home and community based health care came from both the health insurance and locally funded social assistance schemes. In many cases this organizational division continues and also applies to the newly established schemes. This also applies to Japan, whereas in Australia, New Zealand, the Netherlands and Sweden funding of home and community based health care is integrated. Furthermore, there tends to be formal or de facto limits to the scope of collective consumption. Instead private consumption in the form of private payments for formal services and informal care paid by lost income are important complementary aspects of consumption. The last aspect even applies to countries like Sweden, where the level of publicly funded services is relatively high. A study in the mid 1980s for example found that informal care accounted for 64 per cent of the total care time (OECD 1996: 166).

There are even more extensive limitations in relation to applying the definitions of the governance of provision. Hospitals as settings of care provision and doctors as providers of care are of little importance. Instead, care workers such as community nurses, care assistants and social workers together with informal carers, all working in home and community based settings, are central for the provision of this type of health care. Taken together this suggests that shared values and beliefs (and corresponding practices) are important for understanding non-medical health policies. Freeman and Ruskin (1999) refer to this as 'cultural embeddedness' and thereby point to diversity beyond the macrolevel and, notably, a type of diversity that is shaped by organizational bases that are ethnic, gendered, local and personal, rather than national and public.

Where does this leave capturing institutional arrangements as they apply to home and community based health care and explaining corresponding non-medical health policies across our countries? The concept of the health system is of some use, notably to the extent to which home and community based health care is part the organization of medical health care. However, beyond that, using the concept of the health system has clear limits, as some institutions do not have the same importance, whereas others not included in the definition are central for understanding non-medical health policies. Instead, different aspects of institutional context need to be taken into consideration. This requires two things: first, redefining the institutions related to the governing of funding and provision so as to reflect the specific characteristics of home and community based health care (and, where applicable, across the health and social care divide); and second, to include gender as a set of social and cultural institutions. In this respect Pfau-Effinger's (2004) concept of 'gender arrangements' is particularly useful. The concept consists of two components. Gender order describes existing structures of gender relations not least as reflected in gendered divisions of labour. Gender culture for its part refers to deeply embedded beliefs and ideas about the relations between the generations in the family and the obligations associated with such relations.

Against this background one way forward would be to combine the different, yet complementary aspects of institutional context discussed above as part of an 'organizing framework'. In the context of their study of multilevel governance Bache and Flinders (2004: 94) define this as an analytical framework that provides a map of how things relate and that leads to a set of research questions. The value of such an approach is that it helps to explore complex issues and identifies interesting areas for further research.

Possibilities and limitations for cross-national learning

The discussion above concerning the extent to which the typology of health systems helps to explain health policy suggests three things. First, modelled on paradigmatic cases the concept of the health system holds as an ideal type. Second, as such the health system provides a useful springboard for the analysis of health policy, but one which needs to be complemented by more specific institutional explanations. Third, the concept of the health system is less applicable to increasingly important, non-medical areas of health policy. Instead, different aspects of institutional context come into play and they can be combined as part of a looser 'organizing framework'.

Nevertheless, cross-country comparison remains an attractive strategy for social enquiry, not least as it can also provide a basis for identifying the variety of policy options that exist in health policy. As such, comparison holds the implicit promise of learning from other countries and their policy successes and failures. Health policy learning occurs naturally as information about other countries has become more readily available as part of the process of globalization. Policy learning is also explicitly encouraged by international organizations such as the OECD and the WHO when they disseminate information about health systems and reforms in different countries. To policy makers, cross-country comparison and the opportunity to identify which health policy/system works 'best' is attractive for several reasons. Looking at other countries offers a virtual 'test' of different policy options and as such promises 'evidence-based' policy making, policy innovation and, above all, policy success (Stone, 1999).

However, there are in fact different models of policy learning as Freeman (2005, 2006) argues, two of which are particularly relevant in the present context. First, policy learning as transfer is based on a rationalist conception that policy input and policy output relate to each other as cause and effect. Policy learning emerges as an instrumental process that is based on evidence. In other words: policy makers learn in order to address specific problems and policies easily transfer from one country to the other. In contrast and second, policy learning as transplant is based on an institutionalist perspective and governments are seen to show different capacities for learning. The process of learning itself is related to experience and experiment. In other words, policy makers learn in an iterative way through trial and error, and the travel of policies from one country to the next is contingent upon there being a special institutional context.

The work of the OECD and its recent OECD Health Project powerfully represents a model of policy learning that is based on transfer. For example, in the foreword to the final report, the Direct General of the OECD stresses that the Project offers a means for member countries to learn from each other, drawing on 'the best expertise' that exists (OECD, 2005: 3). Consequently, the report lists goals of health systems as generic to health policy and which, as such, are applicable across different countries. Similarly, the report presents policy initiatives in individual countries as equally possible policy options. In short, this is about evaluating health reforms to identify best practice for transfer, where the capacity of governments to learn is assumed. The analysis presented in the preceding chapters more or less explicitly challenges this model of policy learning that assumes that identifying what is 'best' and transferring what is 'best' from one country to another is straightforward. The complexity of health systems and policies in different countries emerging from our analysis suggests otherwise. There are many definitions of what are 'best' health policies/systems, and transferring best practices across countries is difficult because health policies are deeply embedded in country-specific contexts.

Health policy making is a complex process. Chapter 4 identifies quality, equity/access and cost containment/efficiency as the central goals of health policy. The three goals represent different and potentially competing ideas about what is the 'best' health policy/system. This makes learning from other countries a value-laden exercise, which is further complicated by the fact that different actors in health care have different ideas of what is 'best'. Thus, what is the 'best' health policy/system also depends on whom you ask. Importantly, the institutional set-up of different health systems means that actors enjoy different degrees of power. For example, providers are often particularly influential in private insurance systems, as the example of the USA demonstrates, whereas their power is more limited in national health services, as the example of the UK suggests. The same applies to patients, although in the USA the selective access to health insurance constrains the potential influence of patients.

As Figure 8.1 suggests, there are four sets of actors in health care: users, payers (including both third-party payers and the public), providers and the state. Significantly, the different actors in health care often support different goals of health policy and as such have different ideas about what the 'best' health system or policy is. Payers are primarily concerned with cost containment and efficiency, whereas for providers quality of health care is the key. In contrast, the goal orientation of the public is ambivalent; as patients the public puts quality and access/equality first, whereas as payers the public has a predominant interest in cost containment/efficiency. Importantly, the different actors in health care may also have different ideas about the same goal. For users of health care, quality means a well-funded health system that allows for patient choice and fast access to medical technology. This definition of quality is shared by providers of health care, who also emphasize the importance of autonomy in the provision of health care services. In contrast, states are more likely to highlight the public health aspects of quality.

		Actors in Health Care			
		Users	*Payers*	*Providers*	*The State*
Goals of Health Policy	*Quality*	X		X	X
	Equity/Access	X		X	
	Cost Containment/ Efficiency		X		X

Figure 8.1   *The goal orientation of actors in health care*

The discussion above suggests that health systems/policies are 'best' in relation to specific goals, and that the importance attached to the individual goals (and ideas about what is 'best') varies between different actors in health care. Figure 8.2 offers an overview of the 'best' health systems in relation to the goals of quality, equity/access and cost containment/efficiency for our countries. It also includes several definitions (or indicators) of each health policy goal. Considering the complexity of health care this overview uses selected indicators and examples and does not claim to be comprehensive.

Quality of health care is often measured in terms of the financial resources spent on health care. Based on the measure of the percentage of GDP spent on health care, the USA, Germany and France are the 'best' health systems. Other measures of quality relate to the technical and human resources of health systems such as the speed of access to medical technology and the number of doctors, respectively. Subsidiary policy goals are patient choice and commitment to public health. The assumption is that the more money spent, the better the technical and human resources of health systems. Countries such as Germany and Britain support this assumption, although the relationship between different indicators of quality is more complex than this. For example, while the health system in Singapore ranks very low in terms of the level of health care spending and the number of doctors, quality in terms of the extent of patient choice and commitment to public health is high. Other cases highlight the tradeoffs between different indicators of quality. Germany, for example, does very well on all indicators except commitment to public health, suggesting that quality is primarily defined as high-tech medical care.

The share of health care expenditure coming from public sources is an important indicator of equity/access in health systems. Public funding in the form of taxes or social insurance contributions is underpinned by the principles of universality and social solidarity, respectively, and as such makes for universal or near universal (and in principle equitable) access

Quality
Defined as . . .

Level of health care spending (percentage of GDP)	*High*: USA, Germany and France *Low*: Singapore, Britain, Japan
Speed of access to medical technology	*Fast*: USA, Germany *Slow*: Britain, Netherlands
Number of doctors (per 1,000 inhabitants)	*High*: Italy, Germany and Sweden *Low*: Singapore, Britain and Japan
Extent of patient choice	*High*: Singapore, USA *Medium*: Germany and Sweden *Low*: Australia, Britain, Netherlands, New Zealand
Commitment to public health	*High*: Singapore, Sweden *Low*: Germany, USA

Access/Equity
Defined as . . .

Public funding of health care (percentage of total expenditure)	*High*: Sweden, Britain, Japan *Low*: Singapore, USA, Italy
Coverage of population	*High*: Britain (universality), Japan (social solidarity) *Low*: USA

Cost Containment/Efficiency
Defined as . . .

Control of costs	*High (direct budget control)*: Britain, Japan, New Zealand, Sweden *Medium (contractual control)*: Germany, Netherlands *Low (decentralized, market-oriented systems)*: Australia, USA
Supply-side rationing	*High (national health services)*: Britain, New Zealand and Sweden *Low (market-based health systems)*: Singapore, USA

Figure 8.2   *Identifying 'best' health systems*

to health care. On this count, Sweden, Britain and Japan are the three 'best' health systems, whereas the USA is one of the worst. Here, low coverage means that a significant proportion of the population is excluded from what is otherwise a very 'high quality' health system.

Such tradeoffs also exist between the policy goals of cost containment/efficiency and quality. The extent of control of costs is an important indicator of cost containment/efficiency and here the 'best' health systems are characterized by extensive cost control. Direct budget control, such as in Britain, Japan, New Zealand and Sweden, allows for greatest cost control, followed by contractual control as it exists in Germany and the Netherlands. Cost control is weakest in decentralized, market-oriented systems such as Australia and the USA. Health systems with extensive cost controls also make greater use of supply-side rationing. However, this comes at the price of quality in terms of level of health care spending (such as in Japan), speed of access to medical technology (such as in Britain) and the extent of patient choice (such as in New Zealand). Not surprisingly, the 2000 World Health Report by the WHO ranked Britain eighteenth in terms of responsiveness to patients (Laurance and Norton, 2000). The inverse is also true. In the USA and Germany, high quality in terms of level of health care spending and fast access to medical technology come at the price of low to medium control of costs.

Identifying the 'best' health system/policy is a highly complex process that depends on what is defined as 'best': that is, which policy goal is considered to be most important. In an ideal world, all three goals would be equally important. However, as health care resources are ultimately limited, the different policy goals in effect compete with each other. The emphasis put on individual goals and definitions of what is the 'best' health policy/system varies over time as well as between countries. This reflects historical trajectories and the health systems in individual countries together with the balance of power among the different actors in health care.

As such, the lessons policy makers want to learn from other countries also vary among individual health systems. Lesson learning is not necessarily a politically neutral process, but the value of policy lessons lies precisely in their power to bias policy choice (Stone, 1999: 73). Lesson learning is politically motivated and selective and is used to substantiate already made policy choices. Here, Britain is an indicative example. In response to the perceived funding crisis of the British NHS in the late 1980s, the government looked towards the USA and its models of managed care. The strong market orientation of the US health system resonated with the neo-liberal outlook of the Conservative government of the time. The focus on the organization of health services also helped to avoid the politically sensitive issue of making changes to the way in which the NHS is funded.

Moreover, there are only certain lessons policy makers in individual countries can learn, and this points to the limits of transferring 'best practices'. As Chapter 2 emphasizes, health policies are embedded in highly specific historical, cultural and political contexts, and any policy success is ultimately tied to a specific place and point in time. Irrespective of political will, not all policies work everywhere. Successful lesson learning is as much about the substance of policies as it is about the circumstances in which policies succeed (Klein, 1997). For instance, the New Zealand government's attempts to introduce partial charges for users for hospital care in the early 1990s were inspired by a series of reports by US-based health care consultants; but they failed. The policy engendered strong opposition not only from the public but also from the health care professions, which forced the government to withdraw the policy. A possible explanation is that the success of this policy was predicated on a health system that puts great emphasis on individual responsibility (as in the USA) rather than public responsibility (as in New Zealand).

The complexity and contingency of identifying 'best practices' and cross-country learning in health policy does not mean that it cannot or should not be done. Instead, cross-country learning requires sensitivity, notably in two respects. Cross-country learning requires sensitivity towards the different and potentially competing ideas about what are the 'best' health policies/systems. There is no single, universally applicable definition of what is 'best', but rather there are as many definitions as there are goals of health policy. Some health systems are particularly successful in relation to cost containment/efficiency, whereas others score highly on quality as measured in terms of levels of spending and access to medical technology. Importantly, there are tradeoffs between different goals of health policy, and health systems are unlikely to be 'best' in respect to all policy goals. Which health policies are considered 'best' and worthy of lesson learning is ultimately a political decision. Nevertheless, cross-country learning also requires sensitivity towards the specific contexts under which policies succeed.

Contribution to the comparative study of health policy

In many respects the analysis presented in this book has covered familiar ground. Analyses of health systems, doctors and health reform are central topics in the comparative study of health policy. What, then, does the analysis presented in this book contribute to the debate? The contribution of the present analysis lies in the range of countries and policy issues covered. The breadth of the analysis results in a relatively comprehensive map in which specific health policies in individual countries can be located. As such, the analysis offers a basis for more in-depth analyses of a wide range of more specific cases which vary in terms of both countries and policy issues.

The map is based on an analysis that covers a diverse range of countries from the pioneers of publicly funded health systems (such as Germany and Sweden) to health systems that put individual responsibility first (such as Singapore and the USA) and hybrids (such as Australia); from health systems embedded in Western capitalist democracies to health systems embedded in Asian political systems; and from large health systems such as America's which covers 300 million people to small health systems such as New Zealand's which covers only 4 million people. The map is also based on an analysis that includes a diverse range of health policy issues including basic ones such as the funding and provision of health care, health policy issues that are high on the political agenda such as those relating to the allocation of health care resources, and health policy issues that are located on the margins of the health systems such as home care and public health. However, no matter how inclusive, such a loose framework has its own limitations. As Mabbett and Bolderson (1999) argue, the deconstruction of broad-brush categorizations and typologies makes all encompassing cross-country comparison and contrast more difficult.

Nevertheless, by offering a comprehensive map in which specific health policies in individual countries can be located, the analysis presented in this book contributes to the comparative study of health policy in another way. The map offers one way of moving away from the notion that health policies across countries are either different or similar and that they will either continue to be embedded in country-specific contexts or will be submerged by convergence. Over time, health policies across countries will be both different and similar in differing degrees and in different respects. Adopting a map also means embracing complexity, exploring differences in health policy within the same country, and analysing the interfaces with other, related policies. In short, using a map acknowledges the existence of similarities within differences and differences within similarities, and acknowledges that health policy includes more than just health systems. Although this more complex and dynamic view of health policy might lack the comfort that comes with the typology of health systems, the analysis in the earlier chapters demonstrates that it better reflects the real world of health care.

Glossary

Acute Care: Medical treatment rendered to people whose illnesses or medical problems are short-term or don't require long-term continuing care. Acute care facilities are hospitals that mainly treat people with short-term health problems.

All-payer System: A health care system in which, no matter who is paying, prices for health services and payment methods are the same whether federal or state government, private insurance company, a self-insured employer plan, an individual, or any other payer. Also called multiple-payer system.

Ambulatory Care: All health services delivered outside hospitals (that is, in primary care settings).

Capitation: A payment system based on a fixed pre-payment, per patient, covered by a health care provider to deliver medical services to a particular group of patients. The payment is the same no matter how many services or what type of services each patient actually gets.

Case Management: Intended to improve health outcomes or control costs by tailoring services to a patient's needs.

Catastrophic Health Insurance: Health insurance that provides coverage for treating severe or lengthy illnesses or disability.

Chronic Illnesses: Health problems that are long-term and continuing. Nursing homes, mental hospitals and rehabilitation facilities are examples of chronic care facilities.

Clinical Care Guidelines: Carefully developed information on diagnosing and treating specific medical conditions. Guidelines are usually based on clinical literature and expert consensus, are designed to help physicians make decisions and to help funding organizations evaluate appropriateness and medical necessity of care.

Co-payments: Flat fees or payments that a patient pays for each doctor visit or prescription or other health care service.

Core Services: A package of health care services deemed basic for all citizens.

Cost Containment: The method of constraining health care costs from increasing beyond a set level by controlling or reducing inefficiency and waste in the health care system.

Cost Sharing: The requirement that the patient pay a portion of the costs of covered services. Deductibles, co-insurance and co-payments are cost sharing techniques.

Cost Shifting: When one group of patients does not pay the full cost for a service, health care providers pass on the costs for these services to other groups of patients.

Coverage: A person's health care costs are paid by their insurance or by the government.

Covered Services: Treatments or other services for which a health plan pays at least part of the charge.

Deductible: The amount of money, or value of certain services (such as one physician visit) a patient or family must pay before costs (or percentages of costs) are covered by the health plan or insurance company, usually per year.

Diagnostic-Related Groups (DRGs): A system for classifying hospital stays according to the diagnosis of the medical problem being treated for the purposes of payment.

Disease Management: Programmes for persons who have chronic illnesses such as asthma or diabetes that encourage them to live a healthy lifestyle and take medications as prescribed.

Effectiveness: A measure of the extent to which a specific intervention, procedure, regimen or service, when deployed in the field in routine circumstances, does what it is intended to do for a specified population.

Elective: A health care procedure that is not an emergency and that the patient and doctor plan in advance.

Fee-for-Service: The traditional payment method where the insurer (patient, insurance plan or government) pays providers per services rendered. The doctor charges a fee for each service provided.

Gatekeeper: A primary care physician responsible for overseeing and coordinating all aspects of a patient's medical care. The gatekeeper usually has to pre-authorize other specialty care, diagnostic tests or hospital admission.

General Practitioners: Physicians without specialty training who provide a wide range of primary health care services to patients.

Global Budgets: Budgets set to contain health care costs. Common in national health systems that annually set the maximum amount of money that will be spent on health care.

Group Insurance: Health insurance offered through business, union trusts or other groups and associations. The most common system of health insurance in the USA is the one in which the cost of insurance is based on the age, sex, health status and occupation of the people in the group.

Health Indicator: An indicator applicable to a health or health-related situation.

Health Insurance: Financial protection against the health care costs caused by treating disease or accidental injury. A system of risk sharing through pooled resources.

Health Maintenance Organization (HMO): A health plan providing comprehensive medical services to its members for a fixed, prepaid premium. Members must use participating providers and are enrolled for a fixed period of time. HMOs can be either for-profit or not-for-profit. Most HMOs provide care through a network of doctors, hospitals and other medical professionals that their members must use in order to be covered for that care.

Health Outcomes: Measures of the effectiveness of particular kinds of medical treatment. This refers to research-based information that asks what difference a drug, procedure or other health care intervention really makes to a patient's health.

Health Sector: Part of the economy dealing with health-related issues in society.

Health System: The people, institutions and resources, arranged together in accordance with established policies, to improve the health of the population they serve, while responding to people's legitimate expectations and protecting them against the cost of ill-health through a variety of activities whose primary intent is to improve health. The set of elements and their relations in a complex whole, designed to serve the health needs of the population.

Home Health Care: Skilled nurses and trained aides who provide nursing services and related care to someone in his or her home.

In-patient Care: Care for a person who has been admitted to a hospital or other health facility for a period of at least 24 hours.

Long-term Care: Health care, personal care and social services provided to people who have a chronic illness or disability and do not have full functional capacity. This care can take place in an institution or at home on a long-term basis.

Malpractice Insurance: Coverage for medical professionals which pays the costs of legal fees and/or any damages assessed by a court in a lawsuit brought against a professional who has been charged with negligence. Endemic in the USA.

Managed Care Organization: An umbrella term for HMOs and all health plans that provide health care in return for pre-set monthly payments and coordinate care through a defined network of primary care physicians and hospitals. Prepaid medical plans that attempt to control health care costs through a preventative health care approach.

Means Test: An assessment of a person's or family's income or assets so that it can be determined if they are eligible to receive public support.

Out-of-Pocket Costs or Expenditures: The amount of money that a person must pay for his or her health care, including: deductibles, co-payments, payments for services that are not covered, and/or in the US health insurance premiums that are not paid by his or her employer.

Out-patient Care: Health care services that do not require a patient to receive overnight care in a hospital (such as day surgery).

Preventive Health Care: An approach to medicine that attempts to promote and maintain the health of people by preventing disease or its consequences. It includes primary prevention to keep people from getting sick (such as immunizations), secondary prevention to detect early disease (such as Pap smears) and tertiary prevention to keep ill people or those at high risk of disease from getting sicker (such as helping someone with lung disease to quit smoking).

Primary Care: Preventive health care and routine medical care that is typically provided by a doctor trained in internal medicine, paediatrics or family practice, or by a nurse, nurse practitioner or physician's assistant.

Primary Care Provider: The health professional who provides basic health care services and may control patients' access to the rest of the health care system through referrals.

Private Insurance: Health insurance that is provided by commercial insurance companies and where insurance premiums are risk-based.

Quality Assessment/Assurance: A systematic process to improve the quality of health care by monitoring quality, finding out what is not working and fixing the problems of health care delivery.

Rationing: The denial of a treatment to a particular patient who would benefit from it.

Referral System: The process through which a primary care provider authorizes a patient to see a specialist to receive additional care.

Single Payer System: A health care system in which costs are paid by taxes or compulsory contributions to sickness funds or social insurance plans rather than by the employer and employee.

Third Party Payer: An organization other than the patient or health care provider involved in the financing of personal health services.

Uncompensated Care: Health care provided to people who cannot pay for it and who are not covered by any insurance. This includes both charity care which is not billed and the cost of services that were billed but never paid.

Universal Coverage: This refers to health systems that guarantee health care to all people regardless of the way that the system is financed.

Waiting List Time: The amount of time a person must wait from the date he or she is deemed to need a procedure to the date they actually receive it.

Guide to Further Reading

1   Comparative health policy: an introduction

There are many useful books on comparative health systems and health policy for readers to explore for more information. Matcha (2003) provides an analysis of health care systems in Canada, Germany, Sweden, Japan, UK and the USA, including the history, financing and delivery of services. Raffel (1997), DeVoe (2001), Ham (1997a and b) and Powell and Wessen (1999) specifically look at health reform in an international context. Saltman *et al.* (1998) examine critical challenges for health care reform in Europe. Freeman (2000) offers a good overview of the politics of health in Europe as does Moran (1999). Coulter and Ham (2000) specifically discuss the global challenge of rationing, and Ham and Robert (2003) place it in the international context. Green and Thorogood (1998) analyse health policies across nations while Blank and Merrick (2005) examine end-of-life policies in 12 countries. Ranade (1998), Callahan and Wasunna (2006) and Harrison (2004) offer valuable comparative analyses of the role of markets. Scott (2001) specifically compares private and public roles in health systems, while Schwartz (1997) analyses seven countries in Europe and North America as regards budgets and management. Behan (2006) explores American health care policy failure by looking at the policies of Canada and Australia and offers a systematic comparison of these three countries while Lee *et al.* (2002) explore the global dimensions of health policy. For a look at how health care in developing countries differs from the countries analysed here, see Green (1999) and Mills *et al.* (2001).

2   The context of health care

There are many valuable resources on the context of health care for our countries. The Guide to Websites contains the most useful current data as well as contextual information. For Australia, the key books are Duckett (2004a), Gardner (1995) and Palmer and Short (2000). A very useful contextual book on New Zealand health care is Davis and Dew (2000), while Blank (1994) and Gauld (2001) provide good overviews of the health care system. There are numerous books on US society as it relates to health policy including an excellent historical perspective in Weissert and Weissert (2002). For a good analysis of the US legal context see Sage and Kersh (2006). Also, valuable insights into the unique US value context are found in Musgrave (2006), Kleinke (2001) and Blank (1997). Still an excellent source on Japanese culture and health care is Ohnuki-Tiernev (1984). More recent books on Japanese health policy and society include Campbell and Ikegami (1998) and E. Feldman (2000). Ham (2001)

238

provides a useful article on values and health policy in Singapore and the work of Quah (2003) and Lim (2004) are most helpful in understanding the Singapore system. Klein (2001) provides a detailed analysis of the politics of the British NHS since it was established, while Twaddle (1999) focuses on policies of health reform in Sweden. Marmot and Wilkinson (1999) offer a contemporary review of the social determinants of health and Kawachi *et al.* (1999) delve more deeply into the relationship between inequality and poor health.

3   Funding, provision and governance

Suggestions for further reading on the funding, provision and governance of health care must necessarily be highly selective. Scott (2001) examines public and private sector roles in health care funding, provision and regulation, drawing on the experiences of Australia, Canada, Germany, Netherlands, New Zealand, the UK and the USA. Henderson and Peterson (2002) explore the diverse meanings and applications of the term 'consumer' in the health systems of Australia, the UK and Canada. The edited volumes by Altenstetter and Björkman (1997), Ham (1997a), Mossialos and Le Grand (1999) and Ranade (1998) together with a special issue of the *Journal of Health Politics, Policy and Law* (2005, volume 20, numbers 1–2) contain chapters on European countries, focusing on health policy from the perspective of reform. In contrast, the reports by the European Observatory offer detailed overviews of the health systems in Britain (1999), Germany (Busse and Riesberg, 2004), the Netherlands (Exter *et al.*, 2004) and Sweden (Glenngård *et al.*, 2005). For the Netherlands see Okma (2001). Davis and Ashton (2001) provide a detailed account of New Zealand health reforms while Ashton (2005) provides a useful summary of recent changes in funding. A good general work on Australia is Palmer and Short (2000), while Gardner (1997) provides a comprehensive introduction to health policy in that country. Among the countless books on US health policy are R. Feldman (2000), Jonas (2003), Porter and Teisberg (2006) and Musgrave (2006). The publication on affordable health care published by the Singapore Ministry of Health (1995) is invaluable in explaining its unique system. For good summaries of the Japanese health care system, see Ikegami and Campbell (1999), Imai (2002) and especially the Japanese Ministry of Health (2000).

4   Setting priorities and allocating resources

Twaddle (2002) looks at market-oriented health care reforms in numerous countries and analyses the recent concern with the efficiency of medical care while Jacobs *et al.* (2006) examine the pursuit of efficiency across health systems and the techniques available to measure it. General books on rationing medicine include Lamm and Blank (2007) and Ubel (2001). R. Busse (1999) and Perleth *et al.* (1999) specifically focus on issues of rationing and the regulation of medical technology assessment in Germany, whereas Locock (2000) deals with rationing in Britain. Coulter and Ham (2000) and Ham and Robert (2003) provide very useful comparative analyses of rationing and argue it is a global issue, whereas Ham (1997b) specifically focuses on priority setting. Ranade's (1998) and Harrison's (2004) comparative analyses of health care markets are a good introduction to the topic. Ikegami and Campbell (1999) provide an important analysis of cost containment in Japan, and Campbell and Ikegami (1998) extend this analysis to priority setting. More technical books on health allocation techniques include Drummond *et al.*, (1997) and, especially, McKie *et al.* (1998).

5   The medical profession

Johnson (1995) and Light (1995) provide useful introductions to the conceptual issues surrounding doctors and health policy, as do Moran and Wood (1993) and Moran (1999) in their comparative analyses of Britain, Germany and the USA. The edited collection by Bovens *et al.* (2001) contains chapters on recent medical reform in our European countries. Harrison (2001) and Harrison *et al.* (2002) have written widely about doctors in Britain, whereas Garpenby (1997, 1999, 2001) has focused on Sweden. Allsop and Saks (2003) offer a critical perspective on regulation of the medical profession in the UK. Yoshikawa *et al.* (1996) provide good coverage of the medical profession in Japan. A good introduction to the medical profession in the USA is provided by Badasch (1993), while Birenbaum (2002) looks at the impact of managed care on US doctors.

6   Beyond the hospital: health care in the home

Although few works focus specifically on home care, there are a number that offer introductions to key issues and concepts for comparing home care including Alber and Kohler (2006), Anttonen *et al.* (2003), and Tester (1998). Glenndinning (1998a), Hutten and Kerkstra (1996) and Tester (1996) include useful overviews of our European countries, whereas Duff (2001) and OECD (2005b) adopt a broader international perspective and Lundsgaard (2004) focuses on payments of informal carers. More specific country perspectives include the works by Gibson and Means (2000) on Britain and Australia, Campbell and Morgan (2005) on Germany and the USA, Wenger (2001) and Theobald (2004) on Germany, Ashton (2000) and Davey and Keeling (2004) on New Zealand, Means *et al.* (2003) on Britain and Trydegard (2003) on Sweden. Campbell and Ikegami (2003), Izuhara (2003) and Naguchi and Shimizutani (2005) provide a useful range of perspectives on home care policy in Japan. Watson and Mears (1999) book on women and care of the elderly is a good overview of the social issues surrounding home care in Australia. The encyclopaedia of home care for the elderly by Romaine-Davis *et al.* (1995) is a valuable sourcebook while Kitchener *et al.* (2005) and CMS (2003) review Medicaid home and community-based services in the USA.

7 Public health

Since public health comprises such a broad range of areas, many of which fall outside the scope of health care, the resources here are expansive. Among the best recent general works on public health per se are Turnock (2004), Schneider (2005), Merson (2004), Henderson *et al.* (2001) and Garrett (2000). Beauchamp and Steinbock (1999) offer constructive insights on the ethical aspects of public health, while Mackenzie (1998) presents an holistic approach to public health policy. One of the best general books on health promotion is DiClemente *et al.* (2002). For a comprehensive guide to the frameworks, theories and methods used to evaluate health promotion programmes see Valente (2002). More specific country perspectives on public health include books on Europe by Holland and Mossialos (1999), the USA by Milio (2000) and Calman (1998), Australia by Leeder (1999) and Hancock (1999), Britain by Baggott (2000) and Japan by Okamoto (2001). Recent books on environmental and global health include Ball (2006), Moeller (2004) and the massive edited collections of Merson *et al.* (2001) and Koop *et al.* (2002).

Guide to Websites

In the light of the growing importance of the Internet for transferring health policy information, below is a selection of health-related websites for our countries and for key international health organizations. Where possible, we have included English language sites; otherwise an English option is often available. This list of websites is also available online at www.palgrave.com/politics/blank where it will be updated periodically.

Australia

Bureau of Statistics: www.abs.gov.au
Commonwealth Government: www.australia.gov.au
Department of Health and Ageing: www.health.gov.au
Department of Health, Australian Capital Territory: www.health.act.gov.au
Health Communication Network: www.hcn.net.au
Health Insurance Commission: www.hic.gov.au
Institute of Health and Welfare: www.aihw.gov.au
Public Health Association of Australia: www.phaa.net.au

Germany

Expert Panel for the Evaluation of Developments in the Health System (*Sachverständigenrat zur Begutachtung der Entwicklung im Gesundheitswesen*): www.svr-gesundheit.de
Federal Association of Insurance Fund Doctors (*Kassenärztliche Bundesvereinigung*): www.kbv.de
Federal Association of Welfare Organizations (*Bundesarbeitsgemeinschaft der Freien Wohlfahrtspflege*): www.bagfw.de
Federal Centre for Health Education (*Bundeszentrale für Gesundheitliche Aufklärung*): www.bzga.de
Federal Chamber of Doctors (*Bundesärztekammer*): www.bundesaerztekammer.de
Federal Ministry for Health (*Bundesministerium für Gesundheit*): www.bmgesundheit.de
Federal Ministry of Labour and Social Affairs *(Bundesministerium für Arbeit und Soziales)*: www.bmas.bund.de
German Hospital Association (*Deutsche Krankenhaus Gesellschaft*): www.dkgev.de

Japan

Ministry of Health, Labour and Welfare: www.mhlw.go.jp/english

The Netherlands

Association of Dutch Municipalities (*Vereniging van Nederlandse Gemeenten*): www.vng.nl

Association of Municipal Health Services (*Vereniging vor GGD'en*): www.ggd.nl

Central Agency for Health Care Tariffs (*College Tarieven Gezondheidszorg*): www.ctg-zaio.nl/index.php

Ministry for Health, Welfare and Sport (*Ministerie van Volksgezondheid, Welzijn en Sport*): www.minvws.nl

Statistics Netherlands (*Centraal Bureau voor de Statistiek*): www.cbs.nl

Royal Dutch Medical Association (*Koninklijke Nederlansche Maatschappij tot bevordering der Geneeskunst*): www.knmg.nl

New Zealand

Maori Health Policy: www.nzgg.org.nz/maori_health.cfm

Ministry of Health: www.moh.govt.nz

New Zealand Health Information System: www.nzhis.govt.nz

New Zealand Health Network: www.nzhealth.net.nz

New Zealand Health Technology Assessment: nzhta.chmeds.ac.nz

Singapore

Health Sciences Authority: www.hsa.gov.sg

Ministry of Health: www.moh.gov.sg

National Centre for Policy Analysis: www.ncpa.org

Sweden

Medical Responsibility Board (*Hälso- och sjukvårdens ansvarsnåmnd*): www.hsan.se

Ministry for Health and Social Affairs (*Socialdepartementet*): www.regeringen.se/sb/d/1474

National Board of Health and Welfare (*Socialstyrelsen*): www.sos.se

National Institute for Public Health (*Statens Folkhälsoinstitutet*): www.fhi.se

Swedish Association of Local Authorities and Regions (*Sveriges Kommuner och Landsting*): www.skl.se

Swedish Medical Association (*Sveriges läkarförbund*): www.slf.se

UK

British Medical Association: www.bma.org.uk
Department of Health: www.doh.gov.uk
General Medical Council: www.gmc-uk.org
Healthcare Commission: www.chi.nhs.uk
The King's Fund: www.kingsfund.org.uk
National Institute for Health and Clinical Excellence: www.nice.org.uk
NHS Confederation: www.nhsconfed.org
Office of Public Sector Information: www.opsi.gov.uk

USA

Agency for Healthcare Research and Quality: www.ahcpr.gov
American Hospital Association: www.aha.org
Center for Disease Control and Prevention: www.cdc.gov
Center for Medicare and Medicaid Services: www.medicare.gov
Department of Health and Human Services: www.hhs.gov
Department of Veterans Affairs: www.va.gov
Health Resources and Services Administration: www.hrsa.gov
Institute of Medicine: www.iom.edu
National Center for Health Statistics: www.cdc.gov/nchs
National Institutes of Health: www.nih.gov
National Library of Medicine/National Institutes of Health: www.nlm.nih.gov

International organizations

European Observatory on Health Care Systems and Policies: www.euro.who.int/
    observatory
Organisation for Economic Co-operation and Development: www.oecd.org
World Health Organization: www.who.org
World Health Organization, Regional Office for Europe: www.who.dk

Bibliography

Aaron, H.J. (2003) 'Should Public Policy Seek to Control the Growth of Health Care Spending?', *Health Affairs*, 8 January.

Abel-Smith, B. (1984) *Cost Containment in Health Care: The Experience of 12 European Countries 1977–83*. Luxembourg: Commission of European Countries.

Abrams, J. (2002) 'Divided Congress Puts off Many Issues Until after the Election', *Associated Press*, 17 October.

Alber, J. (1995) 'A Framework for the Comparative Study of Social Services', *Journal of European Social Policy* 5 (2): 131–49.

Alber, J. and U. Kohler (2004) *Health and Care in an Enlarged Europe*. Luxembourg: European Foundation for the Improvement of Working Conditions, www.fr.eurofound.eu.int/publications/files/EF03107EN.pdf

Alber, J. and U. Kohler (2006) *Health and Care in an Enlarged Europe*, Luxembourg, Official Publications of the European Communities, European Foundation for the Improvement Working Conditions, www.fr.eurofound. eu.int/publications/files/EF03107EN.pdf, 10 July.

Alber, J. and M. Schölkopf (1999) *Seniorenpolitik. Die soziale Lage älterer Menschen in Deutschland und Europa*. Berlin: Verlag Fakultas.

Allsop, J. and M. Saks (2003) *Regulating the Health Profession*. London: SAGE.

Altenstetter, C. and J.W. Björkman (eds) (1977) *Health Policy Reform, National Variations and Globalization*. London: Macmillan.

Altenstetter, C. and R. Busse (2005) 'Health Care Reform in Germany: Patchwork Change within Established Governance Structures', *Journal of Health Politics, Policy and Law* 30: 121–42.

Altman, S.H., C.P. Tompkins, E. Eilat and M.P.V. Glavin (2003) 'Escalating Health Care Spending: Is It Desirable or Inevitable?', *Health Affairs*, 8 January.

Amelung, V., S. Glied and A. Topan (2003) 'Health Care and the Labor Market: Learning from the German Experience', *Journal of Health Politics, Policy and Law* 28 (4): 693–714.

American Hospital Association (2002) 'Fast Facts on U.S. Hospitals from Hospital Statistics', www.aha.org

American Obesity Association (2006) 'Disability Due to Obesity', http://www.obesity.org/subs/disability/NIDDR_Obesityincluded.shtml

American Society of Bariatric Surgery (2006) 'Rationale for the Surgical Treatment of Morbid Obesity', http://asbs.org/html/rationalerationale.html

Anderson, G.F., B.K. Frogner, R.A. Johns and U.E. Reinhardt (2006) 'Health Care Spending and Use of Information Technology in OECD Countries', *Health Affairs* 25 (3): 819–31.

Anell, A. and P. Svarvar (1999) 'Health Care Reforms and Cost Containment in Sweden', in E. Mossialos and J. Le Grand (eds) *Health Care and Cost Containment in the European Union*. Aldershot: Ashgate.

Angell, M. (1993) 'Privilege and Health – What is the Connection?', *New England Journal of Medicine* 329 (2): 126–7.

Anttonen, A., J. Baldock and J. Sipilä (eds) (2003) *The Young, the Old and the State. Social Care Systems in Five Industrial Nations*. Cheltenham: Edward Elgar.

Antonnen, A., J. Sipilä and J. Baldock (2003) 'Patterns of Social Care in Five Industrial Societies: Explaining Diversity', in A. Antonnen, J. Baldock and J. Sipilä (eds.) *The Young, the Old and the State. Social Care Systems in Five Industrial Nations*. Cheltenham: Edward Elgar.

Appleby, J. (1992) *Financing Health Care in the 1990s*. Buckingham: Open University Press.

Aron, J.L. and J.A. Patz (2001) *Ecosystem Change and Public Health: A Global Perspective*. Baltimore: Johns Hopkins University Press.

Arts, W. and J. Glissen (2002) 'Three Worlds of Welfare Capitalism or More? A State-of-the-Art Report', *Journal of European Social Policy* 12: 137–48.

Ashton, T. (2000) 'New Zealand: Long-Term Care in a Decade of Change', *Health Affairs*, 19 (3): 72–81.

Ashton, T. (2005) 'Recent Developments in the Funding and Organisation of the New Zealand Health System', *Australia and New Zealand Health Policy* 2 (9), http://www.anzhealthpolicy.com/content/2/1/9

Associated Press (2006) 'Singapore Takes Strict Steps against Obesity', www.msnbc.msn.com/id/6124732 (12 October).

Australian Department of Health and Ageing (2002) *A Summary of the National Program Guidelines for the Home and Community Care Program 2002*. Canberra: Commonwealth of Australia.

Australian Department of Health and Ageing (2003) 'Home and Community Care', www.health.gov.au/acc/hacc/index.htm

Australian Department of Health and Ageing (2004) *A New Strategy for Community Care – The Way Forward*. Canberra: Australian Department of Health and Ageing.

Australian Department of Health and Ageing (2006a) 'Home and Community Care Programme', www.health.gov.au/acc/hacc/index.htm

Australian Department of Health and Ageing (2006b) 'Evaluation of the Home and Community Care Program: National Standards Three Year Appraisal', http://www.health.gov.au/internet/wcms/publishing.nsf/Content/ageing-hacc-haccevaluation-standards.htm

Babcock, L. and A. Belotti (1994) 'Defining and Measuring Health over Life', in G. Tolley, D. Kenkel and R. Fabian (eds) *Valuing Health for Policy: An Economic Approach*. Chicago: University of Chicago Press.

Bache, I. and M. Flinders (2004) 'Multi-level Governance and British Politics', in I. Bache and M. Flinders (eds) *Multi-level Governance*. Oxford: Oxford University Press.

Badasch, S.A. (1993) *Introduction to Health Occupations*. New York: Regents/Prentice Hall.

Baggott, R. (2000) *Public Health: Policy and Politics*, Basingstoke: Palgrave Macmillan.

Baggott, R. (2004) *Health and Health Care in Britain*, 3rd edn. Basingstoke: Palgrave Macmillan.

Baird, P. (1993) *Proceed with Care: Final Report of the Royal Commission on New Reproductive Technologies*. Ottawa: Minister of Government Services Canada.

Baker, L., H. Birnbaum, J. Geppert, D. Mishol and E. Moyneur (2003) 'The Relationship between Technology Availability and Health Care Spending', *Health Affairs* 5, November.

Baldock, J. (2003) 'Social Care in the United Kingdom: A Pattern of Discretionary Social Administration', in A. Anttonnen, J. Baldock and J. Sipilä (eds) *The Young, the Old and the State. Social Care Systems in Five Industrial Nations*. Cheltenham: Edward Elgar, pp. 109–41.

Ball, D. (2006) *Environmental Health Policy*. Buckingham: Open University Press.

Banks, J., M. Marmot, Z. Oldfield and J.P. Smith (2006) 'Disease and Disadvantage in the United States and in England', *JAMA* 295: 2037–45.

Banta, D. (2002) 'The Development of Health Technology Assessment', *Health Policy* 63 (2): 121–32.

Bäringhausen, T. and R. Sauerborn (2003) 'One Hundred and Eighteen Years of the German Health Insurance System: Are there any Lessons for Middle- and Low-Income Countries?', *Social Science and Medicine* 54: 1559–87.

Barr, M.D. (2001) 'Medical Savings Accounts in Singapore: A Critical Inquiry', *Journal of Health Politics, Policy and Law* 26 (4): 709–26.

Bartholomée, Y. and H. Maarse (2006) 'Health Insurance Reform in the Netherlands', *Eurohealth* 12 (2): 7–9

Barwick, H. (1992) *The Impact of Economic and Social Factors on Health*. Wellington: Public Health Association of New Zealand.

Batty, D. (2001) 'The GMC in Crisis', *The Guardian*, 29 May.

BBC News (2002) 'Being Single Worse Than Smoking', www.news.bbc.co.uk/l/hi/health/2195609.stm

BBC News (2005) 'Obese Patients Denied Operations'. http://news.bbc.co.uk/go/pr/fro/1/hi/england/suffolk/4462310.stm

Beauchamp, D.E. and B. Steinbock (eds) (1999) *New Ethics for Public Health*. New York: Oxford University Press.

Behan, P. (2006) *Solving the Health Care Problem: How Other Countries Have Succeeded and Why the United States Has Failed*. Albany: State University of New York Press.

Belsky, L., R. Lie, A. Mattoo, E.J. Emanuel and G. Sreenivasan (2004) 'The General Agreements on Trade in Services: Implications for Health Policymakers', *Health Affairs* 23 (3): 137–45.

Bennett, C.J. (1991) 'What is Policy Convergence and What Causes It?', *British Journal of Political Science* 21 (2): 215–33.

Bensoussan, A. and S.P. Myers (1996) *Towards a Safer Choice: The Practice of Traditional Chinese Medicine in Australia*. Sydney: University of Western Sydney Press.

Berg, M., K. Horstman, S. Plass and M. van Heusden (2000) 'Guidelines, Professionals and the Production of Objectivity: Standardisation and the Professionalism of Insurance Medicine', *Sociology of Health and Illness* 22 (6): 765–91.

Berk, M.L. and A.C. Monheit (2001) 'The Concentration of Health Care Expenditures Revisited', *Health Affairs* 20 (2): 9–18.

Bertelsmann Foundation (2003a) 'Diagnosis-Based Hospital Reimbursement', Japan Survey No. 1. Gütersloh: Bertelsmann Foundation, www.reformmonitor.org

Bertelsmann Foundation (2003b) 'PHI Incentive Scheme', Australia Survey No. 1. Gütersloh: Bertelsmann Foundation, www.reformmonitor.org

Bertelsmann Foundation (2004a) 'Public Health Legislation', New Zealand Survey No. 3. Gütersloh: Bertelsmann Foundation, www.reformmonitor.org

Bertelsmann Foundation (2004b) 'Oregon Health Plan Cuts', US Survey No. 3. Gütersloh: Bertelsmann Foundation, www.reformmonitor.org

Bertelsmann Foundation (2004c) 'Medicare Safety Net', Australia Survey No. 4. Gütersloh: Bertelsmann Foundation, www.reformmonitor.org

Bertelsmann Foundation (2004d) 'Graphic Health Warning on Cigarette Packs', Singapore Survey No. 4. Gütersloh: Bertelsmann Foundation, www.reformmonitor.org

Bertelsmann Foundation (2004e) 'Australian Primary Care Collaborative Program', Australia Survey No. 4. Gütersloh: Bertelsmann Foundation, www.reformmonitor.org

Bertelsmann Foundation (2005a) 'Global Budget', Singapore Survey No. 5. Gütersloh: Bertelsmann Foundation, www.reformmonitor.org

Bertelsmann Foundation (2005b) 'MediShield Reform', Singapore Survey No. 4. Gütersloh: Bertelsmann Foundation, www.reformmonitor.org

Bertelsmann Foundation (2005c) 'Merger of Municipalities', Japan Survey No. 5. Gütersloh: Bertelsmann Foundation, www.reformmonitor.org

Bertelsmann Foundation (2006) 'Liberalization of Medisave Use', Singapore Survey No. 7. Gütersloh: Bertelsmann Foundation, www.reformmonitor.org

Birenbaum, A. (2002) *Wounded Profession: American Medicine Enters the Age of Managed Care.* Westport, CT: Praeger Press.

Birrell, B. (2002) 'A Bitter Pill for Rural Australia', www.monash.edu.au/pubs/montage/Montage 97-02/pill.htm

Bitton, A. and J.G. Kahn (2003) 'Government Share of Health Care Expenditures', *Journal of the American Medical Association* 289 (9):1165.

Björkman, J.W. and K.G.H. Okma (1997) 'Restructuring Health Care Systems in the Netherlands: The Institutional Heritage of Dutch Health Policy Reforms', in C. Altenstetter and J.W. Björkman (eds) *Health Policy Reform, National Variations and Globalization.* London: Macmillan.

Blank, R.H. (1994) *New Zealand Health Policy: A Comparative Study.* Auckland: Oxford University Press.

Blank, R.H. (1997) *The Price of Life: The Future of American Health Care.* New York: Columbia University Press.

Blank, R.H. (2001) 'Agenda Setting and the Policy Context', in P. Davis and T. Ashton (eds) *Health and Public Policy in New Zealand.* Auckland: Oxford University Press.

Blank, R.H. and V. Burau (2006) 'Setting Health Priorities across Nations: More Convergence than Divergence?', *Journal of Public Health Policy* 27 (3): 265–81.

Blank, R.H. and J.C. Merrick (eds) (2005) *End-of-Life Decision Making: A Cross-National Study.* Cambridge, MA: MIT Press.

Blendon, R.J., M. Kim and J.M. Benson (2001) 'The Public versus the World Health Organization on Health System Performance', *Health Affairs* 20 (3): 10–20.

Blendon, R.J., R. Leitman, R. Morrison and K. Donelan (1990) 'Satisfaction with Health Systems in Ten Nations', *Health Affairs* 9 (2): 188–9.

Blondel, Jean (1990) *Comparative Government: An Introduction*. Hemel Hempstead: Philip Allan.

Bodenheimer, T. (2005) 'High and Rising Health Care Costs. Part 2: Technologic Innovation', *Annals of Internal Medicine* 142 (11): 932–37.

Bodenheimer, T. and A. Fernandez (2005) 'High and Rising Health Care Costs. Part 4: Can Costs Be Controlled While Preserving Quality?', *Annals of Internal Medicine* 143 (1): 26–31.

Boom, H. (2001) 'Dilemmas and Difficulties in Home Nursing: Theoretical Perspectives', paper presented at the Fifth Conference of the European Sociological Association, Helsinki, 28 August–1 September.

Boom, H., F. Stevens and H. Philipsen (2000) 'Cross-cultural Comparison in the Institutionalisation and Professionalisation of Home Care in Six European Countries', paper presented at the Interim Conference of the ISA Research Committee on Sociology of Professional Groups, Lisbon, 13–15 September.

Borgor, C., S. Smith, C. Truffer, S. Keehan, A. Sisko, J. Poisal and M.K. Clemens (2006) 'Health Spending Projections Through 2015: Changes on the Horizon', *Health Affairs* 25 (2): w61–w73.

Boseley, S. (2000) 'Peers Say NHS Could Embrace Alternative Therapies', *The Guardian*, 29 November.

Boseley, S. (2001) 'Organ Horror Report Outcry', *The Guardian*, 30 January.

Bovens, M., P. t'Hart and B.G. Peters (eds) (2001) *Success and Failure in Public Governance. A Comparative Analysis*. Cheltenham: Edward Elgar.

Boxall, A-M. and S.D. Short (2006) 'Political Economy and Population Health: Is Australia Exceptional?', *Australia and New Zealand Health Policy* 3 (6), http://www.anzhealthpolicy.com/content/3/1/6 (accessed 26 October 2006).

Brenner, M.H. (2001) 'Unemployment, Employment Policy and the Public Health', paper presented at European Commission Expert Meeting on Unemployment and Health in Europe, Berlin, 6–7 July.

British United Provident Association (2002) 'Skin Cancer on the Rise', www.bupa.co.uk/health information/html/health news/250602skin.htm

Brodhurst, Sally and Caroline Glendinning (2001) 'The United Kingdom', in Tim Blackmann, Sally Brodhurst and Janet Convery (eds) *Social Care and Social Exclusion. A Comparative Study of Older People's Care in Europe*. Basingstoke: Palgrave.

Bulman, E. (2006) 'WHO: TB Poses Greatest Threat to Europe', Associated Press, 9 October.

Bundesministerium für Gesundheit (2005) *Statistisches Taschbuch. Gesundheit 2005*. Berlin: Bundesministerium für Gesundheit.

Bunker, J.P., H.S. Frazier and F. Mosteller (1994) 'Improving Health: Measuring Effects of Medical Care', *The Milbank Quarterly* 72 (2): 225–55.

Burau, V. (2001) 'Medical Reform in Germany: The 1993 Health Care Legislation as an Impromptu Success', in M. Bovens, P. t'Hart and B.G. Peters (eds) *Success and Failure in Public Governance. A Comparative Analysis*. Cheltenham: Edward Elgar.

Burau, V. (2005) *Medical Governance between Change and Continuity* ('Governing Doctors: A Comparative Analysis of Pathways of Change', Working Paper 1/2005). Aarhus: University of Aarhus.

Burau, V. (forthcoming) 'Comparative Health Research', in M. Saks and J. Allsop (eds) *Researching health*. London: Sage.

Burau, V. and R.H. Blank (2006) 'Comparing Health Policy – An Assessment of Typologies of Health Systems', *Journal of Comparative Policy Analysis* 8 (1): 63–76.

Burau, V., L. Henriksson and S. Wrede (2004) 'Comparing Professional Groups in Health Care: Towards a Context Sensitive Analysis', *Knowledge, Work and Society* 2 (2), 49–68.

Burau, V. and T. Kröger (2004) 'Towards Local Comparisons of Community Care Governance: Exploring the Relationship between Policy and Politics', *Social Policy & Administration* 38 (7): 793–810.

Burau, V., H. Theobald and R.H. Blank (forthcoming) *Governing Home Care: A Cross-National Comparison*. Cheltenham: Edward Elgar.

Burstrom, B. (2004) 'User charges in Sweden', *Euro Observer* 6 (3), 5–6.

Busse, C. (1998) 'Study Shows Foreign-Trained Doctors Can Ease Rural Physician Shortage', *Carolina News Service* 850, 13 November.

Busse, R. (1999) 'Priority-setting and Rationing in German Health Care', *Health Policy* 50: 71–90.

Busse, R. and C. Howorth (1999) 'Cost Containment in Germany: Twenty Years Experience', in E. Mossialos and J. Le Grand (eds) *Health Care and Cost Containment in the European Union*. Aldershot: Ashgate.

Busse, R. and A. Riesberg (2004) *Health Systems in Transition: Germany*. Copenhagen: WHO Regional Office for Europe on behalf of the European Observatory on Health Care Systems.

Butler, P. (2002) 'How Nice Works', *The Guardian*, 22 March.

Califano, J.A., Jr. (1992) 'Rationing Health Care: The Unnecessary Solution', *University of Pennsylvania Law Review* 140 (5): 1525–38.

Callahan, D. (1987) *Setting Limits: Medical Goals in an Aging Society*. New York: Simon & Schuster.

Callahan, D. (1990) *What Kind of Life? The Limits of Medical Progress*. New York: Simon & Schuster.

Callahan, D. and A.A. Wasunna (2006) *Medicine and the Market: Equity v. Choice*. Baltimore: The Johns Hopkins University Press.

Calman, K.C. (1998) *Potential for Health*. Oxford: Oxford University Press.

Campbell, J.C. and N. Ikegami (1998) *The Art of Balance in Health Policy: Maintaining Japan's Low-Cost, Egalitarian System*. Cambridge: Cambridge University Press.

Campbell, J.C. and N. Ikegami (2003) 'Japan's Radical Reform of Long-Term Care', *Social Policy and Administration* 37 (1): 21–34.

Campbell, A.L. and K.J. Morgan (2005) 'Federalism and the Politics of Old-Age Care in Germany and the United States', *Comparative Political Studies* 38 (8): 1–28, 997–1014.

Carter, H. (2002) 'Death Recording System "Left Shipman Free to Kill"', *The Guardian*, 8 October.

Carvel, J. (2002a) 'Britons Say Non to C'est la Vie Philosophy', *The Guardian*, 16 October.

Carvel, J. (2002b) 'Homeless Suffer for Want of a GP', *The Guardian*, 9 December.

Casciani, D. (2002) 'Asylum Seeker Health Crisis in London', *BBC News*, 12 November, http://news.bbc.co.uk/1/hi/2453263.stm

Castles, Francis G. (1999) *Comparative Public Policy. Patterns of Post-war Transformation*. Cheltenham: Edward Elgar.

Centers for Disease Control (2003) 'Severe Acute Respiratory Syndrome', www.cdc.gov/ncidod/sars/quarantinega.htm

Centers for Medicare and Medicaid Services (2003) 'Alternatives to Nursing Home Care', www.medicare.gov/Nursing/Alternatives/Other.asp

Centers for Medicare and Medicaid Services (2006) 'Program of All-Inclusive Care for the Elderly', www.cms.hhs.gov/QualityInitiativesGenInfo/10_Pace.asp

Cheah, J. (2001) 'Chronic Disease Management: A Singapore Perspective', *British Medical Journal* 323 (7): 990–3.

Checkland, K. (2004) 'National Service Frameworks and UK General Practitioners: Street-Level Bureaucrats at Work?', *Sociology of Health and Illness* 26 (7): 951–75.

Chernichovsky, D. (1995) 'Health System Reforms in Industrialized Democracies: An Emerging Paradigm', *The Milbank Quarterly* 73 (3): 339–56.

Clasen, J. (ed.) (1999) *Comparative Social Policy*. Oxford: Blackwell.

Collier, D. and J.E. Mahon, Jr. (1993) 'Conceptual "Stretching" Revisited: Adapting Categories in Comparative Analysis', *American Political Science Review* 87: 845–55.

Collier, D. and S. Levitsky (1997) 'Democracy with Adjectives: Conceptual Innovation in Comparative Research', *World Politics* 49: 430–51.

Commonwealth Fund (2000) *The Elderly's Experiences with Health Care in Five Nations*. New York: The Commonwealth Fund.

Coolen, J. and S. Weekers (1998) 'Long-term Care in the Netherlands: Public Funding and Private Provision within a Universalistic Welfare State', in C. Glenndinning (ed.) *Rights and Realities. Comparing New Developments in Long-term Care for Older People*. Bristol: Policy Press.

Coulter, A. and C. Ham (eds) (2000) *The Global Challenge of Health Care Rationing*. Buckingham: Open University Press.

Crampton, P. (2001) 'Policies for General Practice', in P. Davis and T. Ashton (eds) *Health and Public Policy in New Zealand*. Auckland: Oxford University Press.

Crinson, Iain (2005) 'The Direction of Health Policy in New Labour's Third Term', *Critical Social Policy* 25 (4): 507–16.

Cuellar, A.E. and J.M. Wiener (2000) 'Can Social Insurance for Long-term Care Work? The Experience of Germany', *Health Affairs* 19 (3): 8–25.

Culyer, A.J., J.E. Brazier and O. O'Donnell (1988) *Organising Health Service Provision: Drawing on Experience*. London: Institute of Health Services Management.

Cumming, J. and C.D. Scott (1998) 'The Role of Outputs and Outcomes in Purchaser Accountability: Reflecting on New Zealand Experiences', *Health Policy* 46(1): 53–68.

Cundiff, D. and M.E. McCarthy (1994) *The Right Medicine: How to Make Health Care Reform Work Today*. Totowa, NJ: Humana Press.

Daatland, S.O. (1996) 'Adapting the "Scandinavian Model" of Care for Elderly People', in OECD (ed.) *Caring for Frail Elderly People. Policies in Evolution.* Social Policy Studies no. 19. Paris: OECD.

Davey, J.A. and S. Keeling (2004) 'Combining Work and Eldercare: A Neglected Work-Life Balance Issue', *Labour, Employment and Work in New Zealand*, Wellington: Victoria University Institute for Research on Ageing.

Davies, G.P., W. Hu, J. McDonald, J. Furier, E. Harris and M. Harris (2006) 'Developments in Australian General Practice 2000–2002: What Did These Contribute to a Well Functioning and Comprehensive Primary Health Care System?', *Australia and New Zealand Health Policy* 3 (1), http://www.anzhealthpolicy.com/content/3/1/1

Davis, P. and T. Ashton (eds) (2001) *Health and Public Policy in New Zealand.* Auckland: Oxford University Press.

Davis, P. and K. Dew (eds) (2000) *Health and Society in Aotearoa New Zealand.* Auckland: Oxford University Press.

Day, S.E., K. Alford, D. Dunt, S. Peacock, L. Gurrin and D. Voaklander (2005) 'Strengthening Medicare', *Australia and New Zealand Health Policy* 2 (18), http://www.anzhealthpolicy.com/content/2/1/18

De Ferranti, D. (1985) *Paying for Health Services in Developing Countries: An Overview.* Washington, DC: World Bank Staff Working Paper 721.

Deleon, P. and P. Resnick-Terry (1999) 'Comparative Policy Analysis: Déjà vu all over Again?, *Comparative Policy Analysis* 1: 9–22.

Dent, M. (2003) *Remodelling Hospitals and Health Professions in Europe. Medicine, Nursing and the State.* Basingstoke: Palgrave Macmillan.

Department of Health (2006a) Departmental Report. The Health and Personal Services Programmes, Cm 6814. London: The Stationary Office.

Department of Health (2006b) *Review Body on Doctors' and Dentists' Remuneration.* Thirty-fifth report 2006. Chairman: Michael Blair, QC (Cm 6733). London: Her Majesty's Stationery Office.

De Voe, J.E. (2001) *The Politics of Health Care Reform: A Comparative Study of National Health Insurance in Britain and Australia.* Kensington, NSW: School of Health Services Management.

De Voe, J.E. and S.D. Short (2003) 'A Shift in the Historical Trajectory of Medical Dominance: The Case of Medibank and the Australian Doctors Lobby', *Social Science and Medicine* 57(3): 343–53.

DiClemente, R.J., R.A. Crosby and M.C. Kegler (2002) *Emerging Theories in Health Promotion Practice and Research: Strategies for Improving Public Health.* San Francisco: Jossey-Bass.

Dillon, A. (2001) 'NICE Idea. The UK National Institute for Clinical Excellence', *Eurohealth* 7 (1): 32–4.

Docteur, E., H. Suppanz and J. Woo (2003) 'The US Health System: An Assessment and Prospective Directions for Reform', *Economics Department Working Papers* No. 350, www.oecd.org/eco

Döhler, M. (1991) 'Policy Networks, Opportunity Structures and Neo-conservative Reform Strategies in Health Policy', in B. Marin and R. Mayntz (eds) *Policy Networks: Empirical Evidence and Theoretical Considerations.* Boulder, CO: Westview Press.

Doneny, K. (2003) 'Skin Cancer: More than 1 Million New Cases in U.S. This Year', *HealthScoutNews*, 26 May.

Drake, D.F. (1994) *Reforming the Health Care Market*. Washington, DC: Georgetown University Press.

Drummond, M.F. (1993) 'Health Technology Policy and Health Services Research', in M.F. Drummond and A. Maynard (eds) *Purchasing and Providing Cost-Effective Health Care*. London: Churchill Livingstone.

Drummond, M.F., B.J. O'Brien, G.L. Stoddart and G.T.W. Torrance (1997) *Methods for the Economic Evaluation of Health Care Programmes*. Oxford: Oxford University Press.

Duckett, S.J. (2004a) *The Australian Health Care System*, 2nd edn. Melbourne: Oxford University Press.

Duckett, S.J. (2004b) 'The Australian Health Care Agreements, 2003–2008', *Australia and New Zealand Health Policy* 1 (5), http://www.anzhealthpolicy.com/content/1/1/5

Duff, J. (2001) 'Financing to Foster Community Health Care: A Comparative Analysis of Singapore, Europe, North America, and Australia', *Current Sociology* 49 (3): 135–54.

Dunne, R. (2002) 'Analysis: GPs and Asylum Seekers', BBC News, 7 November, http://news.bbc.co.uk/1/hi/health/2414887.stm

Dwyer, J.M. (2004) 'Australian Health System Restructuring: What Problem Is Being Solved?', *Australia and New Zealand Health Policy*, 19 November: 1–6.

Eckerberg, K., B. Fordberg and P. Wickenberg (1998) 'Sweden: Setting the Pace with Pioneers, Municipalities and Schools', in W.M. Lafferty and K. Eckerberg (eds) *From the Earth Summit to Local Agenda 21*. London: Earthscan.

Eddy, D.M. (1991) 'What Care is "Essential"? What Services are "Basic"?', *Journal of the American Medical Association* 265 (6): 782–8.

Elston, M.A. (1991) 'The Politics of Professional Power: Medicine in a Changing Health Service', in J. Gabe, M. Calnan and M. Bury (eds) *The Sociology of the Health Service*. London: Routledge.

Epstein, P.R. (2000) 'Is Global Warming Harmful to Health?', *Scientific American*, 20 August.

Esping-Andersen, G. (1990) *The Three Worlds of Welfare Capitalism*. Oxford: Polity Press.

Eto, M. (2001) 'Public Involvement in Social Policy Reform: Seen from the Perspective of Japan's Elderly-Care Insurance Scheme', *Journal of Social Policy* 30 (1), 17–36.

European Observatory on Health Care Systems (1999) *Health Care Systems in Transition: United Kingdom*. Copenhagen: European Observatory on Health Care Systems.

European Observatory on Health Care Systems (2000) *Health Care Systems in Transition: Germany*. Copenhagen: European Observatory on Health Care Systems.

European Observatory on Health Care Systems (2001) *Health Care Systems in Transition: Sweden*. Copenhagen: European Observatory on Health Care Systems.

Eurostat (1999) '"Profound Consequences" as EU Grows Older', News Release no. 75/99, 29 July.

Evers, A. and I. Svetlik (eds) (1993) *Balancing Pluralism. New Welfare Mixes in Care for the Elderly*. Aldershot: Avebury.

Exter, A. den, H. Hermans, M. Dosljak and R. Busse (2004) *Health Care Systems in Transition: Netherlands*. Copenhagen: WHO Regional Office for Europe on Behalf of the European Observatory on Health Care Systems.

Fattore, G. (1999) 'Cost Containment and Health Care Reforms in the British NHS', in E. Mossialos and J. Le Grand (eds) *Health Care and Cost Containment in the European Union*. Aldershot: Ashgate.

Feldman, E.A. (2000) *The Ritual of Rights in Japan: Law, Society, and Health Policy*. Cambridge: Cambridge University Press.

Feldman, R.D. (ed.) (2000) *American Health Care: Government, Market Processes, and the Public Trust*. New Brunswick: Transaction Books.

Ferguson, J. (2005) 'WHO Says Skin Cancer Incidence Is Rising', *Journal Watch*, http://dermatology.jwatch.org/cgi/content/full/2005/426/1#primary content

Field, M.G. (1999) 'Comparative Health Systems and the Convergence Hypothesis: The Dialectics of Universalism and Particularism', in F.D. Powell and A.F. Wessen (eds) *Health Care Systems in Transition: An International Perspective*. Thousand Oaks, CA: Sage.

Finlayson, M. (2001) 'Policy Implementation and Modification', in P. Davis and T. Ashton (eds) *Health and Public Policy in New Zealand*. Auckland: Oxford University Press.

Fleck, L.M. (2002) 'Rationing: Don't Give Up: It's Not Only Necessary, but Possible, if the Public Can Be Educated', *The Hastings Center Report* 32 (2): 35–38.

Foster, D. (2001) 'Frequent Flyer Racks up Big Bill', *Detroit News*, 10 October.

Franck, M.J. (1996) *Against the Imperial Judiciary. The Supreme Court vs. the Sovereignty of the People*. Lawrence: University of Kansas Press.

Freeman, R. (1998) 'Competition in Context: The Politics of Health Care Reform in Europe', *International Journal of Quality in Health Care* 10 (5): 395–401.

Freeman, R. (1999) 'Institutions, States and Cultures: Health Policy and Politics in Europe', in J. Clasen (ed.) *Comparative Social Policy*. Oxford: Blackwell.

Freeman, R. (2000) *The Politics of Health in Europe*. Manchester: Manchester University Press.

Freeman, R. (2005) *Learning in Health Policy*. Text of a Presentation to the Social Policy Forum, Bogazici University, Istanbul, 17–18 June, 2005, unpublished manuscript, University of Edinburgh, http://www.pol.ed.ac.uk/freeman

Freeman, R. (2006) *Of Transfers, Transplants and Translations: How Health Policy Makers Learn from Abroad*. Presentation at the Dansk Forum for Sundhedstjenesteforskning (Danish Forum for Health Services Research), University of Aarhus, Denmark, 28 November.

Freeman, R. and J. Clasen (1994) 'The German Social State: An Introduction', in J. Clasen and R. Freeman (eds) *Social Policy in Germany*. Hemel Hempstead: Harvester Wheatsheaf.

Freeman, R. and M. Ruskin (1999) 'Introduction: Welfare, Culture and Europe', in P. Chamberlayne *et al.* (eds) *Welfare and Culture in Europe: Towards a New Paradigm in Social Policy*. London: Jessica Kingsley.

Freidson, E. (1994) *Professionalism Reborn. Theory, Prophecy and Policy*. Cambridge: Polity.

Fries, J.F., C. Everett Koop, C.E. Beadle, P.P. Cooper, M.J. England, R.F. Greaves, J.J. Sokolov and D. Wright (1993) 'Reducing Health Care Costs by Reducing the Need and Demand for Medical Services', *The New England Journal of Medicine* 329 (5): 321–5.

Fuchs, V.R. (1994) 'The Clinton Plan: A Researcher Examines Reform', *Health Affairs* 13(2): 102–14.

Fuchs, V.R. (2004). 'Reflections on the Socio-economic Correlates of Health', *Journal of Health Economics* 23 (4): 653–61.

Fuchs, V.R. (2005) 'Health Care Expenditures Reexamined', *Annals of Internal Medicine* 143 (1): 76–78.

Fukuda, Y., K. Nakamura and T. Takano (2004) 'Wide Range of Socioeconomic Factors Associated with Mortality Among Cities in Japan', *Health Promotion International* 19 (2): 177–87.

Fuller, B.F. (1994) *American Health Care: Rebirth or Suicide?* Springfield, IL: Thomas.

Furuse, T. (1996) 'Changing the Balance of Care: Japan', in OECD (ed.) *Caring for Frail Elderly People*. Paris: OECD.

Gardner, H. (1995) *Politics of Health: The Australian Experience*, 2nd edn. Philadelphia: W.B. Saunders Company.

Gardner, H. (ed.) (1997) *Health Policy in Australia*. New York: Oxford University Press.

Garpenby, P. (1997) 'Implementing Quality Programmes in Three Swedish County Councils: The Views of Politicians, Managers and Doctors', *Health Policy* 39(2): 195–206.

Garpenby, P. (1999) 'Resource Dependency, Doctors and the State: Quality Control in Sweden', *Social Science and Medicine* 49: 405–24.

Garpenby, P. (2001) 'Making Health Policy in Sweden: The Rise and Fall of the 1994 Family Doctor Scheme', in M. Bovens, P. t'Hart and B.G. Peters (eds) *Success and Failure in Public Governance. A Comparative Analysis*. Cheltenham: Edward Elgar.

Garrett, L. (2000) *Betrayal of Trust: The Collapse of Global Public Health*. New York: Hyperion.

Garvin, T. and J. Eyles (2001) 'Public Health Responses for Skin Cancer Prevention: The Policy Framing of Sun Safety in Australia, Canada and England', *Social Science and Medicine* 53 (9): 1175–89.

Gauld, R. (2001) *Revolving Doors: New Zealand's Health Reforms*. Wellington: Institute of Policy Studies and Health Services Research Centre.

Gerdtham, U-G., B. Jönsson, M. MacFarlan and H. Oxley (1998) 'The Determinants of Health Care Expenditure in OECD Countries: A Pooled Data Analysis', *Developments in Health Economics and Public Policy* 6: 113–34.

Giamo, S. (2002) *Markets and Medicine: The Politics of Health Care Reform in Britain, Germany and the United States*. Ann Arbor: The University of Michigan Press.

Giamo, S. and P. Manow (1999) 'Adapting the Welfare State: The Case of Health Care Reform in Britain, Germany, and the United States', *Comparative Political Studies* 32 (8): 967–1000.

Gibson, D. and R. Means (2000) 'Policy Convergence: Restructuring Long-term Care in Australia and the UK', *Policy and Politics* 29 (1): 43–58.

Glenndinning, C. (1998a) 'Health and Social Care Services for Frail Older People in the UK: Changing Responsibilities and New Developments', in C. Glenndinning (ed.) *Rights and Realities. Comparing New Developments in Long-term Care for Older People.* Bristol: Policy Press.

Glenndinning, C. (ed.) (1998b) *Rights and Realities. Comparing New Developments in Long-term Care for Older People.* Bristol: Policy Press.

Glenngård, A.H, F. Hjalte, M. Svensson, A. Anell and V. Bankauskaite (2005) *Health Systems in Transition: Sweden.* Copenhagen: WHO Regional Office for Europe on behalf of the European Observatory on Health Care Systems.

Glover, J.D., D.M.S. Hetzel and S.K. Tennant (2004) 'The Socioeconomic Gradient and Chronic Illness and Associated Risk Factors in Australia', *Australia and New Zealand Health Policy* 1 (8).

Goodin, R.E. and A. Smitsman (2000) 'Placing Welfare States: The Netherlands as a Crucial Test', *Journal of Comparative Public Policy* 2: 39–64.

Gough, R. (1994) 'Från hembiträden till social hemtjänst', in A. Baude and C. Rundström (eds) *Kvinnans plats i det tidiga välfärdssamhället.* Stockholm: Carlsson, pp. 39–56.

Green, A. (1999) *An Introduction to Health Planning in Developing Countries.* Oxford: Oxford University Press.

Green, J. and N. Thorogood (1998) *Analysing Health Policy: A Sociological Approach.* London: Longman.

Greener, I. (2004) 'The Three Moments of New Labour's Health Policy Discourse', *Policy and Politics*, 32 (3): 303–16.

Greenlee, G. (2003) 'Singapore is Right to Get Tough', www.ctnow.com/news/opinion/op ed

Greiner, W. and J.-M. Graf von der Schulenburg (1997) 'Germany', in M.W. Raffel (ed.) *Health Care and Reform in Industrialized Countries.* University Park, PA: Pennsylvania State University Press.

Greß, S., S. Gildemeister and J. Wasem (2004) 'The Social Transformation of American Medicine: A Comparative View from Germany', *Journal of Health Politics, Policy and Law* 29 (4–5): 659–99.

Greß, S., P. Groenewegen, J. Kerssens, B. Braun and J. Wasem (2002) 'Free Choice of Sickness Funds in Regulated Competition: Evidence from Germany and the Netherlands', *Health Policy* 60: 235–54.

Griffiths, P. (2006) 'Alcohol Deaths Soar among Middle-Aged Men', *Reuters*, 7 November.

Hacker, J.S. (1998) 'The Historical Logic of National Health Insurance: Structure and Sequence in the Development of British, Canadian, and U.S. Medical Policy', *Studies of American Political Development* 12: 57–130.

Hacker, J.S. (2004) 'Review Article: Dismantling the Health Care State? Political Institutions, Public Policies and the Comparative Politics of Health Reform', *British Journal of Political Science* 34: 1–32.

Haddon, K. (2006) 'Britain is Fattest Country in Europe', *Agence France Presse*, 10 October.

Håkansson, S. and S. Nordling (1997) 'Sweden', in M.W. Raffel (ed.) *Health Care and Reform in Industrialized Countries.* University Park, PA: Pennsylvania State University Press.

Hall, J. (1999) 'Incremental Change in the Australian Health Care System', *Health Affairs* 18 (3): 95–113.

Ham, C. (ed.) (1997a) *Health Care Reform: Learning from International Experience.* Buckingham: Open University Press.

Ham, C. (1997b) 'Priority Setting in Health Care: Learning from International Experience', *Health Policy* 42(1): 49–66.

Ham, C. (1999) *Health Policy in Britain,* 4th edn. London: Macmillan.

Ham, C. (2001) 'Values and Health Policy: The Case of Singapore', *Journal of Health Politics, Policy and Law* 26 (4): 739–45.

Ham, C. (2004) *Health Policy in Britain,* 5th edn. Basingstoke: Palgrave Macmillan.

Ham, C. and G. Robert (eds) (2003) *Reasonable Rationing: International Experience of Priority Setting in Health Care.* Buckingham: Open University Press.

Hamilton, C. (2001) 'Putting Doctors where They are Needed', *The Australia Institute,* 27 June.

Hancock, L. (ed.) (1999) *Health Policy in the Market State.* St Leonard's, NSW: Allen & Unwin.

Hantrais, L. and Steen Mangen (eds) (1996) *Cross-national Research Methods in the Social Sciences.* London: Pinter.

Harrison, M.I. (2004) *Implementing Change in Health Systems. Market Reforms in the United Kingdom, Sweden and the Netherlands.* London: Sage.

Harrison, M.I. and J. Calltrop (2000) 'The Reorientation of Market-Oriented Reforms in Swedish Health Care', *Health Policy* 50: 219–40.

Harrison, S. (1998) 'The Politics of Evidence-based Medicine in the United Kingdom', *Policy and Politics* 26 (1): 15–31.

Harrison, S. (2001) 'Reforming the Medical Profession in the United Kingdom, 1989–97: Structural Interests in Health Care', in M. Bovens, P. t'Hart and B.G. Peters (eds) *Success and Failure in Public Governance. A Comparative Analysis.* Cheltenham: Edward Elgar.

Harrison, S. (2002) 'New Labour, Modernisation and the Medical Labour Process', *Journal of Social Policy* 31 (3): 465–85.

Harrison, S. and J.N.W. Lim (2000) 'Clinical Governance and Primary Care in the English National Health Service: Some Issues of Organization and Rules', *Critical Public Health* 10 (3): 321–9.

Harrison, S., M. Moran and B. Wood (2002) 'Policy Emergence and Policy Convergence: The Case of "Scientific-bureaucratic Medicine" in the United States and United Kingdom', *British Journal of Politics and International Relations* 4 (1): 1–24.

Harrison, S. and C. Pollitt (1994) *Controlling Health Professionals. The Future of Work and Organization in the NHS.* Buckingham: Open University.

Harrop, M. (1992) 'Introduction', in M. Harrop (ed.) *Power and Policy in Liberal Democracies.* Cambridge: Cambridge University Press.

Havighurst, C.C. (2000) 'Freedom of Contract: The Unexplored Path to Health Care Reform', in R.D. Feldman (ed.) *American Health Care.* New Brunswick: Transaction, 145–67.

Health Care Financing Administration (2000) *Highlights: National Health Expenditures, 2000.* Washington, DC: HFCA.

Henderson, J.N., J. Coreil and C. Bryant (2001) *Social and Behavioural Foundations of Public Health*. London: Sage.

Henderson, S. and A. Peterson (2002) *Consuming Health: The Commodification of Health Care*. London: Routledge.

Herk, R. van, N.S. Klazinga, R.M.J. Schepers and A.F. Casparie (2001) 'Medical Audit: Threat or Opportunity. A Comparative Study of Medical Audit among Medical Specialists in General Hospitals in the Netherlands and England, 1970–1999', *Social Science and Medicine* 53(12): 1721–32.

Herper, M. (2004) 'Cancer's Cost Crisis', *Forbes*, 8 June.

Heywood, A. (2002) *Politics*. Basingstoke: Palgrave.

Hilless, M. and J. Healy (2001) *Health Care Systems in Transition: Australia*. Copenhagen: The European Observatory on Health Care Systems.

Hochschild, A.R. (1995) 'The Culture of Politics: Traditional, Post-Modern, Cold-Modern and Warm-Modern Ideals of Care', *Social Politics* 2 (3): 333–46.

Holland, W. and E. Mossialos (eds) (1999) *Public Health Policies in the European Union*. Aldershot: Ashgate.

Howell, B. (2005) 'Restructuring Primary Health Care Markets in New Zealand: From Welfare Benefits to Insurance Markets', *Australia and New Zealand Health Policy* 2 (2), http://www.anzhealthpolicy.com/content/2/1/20

Howlett, M. and M. Ramesh (2003) *Studying Public Policy: Policy Cycles and Policy Subsystems*. Oxford: Oxford University Press.

Howse, G. (2004) 'Managing Emerging Infectious Diseases: Is a Federal System an Impediment to Effective Laws?', *Australia and New Zealand Health Policy* 1 (7), http://www.anzhealthpolicy.com/content/1/1/7

Hrebenar, R.J., A. Nakainura and A. Nakamura (1998), 'Lobby Regulation in the Japanese Diet', *Parliamentary Affairs* 51: 551–8.

Huggins, C.E. (2002) 'Poor Face Multitude of Environmental Health Threats', Reuters, 17 October.

Hummelgaard, H., M. Baadsgaard and J.B. Nielsen (1998) *Unemployment and Marginalisation in Danish Municipalities*. Copenhagen: Institute of Local Government Studies.

Hurowitz, J.C. (1993) 'Toward a Social Policy for Health', *New England Journal of Medicine* 329 (2): 130–3.

Hurst, J. and J.-P. Poullier (1993) 'Paths to Health Reform', *OECD Observer* 179: 4–7.

Hutten, Jack B.F. and Ada Kerkstra (1996) (eds), *Home Care in Europe: Country-Specific Guide to its Organization and Financing*. Aldershot: Ashgate.

Iglehart, J.K. (1999) 'The American Health Care System: Medicaid', *New England Journal of Medicine* 340 (5): 393–5.

Ikegami, N. (1992) 'Japan: Maintaining Equity through Regulated Fees', *Journal of Health Politics, Policy and Law* 17 (4): 689–713.

Ikegami, N. and J.C. Campbell (1999) 'Health Care Reform in Japan: The Virtues of Muddling Through', *Health Affairs* 18 (3): 56–75.

Ikegami, N., K. Yamauchi and Y. Yamada (2003) 'The Long Term Care Insurance Law in Japan: Impact on Institutional Care Facilities', *International Journal of Geriatric Psychiatry* 18: 217–21.

Iliffe, S. and J. Munro (2000) 'New Labour and Britain's National Health Service: An Overview of Current Reforms', *International Journal of Health Services* 30 (2): 309–34.

Illich, I. (1976) *Limits to Medicine: Medical Nemesis: The Expropriation of Health*. Harmondsworth: Penguin Books.

Imai, Y. (2002) 'Health Care Reform in Japan', *Economics Working Papers* no. 321. Paris: OECD.

Immergut, E.M. (1992) *Health Politics: Interests and Institutions in Western Europe*. Cambridge: Cambridge University Press.

Inagaki, Kana (2006) 'Japan Battles Rising Obesity: Frets Disease May Cut World-Class Longevity', www.ABCNews.go.com

Institute of Alcohol Studies (2002) 'Alcohol Consumption and Harm in the UK and EU', www.ias.org.uk/factsheets/default.htm

Institute of Medicine (1993) *Access to Health Care in America*. Washington, DC: National Academy Press.

Institute of Medicine (2002) *The Future of the Public's Health in the 21st Century*. Washington, DC: Institute of Medicine.

INSWorld (2002) 'Medical Malpractice Costs Skyrocket', www.insworld.com/web/broker/assurex-global/archive/ebmay02.asp

Izuhara, M. (2003) 'Social Inequality under a New Social Contract: Long-Term Care in Japan', *Social Policy and Administration* 37 (4): 395–410.

Jacobs, A. (1998) 'Seeing Difference: Market Health Reform in Europe', *Journal of Health Politics, Policy and Law* 23 (1): 1–33.

Jacobs, R., P.C. Smith and A. Street (2006) *Measuring Efficiency in Health Care: Analytic Techniques and Health Policy*. Cambridge: Cambridge University Press.

Jacobzone, S. (1999) *Ageing and Care for Frail Elderly Persons: An Overview of International Perspectives*. Labour Market and Social Policy Occasional Papers no. 38. Paris: OECD.

Jacobzone, S., E. Cambois, E. Chaplain and J.M. Robine (1999) *The Health of Older Persons in OECD Countries: Is it Improving Fast Enough to Compensate for Population Ageing?* Labour Market and Social Policy Occasional Paper no. 37. Paris: OECD.

Jamieson, A. (1996) 'Issues in Home Care Services', in OECD (ed.) *Caring for Frail Elderly People. Policies in Evolution*. Social Policy Studies no. 19. Paris: OECD.

Japan Ministry of Health, Labour and Welfare (1999) *Annual Report on Health and Welfare: Social Security and National Life*. Tokyo: Ministry of Health, Labour and Welfare.

Japan Ministry of Health, Labour and Welfare (2000) 'Establishing a Reliable and Stable Medical System', White Paper: *Annual Report on Health and Welfare*. Tokyo: Ministry of Health, Labour and Welfare.

Japan Ministry of Health, Labour and Welfare (2004), *Direction of Health and Welfare Policies for the Elderly over the Next 5 Years*. Tokyo: Ministry of Health, Labour and Welfare.

Jegers, M., K. Kesteloot, D. De Graeve and W. Gilles (2002) 'A Typology for Provider Payment Systems in Health Care', *Health Policy* 60: 255–73.

Jenson, J. and S. Jacobzone (2000) *Care Allowances for the Frail Elderly and Their Impact on Women Care-givers*. Labour Market and Social Policy Occasional Papers no. 41. Paris: OECD.

Johansson, S. (2000) 'Women's Paradise Lost? Social Services and Care in the Quasi-Markets in Sweden' in B. Hobson (eds) *Gender and Citizenship in Transition*. Basingstoke: Palgrave Macmillan.

Johnson, M. and L. Cullen (2000) 'Solidarity Put to the Test. Health and Social Care in the UK', *International Journal of Social Welfare* 9(4): 228–37.

Johnson, T. (1995) 'Governmentality and the Institutionalization of Expertise', in T. Johnson, G. Larkin and M. Saks (eds) *Health Professions and the State in Europe*. London: Routledge.

Jonas, S. (2003) *An Introduction to the U.S. Health Care System,* 5th edn. New York: Springer Publishers.

Joung, I.M., H. van der Mheen, K. Stranks, F.W. van Poppel and J.P. Mackenbach (1994) 'Differences in Self-Reported Morbidity by Marital Status and Living Arrangement', *International Journal of Epidemiology* 23: 91–7.

Kassler, J. (1994) *Bitter Medicine: Greed and Chaos in American Health Care.* New York: Birch Lane Press.

Kawachi, I., B.P. Kennedy and R.G. Wilkinson (eds) (1999) *The Society and Population Health Reader: Income Inequality and Health*. New York: New Press.

Kay, A. (2001) 'Beyond Policy Community. The Case of the GP Fundholding Scheme', *Public Administration* 79 (3): 561–77.

Keatinge, W.R. and G.C. Donaldson (2004) 'The Impact of Global Warming on Health and Mortality', *Southern Medical Journal* 97 (11): 1093–1100.

Kelly, E. and J. Hurst (2006) *Health Care Quality Indicators Project: Initial Indicators Report*. Paris: OECD.

Kenner, D. (2001) 'The Role of Traditional Herbal Medicine in Modern Japan', *Acupuncture Today,* August.

Kerkstra, A. (1996) 'Netherlands', in J.B.F. Hutten and A. Kerkstra (eds) *Home Care in Europe: Country-Specific Guide to its Organization and Financing*. Aldershot: Ashgate.

Kersh, R. and J. Morone (2002) 'The Politics of Obesity: Seven Steps to Government Action', *Health Affairs* 21 (November/December): 142–53.

Kitchener, M., T. Ng, N. Miller and C. Harrington (2005) 'Medicaid Home and Community-Based Services: National Program Trends', *Health Affairs* 24 (1): 206–12.

Klein, R. (1997) 'Learning from Others: Shall the Last Be the First?', *Journal of Health Politics, Policy and Law* 22 (5): 1267–78.

Klein, R. (2001) *The New Politics of the NHS,* 4th edn. Harlow: Prentice Hall.

Klein, R. (2005) 'A Middle Way for Rationing Healthcare Resources', *British Medical Journal* 330: 1340–41.

Klein, R. and A. Williams (2000) 'Setting Priorities: What is Holding Us Back – Inadequate Information or Inadequate Institutions?', in A. Coulter and C. Ham (eds) *The Global Challenge of Health Care Rationing*. Buckingham: Open University Press, 15–26.

Kleinke, J.D. (2001) *Oxymorons: The Myth of a U.S. Health Care System.* San Francisco: Josey-Bass.

Knijn, T. (1998) 'Social Care in the Netherlands', in J. Lewis (ed.) *Gender, Social Care and Welfare State Restructuring in Europe*. Aldershot: Ashgate.

Knijn, T. (2000) 'Marketization and the Struggling Logics of (Home) Care in the Netherlands', in M.H. Meyer (ed.) *Care Work: Gender, Labor and the Welfare State*. New York: Routledge.

Knijn, T. (2001) 'Care Work: Innovations in the Netherlands', in M. Daly (ed.) *Care Work: The Quest of Security*. Geneva: International Labour Office.

Kobayashi, Y. and M.R. Reich (1993) 'Health Care Financing for the Elderly in Japan', *Social Science and Medicine* 37 (3): 343–53.

Kohn, L., J. Corrigan and M. Donaldson (eds) (1999) *To Err is Human: Building a Safer Health System*. Washington, DC: National Academy Press.

Konrad, R. (2006) 'E. coli Fears Prompt Recall of Lettuce', *Associated Press*, October 7.

Koop, C.E., C. Pearson, and M.R. Schwartz (eds) (2002) *Critical Issues in Global Health*. San Francisco: Jossey-Bass.

Kremer, M. (2005) 'Consumers in Charge of Care: The Dutch Personal Care Budget (PGB) and Its Impact on The Market, Professionals and the Family', unpublished manuscript.

Kröger, T. (2001) *Comparative Research on Social Care. The State of the Art*. Brussels: European Commission.

Krugman, Paul, and Robin Wells (2006) 'The Health Care Crisis and What to Do About It', *New York Review of Books*, 23 March.

Kuhlmann, E. (2006) *Modernising Health Care. Reinventing Professions, the State and the Public*. Bristol: Policy Press.

Lamm, R.D. (2003) *The Brave New World of Health Care*. Golden, CO: Fulcrum Press.

Lamm, R.D. and R.H. Blank (2007) *Condition Critical: A New Moral Vision for U.S. Health Care*. Golden, CO: Fulcrum Press.

Lancet, The (ed.) (2006) 'Rationing is Essential in Tax-Funded Health Systems', *The Lancet* 368 (9545): 1394.

Lang, T. and G. Rayner (2005) 'Obesity: A Growing Issue for European Policy?' *Journal of European Social Policy* 15 (4): 301–32.

Lasser, K.E., D.U. Hmmelstein and S. Woolhandler (2006) 'Access to Care, Health Status and Health Disparities in the United States and Canada: Results of a Cross-National Population-Based Survey', *American Journal of Public Health* 96: 1300–7.

Laurance, J. and C. Norton (2000) ' "Unresponsive" NHS Ranked 18th in the World', *The Independent*, 21 June.

Lee, K., K. Buse and S. Fustukian (eds) (2002) *Health Policy in a Globalising World*. Cambridge: Cambridge University Press.

Leeder, S.R. (1999) *Healthy Medicine: Challenges Facing Australia's Health Services*. St Leonard's, NSW: Allen & Unwin.

Leichter, H.M. (1991) *Free to be Foolish: Politics and Health Promotion in the United States and Great Britain*. Princeton, NJ: Princeton University Press.

Leutwyler, K. (1995) 'The Price of Prevention', *Scientific American*, April: 124–9.

Lewis, J. (2001) 'Older People and the Health-Social Care Boundary in the UK: Half a Century of Hidden Policy Conflict', *Social Policy and Administration* 35 (4): 343–59.

Lian, O.S. (2003) 'Convergence or Divergence? Reforming Primary Care in Norway and Britain', *The Milbank Quarterly* 81 (2): 305–30.

Lieverdink, H. and J.H. van der Made (1997) 'The Reform of Health Insurance Systems in the Netherlands and Germany: Dutch Gold and German Silver', in C. Altenstetter and J.W. Björkam (eds) *Health Policy Reform, National Variations and Globalization.* London: Macmillan.

Light, D. (1995) 'Countervailing Powers: A Framework for Professions in Transition', in T. Johnson, G. Larkin and M. Saks (eds) *Health Professions and the State in Europe.* London: Routledge.

Lijphart, A. (1999) *Patterns of Democracy.* New Haven, CT: Yale University Press.

Lim, Meng-Kim (1998) 'Health Care Systems in Transition II. Singapore, Part I.', *Journal of Public Health Medicine* 20 (1): 16–22.

Lim, Meng-Kim (2004) 'Shifting the Burden of Health Care Finance: A Case Study of Public–Private Partnership in Singapore', *Health Policy* 69: 83–92.

Lin, V. and P. Robinson (2005) 'Australian Public Health Policy in 2003–2004', *Australia and New Zealand Health Policy* 2 (7), http://www.anzhealthpolicy.com/content/2/1/7

Lin, Y.Y. (2006) 'Update on Medishield Reform: Early Results', MOH Information Paper: 2006/013. Singapore: Ministry of Health.

Locock, L. (2000) 'The Changing Nature of Rationing in the UK National Health Service', *Public Administration* 78 (1): 91–109.

Lombarts, M.J.M.H. and N.S. Klazinga (2001) 'A Policy Analysis of the Introduction and Dissemination of External Peer Review (Visitatie) as a Means of Professional Self-regulation amongst Medical Specialists in the Netherlands in the Period 1985–2000', *Health Policy* 58(3): 191–213.

London School of Hygiene and Tropical Medicine (1999) *Rapid Reviews of Public Health for London. Housing and the Built Environment.* London: London School of Hygiene and Tropical Medicine.

Loo, M. van het, J.P. Kahan and K.G.H. Okma (1999) 'Developments in Health Care Cost Containment in the Netherlands', in E. Mossialos and J. Le Grand (eds) *Health Care and Cost Containment in the European Union.* Aldershot: Ashgate.

Low, J.A., W.C. Ng, K.B. Yap and K.M. Chan (2000) 'End-of-life Issues: Preferences and Choices of a Group of Elderly Chinese Subjects', *Annals of the Academy of Medicine* 29 (1): 50–6.

Lowi, T.J. (1966) 'Distribution, Regulation, Redistribution: The Functions of Government', in R.B. Ripley (ed.) *Public Policies and their Politics: Techniques of Government Control.* New York: W.W. Norton.

Lundsgaard, J. (2004) 'Consumer Direction and Choice in Long-Term Care for Older Persons, Including Payments for Informal Care: How Can It Help Improve Care Outcomes, Employment and Fiscal Sustainability?', *Health Working Papers*, No. 20, Paris: OCED.

Luzio, G. di (2004) 'The Irresistible Decline of the Medical Profession? An Empirical Investigation of Its Autonomy and Economic Situation in the Changing German Welfare State', *German Politics* 13 (3): 419–48.

Maarse, H. (2004) 'User Charges in the Netherlands', *Euro Observer* 6 (3): 4–5.

Maarse, H. and A. Paulus (2003) 'Has Solidarity Survived? A Comparative Analysis of the Effect of Social Health Insurance Reforms in Four European Countries', *Journal of Health Politics, Policy and Law* 28 (4): 585–614.

Maarse, J.A.M. (1997) 'Netherlands', in M.W. Raffel (ed.) *Health Care and Reform in Industrialized Countries*. University Park, PA: Pennsylvania State University Press.

Mabbett, D. and H. Bolderson (1999) 'Theories and Methods in Comparative Social Policy', in J. Clasen (ed.) *Comparative Social Policy*. Oxford: Blackwell.

MacDaid, D. (2001) 'European Health Technology Assessment Quo Vadis?', *Eurohealth* 7 (1): 27–8.

Macer, D. (1999) 'Bioethics in and from Asia', *Journal of Medical Ethics* 25: 293–5.

Mackenbach, J.P., A.E. Cavelaars, F. Groenhof and J.J. Geurts (1997) 'Socioeconomic Inequalities in Morbidity and Mortality in Western Europe', *Lancet* 7: 349 (9066):1655–9.

Mackenzie, E.R. (1998) *Healing the Social Body: A Holistic Approach to Public Health Policy*. London: Garland.

Maclennan, A.H., D.H. Wilson and A.W. Taylor (1996) 'Prevalence and Cost of Alternative Medicine in Australia', *Lancet* 347: 569–73.

Malcolm, L. and M. Powell (1996) 'The Development of Individual Practice Associations and Related Groups in New Zealand', *New Zealand Medical Journal* 109: 184–7.

Manning, A. (2003) 'Experts Tackle Global SARS Policy', *USA Today*, 7 May.

Marinker, M. (2002) *Health Targets in Europe: Policy, Progress, and Promise*. London: BMJ Books.

Marmot, M. and R.G. Wilkinson (eds) (1999) *Social Determinants of Health*. Oxford: Oxford University Press.

Marnoch, G. (2003) 'Scottish Devolution: Identity and Impact and The Case of Community Care for the Elderly', *Public Administration* 81 (2): 253–73.

Martin, J. and G. Salmond (2001) 'Policy Making: The "Messy Reality"', in P. Davis and T. Ashton (eds) *Health and Public Policy in New Zealand*. Auckland: Oxford University Press.

Massaro, T.A. and Y.-N. Wong (1996) *Medical Savings Accounts: The Singapore Experience*. Singapore: National Center for Policy Analysis.

Matcha, D.A. (2003) *Health Care Systems of the Developing World: How the United States' System Remains an Outlier*. Westport, CT: Praeger Publishers.

Matsushita, Y., N. Yoshiike, F. Kaneda, K. Yoshita and H. Takimoto (2004) 'Trends in Childhood Obesity in Japan over the Last 25 Years from the National Nutrition Survey', *Obesity Research* 12: 205–14.

Maynard, A. and K. Bloor (2001) 'Our Certain Fate: Rationing in Health Care', Office of Health Economics Briefings Page, www.ohe.org/our.htm

McClellan, M. and D. Kessler (1999) 'A Global Analysis of Technological Change in Health Care: The Case of Heart Attacks', *Health Affairs* 18 (3): 250–5.

McConahy, K. (2002) 'Food Portions Are Positively Related To Energy Intake and Body Weight in Early Childhood', *Journal of Pediatrics* 140 (March): 340–7.

McGinnis, J.M. and W.H. Foege (1993) 'Actual Causes of Death in the United States', *Journal of the American Medical Association* 270: 2207.

McKie, J., J. Richardson, P. Singer and H. Kuhse (1998) *The Allocation of Health Care Resources: An Ethical Evaluation of the 'QALY' Approach*. Aldershot: Dartmouth.

Means, R., S. Richards and R. Smith (2003) *Community Care: Policy and Practice*, 3rd edn. Basingstoke: Palgrave.

Means, R. and R. Smith (1998) *Community Care. Policy and Practice,* 2nd edn. London: Macmillan.

Mechanic, D. (1994) *Inescapable Decisions: The Imperatives of Health Care.* New Brunswick, NJ: Transaction.

Mechanic, David (1999) 'Lessons from Abroad: A Comparative Perspective', in F.D. Powell and A.F. Wessen (eds) *Health Care Systems in Transition: An International Perspective.* Thousand Oaks, CA: Sage.

Medicare and Graduate Medical Education (1995) 'Policy Issues and Questions', www.cbo.gov/showdoc.cfm?index.htm

'Medicare to Pay for Variety of Obesity Surgeries' (2006). MSNBC, 21 February, www.msnbc.msn.com/id/11488309/from/ET/

Mendelson, D.N., R.G. Abramson and R.J. Rubin (1995) 'State Involvement in Medical Technology Assessment', *Health Affairs* 14 (2): 83–98.

Merson, M.H. (2004) *International Public Health.* New York: Jones and Bartlett Publishers.

Merson, M.H., R.E. Black and A.J. Mills (2001) *International Public Health: Diseases, Programs, Systems, and Policies.* Sudbury, MA: Jones & Bartlett.

Meyer, J.A. (1996) *Der Weg zur Pflegeversicherung. Positionen, Akteure, Politikprozesse.* Frankfurt am Main: Mabuse Verlag.

Milio, N. (2000) *Public Health in the Market: Facing Managed Care, Lean Government, and Health Disparities.* Ann Arbor, MI: University of Michigan Press.

Miller, A.S. and A. Hagihara (1997) 'Organ Transplanting in Japan: The Debate Begins', *Public Health* 111: 367–72.

Mills, A., S. Bennett, S. Russell and N. Attanayake (eds) (2001) *The Challenge of Health Sector Reform: What Governments Must Do?* Basingstoke: Palgrave.

Ministry of Health and Social Affairs (2001) 'Towards Public Health on Equal Terms', Fact Sheet no. 3. Stockholm: Ministry of Health and Social Affairs.

Ministry of Health, Welfare and Sports (2005) *Health Insurance in the Netherlands. The New Health Insurance System from 2006.* The Hague: Ministry of Health, Welfare and Sport.

Moeller, D.W. (2004) *Environmental Health,* 3rd edn. Cambridge: Harvard University Press.

Mokdad, A. H., E.S. Ford, B.A. Bowman, W.H. Dietz, F. Vinicor, V.S. Bales and J.S. Marks (2003) 'Prevalence of Obesity, Diabetes, and Obesity-related Health Risk Factors', *Journal of the American Medical Association* 289 (1): 76–9.

Mokdad, A.H., J.S. Marks, D.F. Stroup and J.L. Gerberding (2004) 'Actual Causes of Death in the United States, 2000', *Journal of the American Medical Association* 291:1238–45.

Monheit, Alan C. (2003). 'Persistence in Health Expenditures in the Short Run: Prevalence and Consequences', *Medical Care* 41 (7): III53–III64.

Moran, M. (1999) *Governing the Health Care State: A Comparative Study of the United Kingdom, the United States and Germany.* Manchester: Manchester University Press.

Moran, M. (2000) 'Understanding the Welfare State: The Case of Health Care', *British Journal of Politics and International Relations* 2 (2): 135–60.

Moran, M. and B. Wood (1993) *States, Regulation and the Medical Profession*. Cheltenham: Edward Elgar.

Mossialos, E. and J. Le Grand (eds) (1999) *Health Care and Cost Containment in the European Union*. Aldershot: Ashgate.

Mueller, K.J. (1993) *Health Care Policy in the United States*. Lincoln, NE: University of Nebraska Press.

Mullen, P. (1998) 'Rational Rationing?', *Health Services Management Research* 11: 113–23.

Musgrave, F.W. (2006) *The Economics of U.S. Health Care Policy: The Role of Market Forces*. New York: M.E. Sharpe.

Musgrave, P. R. Zeramdini and G. Carrin (2002) 'Basic Patterns in National Health Expenditure', *Bulletin of the World Health Organization* 80 (2): 1–17.

Nakahara, T. (1997) 'The Health System of Japan', in M.W. Raffel (ed.) *Health Care and Reform in Industrialized Countries*. University Park, PA: Pennsylvania State University Press.

Nathan, S.A., E. Develin, N. Grove and A.B. Zwi (2005) 'An Australian Childhood Obesity Summit: The Role of Data and Evidence in "Public" Policy Making', *Australia and New Zealand Health Policy* 2 (17), http://www.anzhealthpolicy.com/content/2/1/17

National Board of Health and Welfare (2000) *Social Services in Sweden in 1999. Needs – Interventions – Development*. Stockholm: National Board of Health and Welfare.

National Center for Health Care Statistics, Centers for Disease Control and Prevention (2006) *Chartbook on Trends in the Health of Americans*. Washington, DC: Government Printing Office.

National Contract for Public Health (2001) *National Contract for Public Health. Declaration of Intent to Cooperate. 2001–2003*. Leiden, 22 February, www.minvws.nl/documents/ Health/natcontract.pdf

Navarro, V. (1999) 'Health and Equity in the World in the Era of "Globalization"', *International Journal of Health Services* 29 (2): 215–26.

Navarro, V., and L. Shi (2001) 'The Political Context of Social Inequalities and Health', *International Journal of Health Services* 31 (1): 1–21.

Navarro, V., C. Borrell, J. Benach, C. Muntaner, A. Quiroga, M. Rodriquez-Sanz, N. Verges, J. Guma and M.I. Pasarin (2003) 'The Importance of the Political and the Social in Explaining Mortality Differentials among the Countries of the OECD, 1950–1998', *International Journal of Health Services* 33 (3): 419–94.

'New Zealand Bans Fatty, Sugary Foods and Drinks from Schools to Fight Obesity', *The Associated Press*, 21 September 2006.

New Zealand Core Services Committee (1992) *The Core Debate: How We Define the Core*. Wellington: National Advisory Committee on Core Health and Disability Support Services.

New Zealand Ministry of Health (2001) *New Zealand Health Strategy, District Health Board TOOLKIT, Obesity: To Reduce the Rate of Obesity*. Wellington: Ministry of Health.

New Zealand Ministry of Health (2003) *Achieving Health for All People: A Framework for Public Health Action*. Wellington: Ministry of Health.

Noguchi, H. and S. Shimizutani (2005) 'Supplier-Induced Demand in Japan's At-Home Care Industry', *ESRI Discussion Paper Series* 148: 1–131.

OECD (1987) *Financing and Delivering Health Care: A Comparative Analysis of OECD Countries*. Paris: OECD.

OECD (1988) *Ageing Populations: Social Policy Implications*. Paris: OECD.

OECD (1992) *The Reform of Health Care Systems: A Comparative Analysis of Seven OECD Countries*. Paris: OECD.

OECD (1996) *Caring for Frail Elderly People. Policies in Evolution*. Social Policy Studies no. 19. Paris: OECD.

OECD (2001) *OECD Health Data 2001. A Comparative Analysis of 30 Countries*. Paris: OECD.

OECD (2005a) *OECD Health Project*, http://www.oecd.org/document/28/0,2340,en_2649_37407_2536540_1_1_1_37407,00.html

OECD (2005b) *The OECD Health Project: Long-term Care for Older People*, Paris: OECD.

OECD (2006) *OECD Health Data 2006. A Comparative Analysis of 30 Countries*. Paris: OECD. Version: 26 June.

Office of Disease Prevention and Health Promotion (2006) 'Fact Sheet'. http://odphp.osophs.dhhs.gov

Ohnuki-Tiernev, E. (1984) *Illness and Culture in Contemporary Japan: An Anthropological View*. Cambridge: Cambridge University Press.

Okamoto, K. (2001) *Public Health of Japan 2001*. Osaka: National Institute of Public Health.

Okma, K.G.H. (2001) *Health Care, Health Policies and Health Care Reforms in the Netherlands*. International Publication Series Health, Welfare and Sport no. 7. The Hague: Ministry of Health, Welfare and Sport.

O'Malley, S.P. (2006) 'The Australian Experiment: The Use of Evidence Based Medicine for the Reimbursement of Surgical and Diagnostic Procedures (1998–2004)', *Australia and New Zealand Health Policy* 3 (3), http://www.anzhealthpolicy.com/content/3/1/3

O'Neill, M. and P. Simard (2006) 'Choosing Indicators to Evaluate Healthy Cities Projects: A Political Task?', *Health Promotion International* 21 (2): 145–52.

Øvretveit, J. (1998) *Comparative and Cross-cultural Health Research*. Abingdon, UK: Radcliffe Medical Press.

Palmer, G.R. and S.D. Short (2000) *Health Care and Public Policy: An Australian Analysis*, 3rd edn. Melbourne: Macmillan.

Paton, C. (1997) 'The Politics and Economics of Health Care Reform: Britain in a Comparative Context', in C. Altenstetter and J.W. Björkam (eds) *Health Policy Reform, National Variations and Globalization*. London: Macmillan.

Peckham, S. and M. Exworthy (2003) *Primary Care in the UK*. Basingstoke: Palgrave.

Perleth, M., R. Busse and F.W. Schwartz (1999) 'Regulation of Health-related Technologies in Germany', *Health Policy* 46 (2): 105–26.

Peters, B.G. (1998) *Comparative Politics: Theory and Methods*. Basingstoke: Macmillan.

Peterson, C.L. (2006) *Alternatives for Modeling Results from the RAND Health Insurance Experiment*. Washington, DC: Congressional Research Service.

Pfau-Effinger, B. (2004) *Development of Culture, Welfare State and Women's Employment in Europe*. Aldershot: Ashgate.

Pollitt, C. (2002) 'Clarifying Convergence: Striking Similarities and Durable Differences in Public Management Reform', *Public Management Review*, 4 (1): 471–92.

Porter, M.E. and E.O. Teisberg (2006) *Redefining Health Care: Value-Based Competition on Results*. Cambridge, MA: Harvard Business School Press.

Powell, F.D. and A.F. Wessen (eds) (1999) *Health Care Systems in Transition: An International Perspective*. Thousand Oaks: Sage.

Public Citizen (2003) 'Medical Malpractice: Bush & Congress Should Act to Reduce Medical Errors, Not Reduce Compensation to Injured Patients', www.citizen.org

Quah, E. and T.L. Boon (2003) 'The Economic Cost of Particulate Air Pollution on Health in Singapore', *Journal of Asian Economics* 14 (1): 73–90.

Quah, S.R. (2003) 'Traditional Healing Systems and the Ethos of Science', *Social Science and Medicine* 57 (10): 1997–2012.

Raffel, M.W. (ed.) (1997) *Health Care and Reform in Industrialized Countries*. University Park, PA: University of Pennsylvania Press.

Ranade, W. (ed.) (1998) *Markets and Health Care: A Comparative Analysis*. London: Longman.

Rauch, D. (2005) *Institutional Fragmentation and Social Service Variations: A Scandinavian Comparison*. Doctoral thesis, Umeå, Sweden: University of Umeå.

Rehnberg, C. (1997) 'Sweden', in C. Ham (ed.) *Health Care Reform: Learning from International Experience*. Buckingham: Open University Press.

Reidpath, D.D., D. Crawford, L. Tilgner and C. Gibbons (2002) 'Relationship between Body Mass Index and the Use of Healthcare Services in Australia', *Obesity Research* 10: 526–31.

Reinhardt, W.E. (1990) 'Commentary', in OECD (ed.), *Health Care Systems in Transition: The Search for Efficiency*. Paris: OECD.

Reiss, C. (2003) 'Malpractice Debate Now A Blame Game', *Sarasota Herald Tribune* 13 January, p. 1A.

Reuters (2005) 'Expert Sees Obesity Hitting U.S. Life Expectancy', http://news.yahoo.com/news?tmpl=story&cid=571&u=/nm/20050202/html

Reuters (2006) 'Hospitals Prepare for Growing Ranks of Obese', 6 June.

Richmond, J.B. and R. Fein (1995) 'The Health Care Mess: A Bit of History', *Journal of the American Medical Association* 273(1): 69–71.

Rico, A., R.B. Saltman and W.G.W. Boerma (2003) 'Organizational Restructuring in European Health Systems: The Role of Primary Care', *Social Policy and Administration* 37(6): 592–608.

Riska, E. and K. Wegar (1995) 'The Medical Profession in the Nordic Countries. Medical Uncertainty and Gender-based Work', in T. Johnson, G. Larkin and M. Saks (eds) *Health Professions and the State in Europe*. London: Routledge.

Rix, M., A. Owen and K. Eagar (2005) '(Re)form with Substance? Restructuring and Governance in the Australian Health System 2004/05', *Australia and New Zealand Health Policy* 2 (19), http://www.anzhealthpolicy.com/content/2/1/19

Romaine-Davis, A., J. Boondas and A. Lenihan (eds) (1995) *Encyclopedia of Home Care for the Elderly*. Westport, CT: Greenwood Press.

Ros, C.C., P.P. Groenwegen and D.M.J. Delnoij (2000) 'All Rights Reserved, or Can We Just Copy? Cost Sharing Arrangements and Characteristics of Health Care Systems', *Health Policy* 52(1): 1–13.

Rosenbrock, R. and T. Gerlinger (2004) *Gesundheitspolitik. Eine systematische Einführung*. Bern: Verlag Hans Huber.

Ross, E. (2003) 'WHO Links SARS to Three Small Mammals', *Associated Press News Story*, 23 May.

Sage, W.M. and R. Kersh (eds) (2006) *Medical Malpractice and the U.S. Health Care System*. Cambridge, MA: Cambridge University Press.

Salter, B. (2005) 'Governing UK Medical Performance: A Struggle for Policy Dominance', Working Paper 2/2005. Aarhus: University of Aarhus.

Saltman, R.B. (1997) 'Convergence Versus Social Embeddedness. Debating the Future Direction of Health Systems', *European Journal of Public Health* 7 (4): 449–53.

Saltman, R.B. (1998) 'Health Reform in Sweden: The Road Beyond Cost Containment', in W. Ranade (ed.) *Markets and Health Care: A Comparative Analysis*. London: Longman.

Saltman, R.B. (2002) 'Regulating Incentives: The Past and Present Role of the State in Health Care Systems', *Social Science and Medicine* 54 (11): 1677–84.

Saltman, R.B. and V. Bankauskaite (2006) 'Conceptualizing Decentralization in European Health Systems: A Functional Perspective', *Journal of Health Economics, Policy and Law* 1: 127–47.

Saltman, R.B and S.-E. Bergman (2005) 'Renovating the Commons: Swedish Health Care Reforms in Perspective', *Journal of Health Politics, Policy and Law* 30 (1): 253–76.

Saltman, R.B, A. Rico and W. Boerma (eds) (2006) *Primary Care in the Driver's Seat? Organizational Reform in European Primary Care*. Maidenhead: Open University Press.

Saltman, R., J. Figueras and C. Sakellarides (eds) (1998) *Critical Challenges for Health Care Reform in Europe*, Buckingham: Open University Press.

Schneider, M.J. (2005) *Introduction to Public Health*, 2nd edn. New York: Jones and Bartlett Publishers.

Schoen, C., E. Strumpf, K. Davis, R. Osborn, K. Donelan and R.J. Blendon (2000) *The Elderly's Experiences with Health Care in Five Nations*. New York: The Commonwealth Fund.

Schwartz, F.F. (1997) *Fixing Health Budgets: Experience from Europe and North America*. New York: John Wiley.

Schwartz, F.F. and R. Busse (1997) 'Germany', in C. Ham (ed.) *Health Care Reform: Learning from International Experience*. Buckingham: Open University Press.

Scott, C.D. (2001) *Public and Private Roles in Health Care: Experiences from Seven Countries*. Buckingham: Open University Press.

Scott, W.G., H.M. Scott and T.S. Auld (2005) 'Consumer Access to Health Information on the Internet: Health Policy Implications', *Australia and New Zealand Health Policy* 2 (13), http://www.anzhealthpolicy.com/content/2/1/13

Seedhouse, D. (1991) *Liberating Medicine*. Chichester: Wiley.

Sexton, S. (2001) 'Trading Health Care Away? GATS, Public Services and Privatisation', www.thecornerhouse.org.uk/pdf/briefing/23gats.pdf

Shortt, J. (2004) 'Obesity: A Public Health Dilemma', *AORN Journal* 80 (6): 1069–76, 78.

Singapore Ministry of Health (1995) 'Traditional Chinese Medicine', *Report of the Committee on Traditional Chinese Medicine*, October.

Singapore Ministry of Health (2000) *White Paper on 'Affordable Health Care'*. Singapore: MOH.

Singapore Ministry of Health (2001) *Health Care Financing in Singapore*. Singapore: MOH.

Singapore Ministry of Health (2002a) 'Health Care Financing in Singapore', www.gov.sg/scripts/moh/newmoh/ asp/you.html

Singapore Ministry of Health (2002b) *Hospital Statistics*. Singapore: Ministry of Health.

Singapore Ministry of Health (2002c) 'Overview of the Singapore Healthcare System', www.gov.sg/moh/mohinfo/mohinfo-a.html

Singapore Ministry of Health (2006) Singapore: Singapore Ministry of Health, http://www.moh.gov.sg/corp/index.do

Skinner, J.S., D.O. Staiger and E.S. Fisher (2006) 'Is Technological Change in Medicine Always Worth It? The Case of Myocardial Infarction', *Health Affairs* 25: w34–w47.

Sloane, T. (2005), 'The Long-Term Problem', *Modern Healthcare* 35 (30): 18.

Smith, R.D., R. Beaglehole, D. Woodward, N. Drager and T.K. McArthur (2003) *Global Public Goods for Health: Health, Economic, and Public Health Perspectives*. Oxford: Oxford University Press.

Social Insurance Agency (2006) 'Overview of the Social Insurance Systems', www.sia.go.jp/e/index.html

Stanton, G.T. (2003) 'How Marriage Improves Health', www.divorcereform.org/mel/abetterhealth.html

Starfield, B. (2000) 'Is US Health Really the Best in the World?', *Journal of the American Medical Association* 284 (4): 483–5.

Starr, P. and E. Immergut (1987) 'Health Care and the Boundaries of Politics', in C.S Maier (ed.) *Changing Boundaries of the Political. Essays on the Evolving Balance between the State and Society, Public and Private in Europe*. Cambridge: Cambridge University Press.

State Coverage Initiatives (2002) 'Who are the Uninsured in the United States?', www.statecoverage.net/who.html

Steinberg, E.P. and B.R. Luce (2005) 'Evidence Based: Caveat Emptor!', *Health Affairs* 24 (1): 80–93.

Stone, D. (1999) 'Learning Lessons and Transferring Policy across Time, Space and Disciplines', *Politics* 19 (1): 51–9.

Straits Times, The (2000) 'Singapore's Health System is Best in Asia', 21 January.

Stukel, T.A., F. Lee Lucas and D.E. Wennberg (2005) 'Long-term Outcomes of Regional Variations in Intensity of Invasive vs. Medical Management of Medicare Patients with Acute Myocardial Infarction', *Journal of the American Medical Association* 293: 1329–37.

Stunkard, A.J. and J. Sobal (1995) 'Psychological Consequences of Obesity', in K.D. Brownell and C.G. Fairburn (eds) *Eating Disorders and Obesity: A Comprehensive Handbook*. New York: The Guilford Press.

Sullivan, Louis W. (1990) 'Healthy People 2000', *New England Journal of Medicine* 323: 1065–7.

Sultz, H.A. and K.M. Young (1999) *Health Care USA: Understanding its Organisation and Delivery*, 2nd edn. New York: Aspen.

Swerissen, H. (2004) 'Australian Primary Care Policy in 2004: Two Tiers or One for Medicare?', *Australia and New Zealand Health Policy* 1 (2), http://www.anzhealthpolicy.com/content/1/1/2

Syrett, K. (2003) 'A Technocratic Fix to the "Legitimacy Problem"? The Blair Government and Health Care Rationing in the United Kingdom', *Journal of Health Politics, Policy and Law* 28 (4): 715–46.

Szebehely, M. (2005) 'Anhörigas betalda och obetalda äldreomsorgsinsatser', in Statens Offentliga Utredningor (SOU) (2005:66), *Forskingsrapporter till Jämställdhetspolitiska utredningen*, Stockholm: Social Department.

Takano, T. and K. Nakamura (2004) 'Participatory Research to Enhance Vision Sharing for Healthy Town Initiatives in Japan', *Health Promotion International* 19 (3): 299–307.

Tanner, L. (2006) 'U.S. Newborn Survival Rate Ranks Low', AP, 5 May.

Teo, P., A. Chan and P. Straughan (2003) 'Providing Health Care for Older Persons in Singapore', *Health Policy* 64(3): 399–413.

Tester, S. (1996) *Community Care for Older People. A Comparative Perspective*. London: Macmillan.

Tester, S. (1998) 'Comparative Approaches to Long-Term Care for Adults', in J. Clasen (ed.), *Comparative Social Policy: Theories and Methods*, Oxford: Blackwell: 136–58.

Theobald, H. (2003) 'Welfare System, Professionalisation and the Question of Inequality', *International Journal of Sociology and Social Policy* 23 (4/5): 159–85.

Theobald, Hildegard (2004) 'Care Services for the Elderly in Germany. Infrastructure, Access and Utilisation from the Perspective of Different User Groups', discussion paper (SP I 2004-302), Working Group on Public Health Policy. Berlin: Social Science Research Centre (WZB) Berlin.

Thorpe, K.E. (1992) 'Health Care Cost Containment: Results and Lessons from the Past 20 Years', in S.M. Shortell and U.E. Reinhardt (eds) *Improving Health Policy and Management*. Ann Arbor, MI: Health Administration Press.

Thorpe, K.E., C.S. Florence, D.H. Howard and P. Joski (2004a) 'The Impact of Obesity on Rising Medical Spending', *Health Affairs*, 20 October.

Thorpe, K.E., C.S. Florence and P. Joski (2004b) 'Which Medical Conditions Account for the Rise in Health Care Spending?', *Health Affairs*, 25 August.

Timmermans, Arco (2001) 'Arenas as Institutional Sites for Policymaking: Patterns and Effects in Comparative Perspective', *Journal of Comparative Policy Analysis* 3: 311–37.

Tjadens, F. and M. Duijnstee (2000) 'The Netherlands', in F. Tjadens and M. Pijl (eds) *The Support Of Family Carers and Their Organisations in Seven Western-European Countries: State of Affairs in 1998*. Utrecht: Netherlands Institute for Care and Welfare.

Trappenburg, M. and M. De Groot (2001) 'Controlling Medical Specialists in the Netherlands: Delegating the Dirty Work', in M. Bovens, P. t'Hart, and B.G. Peters (eds) *Success and Failure in Public Governance. A Comparative Analysis*. Cheltenham: Edward Elgar.

Trydegard, G.-B. (2000) *Traditions, Change and Variation: Past and Present Trends in Public Old-Age Care*. Dissertation. Stockholm: Department of Social Work, University of Stockholm.

Trydegard, G.-B. (2003) 'Swedish Elderly Care in Transition: Unchanged National Policy but Substantial Changes in Practice', paper presented at the 2003 ESPAnet Conference, 13–15 November, Copenhagen.

Trydegård, G.-B. and M. Thorslund (2001) 'Inequality in the Welfare State? Local Variation in Care of the Elderly – the Case of Sweden', *International Journal of Social Welfare* 10 (3): 174–84.

Turner, J.B. (1995) 'Economic Context and the Health Effects of Unemployment', *Journal of Health and Social Behavior* 36: 213–29.

Turnock, B.J. (2004) *Public Health: What It Is and How It Works*, 3rd edn. New York: Jones and Bartlett Publishers.

Twaddle, A.C. (1999) *Health Care Reform in Sweden, 1980–1994*. London: Auburn House.

Twaddle, A.C. (ed.) (2002). *Health Care Reform around the World*. Westport, CT: Auburn House.

Twigg, J. (1989) 'Models of Carers: How Do Social Care Agencies Conceptualise Their Relationship with Informal Carers?', *Journal of Social Policy* 18 (1): 53–66.

Ubel, P.A. (2001) *Pricing Life: Why it's Time for Health Care Rationing*. Cambridge, MA: MIT Press.

United Nations High Commission for Refugees (2001) 'Asylum Applications in Industrialized Countries: 1980–1999', http://www.unhcr.ch/pubs/ statis-tics/nov2001/ toc2.htm

United Nations Statistics Division (2005) www.unstats.un.org

United States Department of Health and Human Services (2000) *Healthy People 2010*. Washington, DC: US Government Printing Office.

United States Department of Health and Human Services (2001) *The Surgeon General's Call to Action to Prevent and Decrease Overweight and Obesity*. Washington: US Government Printing Office.

United States Department of Health and Human Services (2004) 'HHS Announces Revised Medicare Obesity Coverage Policy', (accessed 10 October 2006).

United States Department of Health and Human Services (2005) *National Guideline for Overweight and Obesity in Children and Adolescents: Assessment, Prevention, and Management*. Washington, DC: US Government Printing Office.

United States Public Health Service (1995) *For a Healthy Nation: Returns on Investment in Public Health*. Washington, DC: US Government Printing Office.

United States Public Health Service (2002) *Healthy People 2010: A Systematic Approach to Health Improvement*. Washington, DC: US Government Printing Office.

Valente, T.W. (2002) *Evaluating Health Promotion Programs*. New York: Oxford University Press.

Vasoo, S. (2001) 'Health Care in Singapore: Policy Issues and Challenges', www.hku.kk/socwork/dept/hepl/hepl.html

Victorian Department of Human Services (1996) *Towards a Safer Choice: The Practice of Traditional Chinese Medicine.* Melbourne: Department of Human Services.

Victorian Ministerial Advisory Committee on Traditional Chinese Medicine (1998) *Traditional Chinese Medicine: Report on Options for Regulation of Practitioners.* Melbourne: Department of Human Services.

Visser-Jansen, G. and C.P.M. Knipscheer (2004) *Eurofamcare: National Background Report for the Netherlands.* Amsterdam: Free University.

Waddan, A. and D. Jaenicke (2006) 'Recent Incremental Health Care Reforms in the US: A Way Forward or False Promise?', *Policy and Politics* 34(2): 241–63.

Wagenaar, A.C. and M. Wolfson (1995) 'Deterring Sales and Provision of Alcohol to Minors: A Study of Enforcement in 295 Counties in Four States', *Public Health Reports* 995 (110): 419–27.

Wall, A. (ed.) (1996) *Health Systems in Liberal Democracies.* London: Routledge.

Ward, L. (2002) 'Health Service Failing Homeless', *The Guardian*, 17 December.

Watson, E.A. and J. Mears (1999) *Women, Work and Care of the Elderly.* Aldershot: Ashgate.

Weale, A. (1998) 'Rationing Health Care', *British Medical Journal* 316: 410–26.

Weber, M. (1949) *The Methodology of the Social Sciences.* New York: Free Press.

Weinstein, M.C. (2001) 'Should Physicians be Gatekeepers of Medical Resources?', *Journal of Medical Ethics* 27: 268–74.

Weissert, C.S. and W.G. Weissert (2002) *Governing Health: The Politics of Health Policy.* Baltimore: The Johns Hopkins University Press.

Wendt, C., H. Rothgang and U. Helmert (2005) *The Self-Regulatory German Health Care System between Growing Competition and State Hierarchy.* TranState Working Papers no 32, Bremen: University of Bremen.

Wenger, E.L. (2001) 'Restructuring Care for the Elderly in Germany', *Current Sociology* 49 (3): 175–88.

Wennberg, J.E. (1998) *Dartmouth Atlas of Health Care.* Chicago, IL: American Hospital Association.

Werkö, L., J. Chamova and J. Adolfson (2001) 'Health Technology Assessment. The Swedish Experience', *Eurohealth* 7 (1): 29–31.

Wessen, A.F. (1999) 'The Comparative Study of Health Care Reform', in F.D. Powell and A.F. Wessen (eds) *Health Care Systems in Transition: An International Perspective.* Thousand Oaks, CA: Sage.

Whitehead, M. (1998) 'Diffusion of Ideas on Social Inequalities in Health: A European Perspective', *The Milbank Quarterly* 76 (3): 469–92.

WHO (1946) 'Preamble to the Constitution of the World Health Organization as adopted by the International Health Conference', New York, 19–22 June, 1946; signed on 22 July 1946 by the representatives of 61 States, and entered into force on 7 April 1948.

WHO (1996) 'Traditional Medicine', Fact Sheet no. 134, September. Geneva: WHO.

WHO (2001) *Global Status Report on Alcohol*. Geneva: WHO, June.

WHO (2002) *Alcohol Control Policies*. Geneva: WHO, www.WHO. int/substance_abuse/PDFfiles/global_alcohol_status_report/8Alcoholcontrol policies.pdf

WHO (2003) *Moving towards a Tobacco-free Europe: The European Report on Tobacco Control Policy, 1997–2002*. European Ministerial Conference for a Tobacco-free Europe Copenhagen: WHO.

WHO (2004) *Global Strategy on Diet, Physical Activity and Health*. Geneva: WHO.

WHO (2005) 'The World Health Organization Recommends That No Person under 18 Should Use a Sunbed', http://www.who.int/mediacentre/news/ notes/2005/np07/en/index.html

WHO, Regional Office for Europe (2003a) *European Environment and Health Committee*, www.euro.who.int/eprise/main/who/progs/eehc/home

WHO Regional Office for Europe (2003b) 'Global Change and Health', www.euro.who.int/eprise/main/who/progs/gch/home

WHO Regional Office for Europe (2003c) 'National Environmental Action Plans', www.euro.who.int/envhealthpolicy/ Plans/20020807_1

WHO, Regional Office for Europe (2004) Declaration. Fourth Ministerial Conference on Environment and Health, 23–25 June 2004, Budapest, (EUR/o4/5046267/06), Copenhagen: WHO, Regional Office for Europe.

WHO, Regional Office for Europe (2006) *European Charter on Counteracting Obesity*. Copenhagen: WHO Regional Office for Europe.

Wiener, J.M. (1992) 'Rationing in America: Overt and Covert', in M.A. Strosberg, J.M. Wiener and R. Baker (eds) *Rationing America's Medical Care: The Oregon Plan and Beyond*. Washington, DC: The Brookings Institution.

Wilensky, Gail R. (2005), 'The Challenges of Medicaid', *Healthcare Financial Management* 59 (6): 34–5.

Wilkinson, R.G. (1992) 'National Mortality Rates: The Impact of Inequality?', *American Journal of Public Health* 82: 1082–4.

Wilkinson, R.G. (1997) *Unhealthy Societies: The Afflictions of Inequality*. London: Routledge.

Williams, B.O. (2000) 'Ageism Helps to Ration Medical Treatment', *Health Bulletin* 58 (3): 198–202.

Wilsford, D. (1994) 'Path Dependency, or Why History Makes it Difficult, but not Impossible to Reform Health Systems in a Big Way', *Journal of Public Policy* 14(3): 285–306.

Winkleby, M.A., D.E. Jatulis, E. Frank, and S.P. Fortmann (1992) 'Socioeconomic Status and Health: How Education, Income, and Occupation Contribute to Risk Factors for Cardiovascular Disease', *American Journal of Public Health* 82 (6): 816–21.

Winslow, R. (2001) '1 Patient, 34 Days, $5 Million', *The Wall Street Journal*, 3 August, p. 1A.

Witherick, M.E. (2002) *States of Health and Welfare*. Cheltenham: Nelson Thornes.

Wong, M. (2003) 'WHO Removes Hong Kong from SARS List', *The Associated Press*, 23 June.

Woodman, R. (2001) 'UK Hospitals Face 3.9 Billion Negligence Bill', *Reuters News*, 4 May, http://dailynews.yahoo.com/h/nm/20010504/hl/hospitals_1.htm

Woods, K.J (2004) 'Political Devolution and the Health Services in Great Britain', *International Journal of Health Services* 34 (2): 323–39.

Wooldridge, M. (2001) 'More Doctors for Rural Australia', Department of Health and Aged Care, Media Release (6 June).

Woolhandler, S. and D.U. Himmelstein (2002) 'Paying for National Health Insurance and Not Getting It', *Health Affairs* 21: 88–98.

World Fact Book, The (2006), www.cia.gov/cia/publications/factbook/rankorder/2004rank.html

Wroe, D. (2003) 'Australia: Home Care Programs for Elderly "In Crisis"', *The Age*, 13 June.

Yahoo News (2003) 'Central China's Henen Province Punishes 800 Officials and Others over SARS', www.story.news.yahoo.com...fp/health

Yoshikawa, A., J. Bhattacharya and W.B. Vogt (eds) (1996) *Health Economics of Japan: Patients, Doctors, and Hospitals under a Universal Health Insurance System*. Tokyo: University of Tokyo Press.

Zwillich, T. (2001) 'Medical Technologies May Drive Up Health Costs', *Reuters News Service*, 6 March.

Zwillich, T. (2003) 'US Spent Record $1.4 Trillion on Health in 2001', *Reuters News Service*, 8 January.

Index

275